ROMANCE OF THE GRAIL

THE COLLECTED WORKS OF JOSEPH CAMPBELL

More titles forthcoming

ROMANCE OF
THE GRAIL

THE MAGIC AND MYSTERY OF
ARTHURIAN MYTH

Joseph Campbell

EDITED BY EVANS LANSING SMITH

JOSEPH CAMPBELL™
FOUNDATION

New World Library
Novato, California

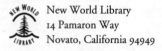

New World Library
14 Pamaron Way
Novato, California 94949

Text design by Tona Pearce Myers

Library of Congress Cataloging-in-Publication Data
Campbell, Joseph, 1904–1987.
Romance of the Grail : the magic and mystery of Arthurian myth / Joseph Campbell ; edited by Evans Lansing Smith.
    pages   cm. — (The collected works of Joseph Campbell)
Includes bibliographical references and index.
ISBN 978-1-60868-828-9 (paperback)
1. Grail—Legends—History and criticism. 2. Arthurian romances—History and criticism.
3. Love—Mythology. 4. Myth. 5. Mythology—Psychological aspects. I. Smith, Evans Lansing, [date] editor. II. Title. III. Title: Magic and mystery of Arthurian myth.
PN686.G7C34 2015
809'.93351—dc23   2015025927

First paperback printing, August 2022
ISBN 978-1-60868-828-9
Printed in Canada on 100% postconsumer-waste recycled paper

New World Library is proud to be a Gold Certified Environmentally Responsible Publisher. Publisher certification awarded by Green Press Initiative. www.greenpressinitiative.org

10   9   8   7   6   5   4   3   2   1

CONTENTS

ABOUT THE COLLECTED WORKS OF
JOSEPH CAMPBELL

AT HIS DEATH in 1987, Joseph Campbell left a significant body of published work that explored his lifelong passion, the complex of universal myths and symbols that he called "Mankind's one great story." He also left, however, a large volume of unreleased work: uncollected articles, notes, letters, and diaries, as well as audio- and videotape-recorded lectures.

The Joseph Campbell Foundation—founded in 1990 to preserve, protect, and perpetuate Campbell's work—has undertaken to create a digital archive of his papers and recordings and to publish *The Collected Works of Joseph Campbell.*

THE COLLECTED WORKS OF JOSEPH CAMPBELL
Robert Walter, Executive Editor
David Kudler, Managing Editor

EDITOR'S FOREWORD

My connection with Joseph Campbell began with a journey, a dream, and a poem. Not knowing what I wanted to do after graduating from Williams College in 1972, I decided to get a degree in creative writing from Antioch International and so went abroad for the first time to spend a year and a half working on a novel and a bunch of poems in London and Dublin. Crossing the Irish Channel, on seas traveled by Tristan and Isolde, I had a powerful dream about a young woman I had met on the journey.

After I told her about the dream, she said that she had a book for me to read, and brought me a copy of *The Hero with a Thousand Faces*. A few months after sharing *The Hero* with me, she gave me a flyer from the Mann Ranch in California announcing a two-week trip to northern France to study the Arthurian romances of the Middle Ages with Joseph Campbell. I signed up and devoured *The Masks of God: Creative Mythology*, and one early September autumn afternoon in 1976 found myself, an ignorant twenty-six-year-old, sitting on a bus beside Joseph Campbell, hearing him tell the story of climbing the belfry at Chartres Cathedral to ring the bells when *he* was twenty-six years old and identifying every single biblical figure in the stained glass and sculpture of that great church. When I walked through the Royal Portal the next morning and moved toward the great octagonal labyrinth on the pavement of the nave, the organist burst into a rehearsal of Bach's famous *Toccata*—it seemed just for me! All the stones in the church trembled resonantly, as if they were about to collapse.

The visit to Chartres came near the end of a terrific week, which had included visits to Rouen, Amiens, Mont Saint-Michel, the standing stones of Carnac, the medieval forests of Brittany, the châteaux country of the Loire River valley, and then on to Paris. On the bus from the Loire River into Chartres at twilight, Campbell had beamed with delight in his window seat beside me, looking out at a host of châteaux entirely invisible to me: he had piercing blue eyes, and knew the terrain well—where to look beneath a cluster of trees or behind a tiny copse in the distance for the noble relics of the Middle Ages.

We'd had lunch on the grounds of one of the châteaux earlier in the day, sitting beside the still pool that surrounded the beautiful building, which was perfectly reflected on the surface of the water: spires, towers, turrets, crenellations, copes, and barbicans—all perfectly replicated, though pointing downward, in the serene mirror of the pool's surface. The castle shimmered, above and below the waterline, a dazzling white surrounded by a bevy of immemorial oaks.

It was as if we had stepped through a hole in the hedge into another world, or as if we had passed through a glass door into the mysterious chambers of Glastonbury Abbey, where Arthur and his court danced the Nine Men's Morris.

Earlier our group had stopped in a little pub in the woods of Brittany to have a cup of cider and some cheese, and to enjoy the fine hospitality of our perfectly darling old French host, a diminutive white-haired dwarf with a mystical sense of humor. After several glasses of cider, we strolled down the long path outside the pub, which led into the woods where Vivian had beguiled Merlin—a picture of which he had carved into the cedar panels of his bar. Stopping beneath a tremendous flowering hawthorn, the old man said to me: "*Il y a beaucoup de choses qui n'existent pas!*" (There are many things that don't exist!)

And I could well believe him.

Deep inside the woods, where our group walked after lunch, we all sat down in a circle, sitting on logs and fallen tree trunks amid the briars and a scattering of *Amanita muscaria* mushrooms.

"Don't eat those," Campbell said, "or we'll never get to Paris!"

He then told the story of Merlin's death.

At the end of his life, the old man fell in love with Vivian (also known as Morgan la Fey), the sorceress who coaxed his magic spells out of him, then used them to imprison the old wizard in a tower of white thorns, in which he remains eternally invisible. Only the sound of his voice—whispering with the wind blowing gently through the trees of the vast forest—comes to those knights who wander through the forests of Brocéliande, in quest of love, or the Holy Grail.

As Campbell finished his story, with hounds bellowing in the distance, the sun broke free from the mist, and its shafts penetrated the copse of tall oak trees surrounding our silent, spellbound group. It continued to shine on the surface of the little pond where we had lunched, Campbell leaning against a standing stone on the shore, with the Lady of the Lake retrieving Excalibur in the water behind him: I imagined I saw her hand extend from beneath the rippling surface, waving the dazzling steel three times in the air, before returning to the depths.

The next day, we drove on to visit Mont Saint-Michel, staying at the little hotel down the road where Eisenhower had set up offices after the Normandy invasion—the beaches of which we had driven by that day. In Rouen I'd seen where machine guns had gouged gaping holes in the cathedral, and an old woman had taken me in to her burned-out courtyard to thank me for liberating France!

On my return, I conveyed her gratitude to my father.

In the peaceful hotel, Campbell sat quietly in a corner after breakfast, before his slide-illustrated lecture, for which he said he was "composing his images." The evening before, a few of us had gone out after dinner to see the Mount at night rising mysteriously above the dark swirl of the treacherous tides, pinnacle and archangel invisible in the darkness above. We drove with a *National Geographic* photographer who was working on a story there, and walked up along the cobbled streets of the village to the colossal arch leading into the monastery and cathedral.

I leaned back against the stone barricades to gaze up at the huge, fluted arches that support the massive weight of the monastery, which eerily dissolved into the intangible darkness of the endless night above.

"It's the impenetrable inner Self," Fred whispered to me, as I stood with thighs trembling in the wind.

Fred was a bandy-legged, feisty little Australian analyst—with a laugh like a Gatling gun—who had received his Jungian calling from a hallucinatory crow, which sat on his right thigh for years, refusing to fly away until Fred began his analysis. (Do you know the Norse myth of the two ravens, named Thought and Memory, perched on Wotan's shoulders?)

My trembling returned later in Paris, when a small group of us walked over to Notre Dame, and then continued down to the Seine, after a lengthy dinner (with lots of wine). The powerful vaulted nave and apse of the cathedral, as seen from the river below, with the flurry of flying buttresses supporting the weight, overwhelmed me. The trembling didn't stop until one of our companions, an older woman who ran a philanthropic foundation in California, simply melted on the stone steps climbing up from the embankment: she'd had far too much wine!

And so I came back to Baltimore a different person, with a new destiny seeded within me. I began to read *Parabola* magazine, in which I saw advertisements about Campbell's lectures in New York at Theatre of the Open Eye, which his wife, Jean Erdman, cofounded; I took the Metroliner up to attend them. At one of the weekend lectures, Campbell was accompanied by Jean Houston. She conducted an imagery session during which we were led to encounter an important guide in our lives. Campbell sat behind me, and when Jean asked him to share his experience, Campbell said he had met James Joyce and that all the churches of the world had collapsed!

On another visit, I went to see Jean Erdman perform Anna Livia Plurabelle in *The Coach with Six Insides*, her extraordinary song and modern dance adaptation of Joyce's *Finnegans Wake*, the subject of Campbell's first book, *A Skeleton Key to Finnegans Wake*, which he cowrote with Henry Morton Robinson. *The Coach with Six Insides* is a remarkable piece. Jean was older, and it was very, very touching to see her dance the part of the dying daughter of the river when she returns to her father, the Irish Sea, at the end of the piece ("a way a lone a last a loved a long the riverrun...").[1]

Sometime after those trips to France (as well as others with Campbell to Egypt and Kenya) and the seminars at the Open Eye, I decided to go to graduate school to study comparative literature, and so I set off across the country to Claremont Graduate University in California, where I stayed for seven years, like Hans Castorp trapped on the Magic Mountain in Thomas Mann's great novel. In the first year—1980, I think it was—I got a flyer from the leader of a Jungian dream group I was in about a weeklong seminar with Campbell at La Casa Maria in Montecito.

I signed up.

During one incredible week, I watched completely amazed as Campbell, then eighty years old, lectured all day long, and then into the evening. During another week at the San Francisco Jung Institute, he went through all of Joyce and Mann, from dawn to dusk, with unflagging delight. He would get up in the morning, speak until lunch, then all afternoon to dinnertime, and then pick up the ball for a couple of hours after dinner. And he kept it up for a solid week, one many of us who were there will never forget. His stamina, at that age, along with the stunning breadth and detail of the information he communicated, with the kind of grace the Italians call *sprezzatura* (making a difficult task look easy), have been the inspiration of my teaching career.

"It's the heart," Campbell had told me. He had kept fit for many years swimming laps at the New York Athletic Club, but he meant more than that.

It's the heart. Words I will always remember and be grateful for having heard.

After that week at Casa Maria, I continued to drive up from Claremont throughout the course of my graduate studies, to hear many more lectures, before getting my doctorate in 1986 and leaving for my first job. After two years of teaching at Franklin College in Lugano, Switzerland, I returned to America in 1988 and turned on the television at my grandparents' summer home on Fire Island to watch, spellbound, as Bill Moyers got Campbell to tell the story about the day he rang the bells of Chartres. Shortly after *The Power of Myth* had finished filming in 1987, Campbell died in Hawaii, the land beyond the waves. After his death, I had a dream about him:

> I was walking down one of the avenues in New York City. When I turned off into a side street, I came to a nondescript doorway with no address and nothing written above it. On a whim I walked up the dark stairway to an empty room on the upper floor, where I found Joseph Campbell and sat down with him. He had a bell jar in his hand, a kind of alchemical beaker, hermetically sealed. A vaporous mist hovered over some dirt on the bottom of the jar, into which we both gazed, Campbell with that marvelous smile of delight that so often lit up his face. As we looked into the jar, the mist slowly swirled around and became animated with the delicate colors of the

rainbow. Campbell pointed to the rainbow—the Cauda Pavonis, or peacock's tail, of the alchemical marriage—and I was led to see in it the emergence of life from the mysterious, invisible forces of the universe, into which the colorful apparition would return at the end of the cycle, evaporated into "thin air," like a dream.

As we watched the phosphorescent mist swirl above the handful of earth at the bottom of the beaker, a tiny couple slowly became visible, two fairy children, with nearly transparent bodies of light. They were joined at the waist, like Siamese twins. Again, I was led to understand, with no words passing between us, that this was an alchemical marriage, a herald of the new life, which was just then beginning for me.

In 2010 I retired from Midwestern State University in Texas and came to serve as core faculty and chair of the Mythological Studies program at the Pacifica Graduate Institute in California. It is the site of a library that holds all of Joseph Campbell's books. The Joseph Campbell Collection (which recently found a home at the New York Public Library) included extensive notes that Campbell used to prepare his lectures and write his books—remarkably detailed and precise, and labeled and beautifully organized into files—as well as handwritten and typed notes from his own readings and from some of the lectures he had attended in Europe.

Appendix B of this work catalogs the books in the library dealing with the Arthurian romances of the Middle Ages. In addition, I have transcribed some of Campbell's marginalia.

Of especial interest to me is the copy, included in the collection, of Campbell's master's thesis, submitted to the Department of English and Comparative Literature at Columbia University, on March 15, 1927. It is titled "A Study of the Dolorous Stroke," a key theme in the Arthurian romances of the Middle Ages, having to do with the origins of the Waste Land. Since it has not been previously published, I include the thesis, as it was originally submitted in 1927, as appendix A. No changes have been made to update the scholarship, spelling, or discourse to suit contemporary audiences. I don't, for example, edit words such as *savage* or *primitive man*, terms that, after all, Claude Lévi-Strauss used (with apparent impunity) four decades later in his classic work, *La Pensée sauvage*.

As I prepared this book, three major points emerged in my reflections on this material, all related to the central idea that Campbell's entire career was generated by his Arthurian studies.

The first point is that those studies opened up the whole rich world of comparative mythology to him. When Campbell left New York for his studies abroad in the summer of 1927, having just completed "A Study of the Dolorous Stroke," his notion was that the origins of the Arthurian romances were to be found in the indigenous world of the Celtic peoples of old Europe (Welsh, Breton, and Irish). Establishing those connections was the life work of his mentor at Columbia, Roger Sherman Loomis. But after a year or so in Paris, where he studied Old French and Provençal, Campbell went to Munich, where a very different approach to the literature of the European Middle Ages had flourished for more than a century. The criticism of the German school, sometimes labeled Orientalist, focused less on the Celtic backgrounds of pre-Roman, pre-Christian Europe and much more on establishing Asian roots for the myths. A variety of scholars were devoted to exploring Persian, Babylonian, Arabic, and Hindu texts as sources for the myths. In doing so they were following in the footsteps of the philosophers of the German Romantic movement (Schopenhauer, the Schlegels, and later Max Müller), and of Theodore Benfey, who in 1859 translated a copy of the *Panchatantra* and demonstrated the infiltration of Hindu myth into the European literature of the Middle Ages via translations into Arabic and Latin.

His time in Munich turned Campbell's eyes eastward, where in many ways they remained focused throughout his career, and led him to begin his studies in Sanskrit. Those studies eventually led to his friendship with the German Indologist Heinrich Zimmer, who fled Nazi Germany in 1938 and by 1940 was lecturing at Columbia University. After Zimmer's untimely death in 1943, Campbell would spend more than a decade translating and editing the four books on Indian mythology and art that Zimmer had left unfinished. As it happens, Zimmer's father had been a famous Celtic studies scholar. Put the two Zimmers together, and you have the essence of Joseph Campbell's approach to discovering the origins of the Arthurian romances—an approach from the perspective of both Celtic and Oriental mythologies. [2]

The second key point is Campbell's idea that the Arthurian myths represent the world's first "secular mythology," by which he meant that the myths were not to be taken literally but to be interpreted as metaphors of the natural stages of spiritual growth and development —symbols of the stages of the individuation process, one might say. [3] It seems that Campbell's discovery of the inner, psychological implications of myths occurred during the critical time of his studies in Munich, beginning in November 1928 and ending in the spring of 1929, when he traveled via Greece to Constantinople—before his return to New York, where he arrived on August 23 of that same year. Later Campbell wrote of the creative synthesis of psychology and myth that began in Munich:

> The discovery of German was a real event in my life.... It was when I was a student in Germany that the metaphysical aspect of what I was studying broke open for me. I'd been working on mythology, and particularly medieval mythology, just in the way of a Western scholar. Then I ran into Goethe, ran into Thomas Mann, ran into Jung, and suddenly I realized what the mythic dimension was of these things, not simply the academic circus. Consequently I have a very deep feeling for that country.[4]

The final point is that Campbell, following Denis de Rougemont's classic book, found in the Arthurian poems the origins of *Love in the Western World*.[5] It was a special kind of love, combining the sexuality of *eros* and the communal service of *agapē*, with a special emphasis on the unique relationship between two individuals that Campbell called *amor*. *Amor* involves two separate individuals whose lives are inspired and nourished by their relationship. Neither is lost in their connection, and both become more fully what they truly are—and more than they could be without each other—without sacrificing their discrete identities.

These three ideas are of central importance to Campbell's work as a whole and emerged from his engagement with the Arthurian materials, so richly gathered together in Pacifica Graduate Institute's special collections library, and in the OPUS Archives. Of special interest to me were Campbell's personal copy of his favorite poem, Wolfram von Eschenbach's *Parzival*, and a copy of Franz Rolf Schröder's little study of the poem entitled *Die Parzivalfrage* (The Parzival question), published in 1925, which Campbell probably bought while he was in Munich. Campbell's copy of Wolfram's poem includes several handwritten notes taken from Schröder's book, along with extensive underlining and marginalia, so I conclude that *Die Parzivalfrage* was important to Campbell, even though I have not found it cited in any of his published works on the Arthurian romances.

I first heard Campbell tell the story of Parzival in the candlelit ambience of a stony hotel on the cold shores of Brittany, one beautiful

night during our trip together in France, after an amazing five-course
dinner that had included oysters culled from the bay we could see
from the dining room. It was a stupendous night, so moving that an
old lawyer from New York broke down in tears while Campbell wove
his inimitable spell over our little group. I must have heard him tell
the story of Parzival twenty-five more times over the course of as many
years, and yet I had a lot to learn from this book by Franz Schröder.

I read *Die Parzivalfrage*, underlining key passages devoted to the
myth of celestial ascent, which I had never associated with Wolfram's
poem or heard Campbell discuss. Schröder argues that the myth is
of Iranian origin, with Hermetic, Neoplatonic, and Gnostic variations having to do with the celestial ascent of the soul after death—or
during ecstatic visionary flights during life. And Schröder points us
toward the story Wolfram tells about the origins of the Grail in the
heavens—a theme that Henry and Renée Kahane have pursued quite
productively in their publications.[6]

Then, when I asked Pacifica's special collections librarian (Richard Buchen, who has been of inestimable help) to send me the photo-
copied pages of Campbell's copy of *Die Parzivalfrage*, complete with
marginalia in an exquisitely fine hand, I found that I had underlined
the same passages that Campbell had. I knew then that I was on the
right track, and that the old master was still speaking to me from
beyond the grave—like Merlin's voice on the wind whistling through
the pines of Brittany after Vivian casts the spell of death upon him,
imprisoning the old wizard in a tower of flowering hawthorns.

In addition to Schröder's *Die Parzivalfrage*, several other key
documents in the Joseph Campbell Collection indicate Campbell's
shift from Celtic to Oriental mythologies in his understanding of the
Arthurian material, a shift that catalyzed the emergence of Campbell's truly global, comparative perspective on myth in general, and
on the Grail romances in particular, that has become the signature
of his unique genius of creative synthesis. This shift can be seen in
several pages of very old notes (with the underlined headnote "Dolorous Stroke,") which indicates the impact of Leo Frobenius's writings
on his work. One page reveals this process at work, showing Campbell's notes in German that suggest parallels between Paleolithic, Erythraean, Inuit, Egyptian, Nordic, and Arthurian myths revolving
around such themes as the Night-Sea Journey (*Nachtmeerfahrt*, from

Frobenius and Jung), Rebirth (*Wiedergeburt*), "The Dolorous Stroke" and "The Bleeding Lance," the Belly of the Whale myths (*Walfisch mythe*), Ritual Regicide (*Rituelle Königsmord*), Battle with the Dragon (*Drachenkampf*), and the Fisher King of the Grail stories. The dating of another page (1927) shows that these amplifications of the motifs from the Grail romances—motifs not yet elaborated in Campbell's master's thesis—were nevertheless percolating at the time Campbell was finishing his work at Columbia. Subsequent pages from the same sequence clearly demonstrate his debt to Frobenius, with quotations copied out in German from *Das Zeitalter des Sonnengottes* and *Und Afrika Sprach*, and by the end of the sequence, a note on Osiris from *Wandlungen und Symbole der Libido* signals that the connection to Jung has already emerged.

Another indication of Campbell's turning eastward during his exploration of the Grail mythologies is a page of notes from a book in French by Basilide, *Essai sûr la tradition celtique*, which suggests that the Chaldean and Celtic Churches ("*l'Église chaldéenne*" and "*l'Église celtique*") were both derived from the Mother Church of Jerusalem ("*l'Église-mère de Jérusalem*") and synthesized ("*le Saint Graal est le lien entre elles*") by the Church of the Holy Grail in Northern Scotland. These parallels among an extraordinary range of mythologies (Neolithic; Bronze Age Cretan, Egyptian, and Near Eastern; Greco-Roman; Celtic; Nordic; Hindu; Buddhist; Christian) would bear rich fruit in Campbell's commentaries and lectures on the Arthurian romances of the Grail. While the thesis of 1927 shows the then-fashionable interest in the anthropological writings of Sir James Frazer and Jessie Weston—which focused on the dying and resurrecting gods of natural cycles of fertility, in season and storm—Campbell's thought dramatically expands to embrace a truly global, multicultural approach to the subject of comparative mythology.

There can be no doubt that this tendency was powerfully reinforced and abetted by Campbell's friendship with Heinrich Zimmer from 1941 to March 1943, during the latter's years of exile from Nazi Germany. Zimmer died quite suddenly of pneumonia (which Campbell thought Zimmer had carried with him since the trenches of the First World War) "to the immense shock and grief of all who loved him."[7] After Zimmer's death, Campbell undertook the heroic endeavor of editing and translating his great mentor's voluminous works—a task that took more than thirteen years of what Campbell called "hellish hard work, but a real, real delight."[8] The most important of these, for our purposes, is *The King and the Corpse*, published on March 26, 1948, Campbell's forty-fourth birthday.[9] This book includes a marvelous chapter called "Four Romances," which exemplifies Zimmer's genius and rich comparative approach to the stories of Gawain, Lancelot, Merlin, and Yvain. It is an approach in which the creative synthesis of Celtic and Oriental mysticism that characterizes Campbell's work on the Arthurian material is masterfully and gracefully executed. Many of Zimmer's typed drafts for the lectures he gave on these stories are also to be found in the Joseph Campbell Collection.

Let me conclude with a note on the sources for the selections from Campbell's work that constitute the stories and commentaries gathered together in the body of this volume. I have drawn from several audio lectures available through Joseph Campbell Foundation's Joseph Campbell Audio Collection: "Arthurian Tradition" (I.6.3), "The Grail Legend" (I.6.4), "The Forest Adventurous" (I.6.5), and "Grail Mythology" (II.1.8). I have also made use of cassette tapes of unreleased lectures stored in the Joseph Campbell Collection: L181 Esalen, L769 Holy Grail 1, and L770 Holy Grail 2, as well as from my personal collection of the cassettes of a seminar entitled "Myths and Mysteries of the Great Goddess," recorded at the Casa Maria in Montecito, California, from April 7, 1983.[10] In addition, I have extracted material from the transcription of a lecture called "Psyche and Symbol," generously provided by David Kudler, as well as portions of Campbell's essay "Indian Reflections in the Castle of the Grail," published in *The Celtic Consciousness*.[11] Finally, I have referred to selections of the outtakes stored in the Joseph Campbell Collection, with transcriptions by Joseph Campbell Foundation. My goal in each case was to preserve not only the integrity of the original lectures but also the coherence of the narratives associated with the individual stories about the various knights in quest. This required some cutting and pasting from the archival materials, so that, for example, the story of Parzival draws from several of the sources named above.

—Evans Lansing Smith

ACKNOWLEDGMENTS

⎯⎯⎯⎯⎯⎯●⎯⎯⎯⎯⎯⎯

THIS BOOK COULD NOT HAVE BEEN WRITTEN without the help and expertise of many people: Bob Walter and David Kudler directed me to the relevant audio recordings of Joseph Campbell's lectures (available on the Joseph Campbell Foundation website at JCF.org/audio) and provided me with transcriptions both of these lectures and of selections from the various notes preserved as outtakes in Joseph Campbell's Archives. Richard Buchen, then librarian of the special collections library at the Pacifica Graduate Institute, was the first to introduce me to the marvelous resources of Joseph Campbell's personal library (annotated in appendix B), and to the typescript of Campbell's master's thesis, "A Study of the Dolorous Stroke" (here published for the first time as appendix A). Dr. Safron Rossi, then the curator of the Joseph Campbell Collection (and editor of Campbell's *Goddesses: Mysteries of the Feminine Divine*), was my Ariadne, my guide into the labyrinthine complexities of the vaults where Campbell's papers are stored. She was indefatigable and enthusiastic, directing me to the heavy boxes (more than 130 of them), which contain the carefully labeled files of Campbell's extraordinary notes, diligently recorded over a lifetime of disciplined scholarship, unique in its breadth and depth.

I began this work ten years ago, in 2005. It could not have been done without the support of steady employment—at Midwestern State University in Wichita Falls, Texas, for twenty years, and now at Pacifica Graduate Institute in Carpinteria, California—and the friendship and interest of my colleagues and friends from both schools. I am particularly grateful to Dr. Jesse Rogers, president; Dr. Sam Watson, dean; Dr. Thomas Galbraith, chair of the English Department; and the Faculty Research and Development Committee at Midwestern State University, for supporting my endeavors, and for providing me with funds for my research at the Bibliothèque nationale in Paris, and in the special collections library and OPUS Archives, housed at the Pacifica Graduate Institute. Finally, I owe an inestimable debt of gratitude to Drs. Dennis Slattery and Patrick Mahaffey, who made it possible for me to retire from twenty years of teaching at Midwestern State University in order to join the marvelous faculty in the Mythological Studies Program.

PART ONE

FOUNDATIONS AND BACKGROUNDS OF THE GRAIL ROMANCES

Figure 1. "Each entered the forest at the spot that he himself had selected." (print, United States, 1913)

CHAPTER I

———•———

Neolithic, Celtic, Roman, and German Backgrounds

THE HIGH PERIOD OF THE ARTHURIAN ROMANCES is exactly that of the building of the cathedrals, the wonderful century from 1150 to 1250 A.D. In my view, this period—Gothic times—is the counterpart to the Homeric period. We have two great Europes: the Europe of Greece and Rome, and the Europe of the Celts and Germans. The stress is on the individual—the individual not as the subject of the state but as a citizen of the state, the state being a vehicle of his or her will. This is a European mind-set.

There have been moments in history when, on this little peninsula of European consciousness, in the field of the great Eurasian-African world mass, the individual has stood forth. In the Greek understanding of what happened at Marathon and Thermopylae, you already have the Greeks appreciating themselves as very different from the whole Orient. There was enormous respect for the Egyptians, but they were Oriental, and in the Orient you don't have individuals, you have people of certain types, certain memberships, certain races, certain strata of society. The principle of *dharma*, and of what Yeats called the primary mask, both of which are put on you by the society, relieve the individual of personal responsibility.

This is the attitude of the soldier: a good soldier is not responsible for what he does; he is responsible for how well he does it—and that's the attitude of Oriental life. When a draft comes along and a Western individual becomes a soldier, very often he has a terrific psychological crisis to face, because he has to move into another order of virtue, where there are no individuals but only agents of an impersonal order. Of course, no one is responsible for the order, either, because that comes down from the ancestors, so no one is responsible for anything, and you have an absolutely cold-blooded situation.

Once when I was in Bombay I asked a gentleman out on the street the way to the post office, and he pointed it out to me. I said, "Thank you very much."

He said, "Oh, it's just my duty," and walked on.

I thought, *Holy God, wouldn't you expect to get a more human response to a little question like that?*

An Oriental religion swept into Europe with real force at the end of the fourth century—namely, Christianity, with all humankind inheriting Adam's sin and all humankind possibly saved by Jesus's deed, with no individual doing anything on his own (the sin wasn't yours in the first place, nor was the salvation). This became the official state religion of the whole of the Roman Empire; people weren't allowed to think anything else. A century or so later, of course, the European portion of the Roman Empire collapsed, and what we called Rome from then on is really Constantinople, which is Byzantium, which is Asia again.

So this totally alien point of view was imposed on Europe. Europe had perfectly good religions and mythologies, and then this other thing was brought in on top of it. And what you got then, in the creative life in Europe throughout the Middle Ages, was an attempt on the part of the European mind to assimilate this Levantine emphasis on the collective and translate it into something like European thinking.

In my view, the pinnacle of that achievement is the moment represented in the Arthurian romances, written down in the twelfth and thirteenth centuries. In these works, you have a Christian vocabulary but completely European forms of consciousness.

In the later thirteenth century, however, after the establishment of the Inquisition, we hear very little of new creative productions in the spirit of the Arthurian romances. We find rewritings of them, translations of them, and so forth—the most important for the

English-speaking world being Malory's *Morte d'Arthur*—but there's no more important creativity after about 1230 A.D.

The roots of this European consciousness go very deep. There has been a recent correction of the carbon 14 datings for Europe that has pushed some of the datings back quite far, so that the emergence of civilized consciousness in Europe in the period of the Great Goddess is now being dated something like 7000 B.C.[1] This is very, very early. The development of agricultural life in Europe is as early as anything taking place in the Near East.

And then we have in eastern Europe a very important development: there may have been a kind of linear writing, a linear script invented—there are a couple of signs of this—in which case it would have been 3,000 years earlier than the Sumerian writing.[2] And then in western Europe you have the emergence of the great megalithic systems: Stonehenge and Woodhenge in England and Newgrange in Ireland and the megaliths all over the Carnac area in Brittany and down into Spain. It's a tremendous development and may go back as far back as 4000 B.C. That's earlier than the pyramids by far; the pyramids were of the fourth dynasty, beginning with the Step Pyramid of around 2600 B.C. The importance, then, of this antiquity of Europe must be recognized, and it's the past chiefly of the Goddess.

What we find is that the basic mythologies of the European consciousness were those of the Goddess from perhaps as early as the preceramic Neolithic on to the later Bronze Age. In Cornwall there were tin mines. In Ireland there was gold floating free in the River Liffey, so one could pan for it. Wherever there was tin in the Bronze Age there would be an important exploiting colony because tin was an important ingredient of bronze and is not found in very many places. And so from an early time, the Irish Sea area—Dublin and Wales and Cornwall, the Isle of Man, and western Scotland—was a matrix of civilized living. This is the background of the Celtic mythologies, and it is the background also of the prominence and power of the Goddess figure in these mythologies. Our fairy godmothers, for instance, are reflexes of all that.

About the first millennium B.C. the Celts begin to come into the British Isles and western France. Now, the Celts are Indo-European

people; the Indo-Europeans have their beginning in the southwest
Russian steppe north of the Black Sea; they're called the Kurgan
people, *Kurgan* being a Russian word for "mound burial." And these
mound burials, which are the mound burials of warrior chieftains,
are the characteristic symptoms of the extent and period of the Indo-
Europeans' early diffusions. Their culture extended in two directions
from that area, one southeastward and the other southwestward.

Southeastward they go into India; as the Indo-Europeans, they're
Vedic people with their warrior chieftains and their cattle herds.
These are the people who had mastered the horse and become thereby
almost invincible. The horse and the war chariot are the counterparts
of the atom bomb today: ancient people just couldn't do anything
about them; these tribes overrode and overran and took charge.

Before that time, with the separation of peoples, everyone was
going on foot, and peoples would go apart and become very closely
linked with the landscape of their new land. With this emergence
of the horse we begin to have significant intercourse back and forth,
almost like what's happening now with the airplane. People who for-
merly had been separated from each other suddenly came into relationship, and we see cross-references and as a result the sometimes
startling parallels between what we find in the Celtic world and the
Chinese world. But they are really not too surprising because there is
this back-and-forth relationship.

Of the various Indo-European peoples and groups moving out of
these centers, one of the most important for the West was the Celtic
community, and the original area of its constellation was southeast
Europe, in the area of Bavaria and Austria. At that place and time
(1000 B.C.) they were part of what is called the Hallstatt culture, with
their heavy wagons, very like the Conestoga wagons that went across
the American plains in the nineteenth century. When the Celts went
into western France, a new brilliance came into the culture, known as
La Tène culture. We find evidence of these brilliant chariot warriors
in their glorious gold work with the clean, graceful designs; they were
a group of ruthless barbarians, but with glorious metal artists. And it
was a group of these people who in various waves moved into the British Isles and over into Ireland.

The earlier Bronze Age inhabitants of the British Isles were mother right people, matrilineal in their descent, with the right to rule passing down from mother to daughter, and the actual governing being done by the queen's brother. (In the Arthurian romances, notice the multitude of important uncle-nephew relationships.) The Celts, however, were patriarchal, and vigorously so. As they moved from Bavaria to France to Great Britain and then to Ireland, the patriarchal accent became less and less emphatic and the continuation of the female accent more and more perceptible, so that by the time you get to Ireland and Wales, the Mother Goddesses are still the most powerful.

The typical Celtic story dating from those periods is in the style and spirit of a legend of the Celtic fairyland, the people of the Sidhe transformed into the ladies and knights of an enchanted castle, the rules of their disenchantment being known to the knights and ladies themselves but not to the one who is expected to arrive one day and release them. The tales are of a young patriarchal warrior type led astray by following some animal or will-o'-the-wisp until he comes to a fairy hill, into which the old Mother Goddess people have retreated since the arrival of the patriarchal invaders, and the queen of the fairy hill becomes his mistress. When he arrives there, he finds the queen in distress; the people of another fairy hill are harassing her, and he becomes her champion and stays with her. And when his work is done, he remains with the fairy queen of the hill in a state of bliss, as in Wagner's Tannhäuser in Venusberg, where the centuries pass as years and there is neither old age, nor sorrow, nor death, nor even boredom. And if by chance he should leave, to return for a brief visit to the historical world, he will have been warned to remain on his magical horse and not to set foot on the ground. In fact, of course, he generally does precisely what he was forbidden to do, and immediately he crumbles to dust and disappears. Such was the fate of one of the members of Bran's company, who returns from the Isle of Women; such, also, of Saint Brendan, when, after a season of only forty days in the Land of Promise, he returns to Ireland, where he immediately dies and, of course, goes straight to heaven.

This becomes a major motif in the later Arthurian romances, and we'll see it time and time again, in which the hero befriends and defends the chatelaine, the lady of a besieged castle, and becomes her consort. This old Celtic Bronze Age theme, combining the male powers and the female, has come rolling right down through the ages.

When you start looking at the entry of Neolithic people into Europe, you find the urn-burial people, and the bell-urn people—one kind after another. Identifying these different peoples who came over into Europe and over into the British Isles becomes extremely complicated. There were almost certainly very important Mediterranean continuities connected with the trans-European Bronze Age tin trade; Irish gold and Irish bronze were distributed all through Europe.

In the Hellenistic period we find the beautifully carved figure of the dying Gaul. This naked Gaelic warrior is wearing an Irish torque (a kind of necklace with two big heavy heads meeting) in Turkey. The trade was strong between the British Isles and the mainland. There were always connections by sea between Spain and Ireland. When he arrived in Gaul, Caesar remarked that the seacoast people had a trade running up and down the coast—trade in gold, trade in tin, trade in bronze, and so forth—which must have come from the islands.

So we have the Neolithic Bronze Age Britons, with their matrilineal accent. Next came these people from the Black Sea, the patrilineal Celts, who swept in (with a stopover in southern Europe), during the first millennium B.C., up through as late as 50 B.C.

What happens next, of course, is that *all of Gaul is divided into three parts.* Julius Caesar fought the Gaelic Wars, and the Romans conquered France. Then, shortly after Caesar's time, the Romans conquered Britain. The conquest of Britain you can date to roughly 50 B.C., and it lasted until around 450 A.D., so there were five hundred years of Roman occupation of what we now call England (then it was Britain). The Roman occupation reached as far as what we now call Scotland and westward almost into Wales. That left Scotland, Wales, Cornwall, the Isle of Man, and Ireland as territory that was outside the Roman conquest but subject to Roman influences. Meanwhile, the Germans were piling up in northern Europe. The Germans were another group of Indo-Europeans, but they settled somewhat eastward and northward of the Celts. The German culture was similar to the Celtic one, and their languages were closely related—they were

FIGURE 2. Dying Gaul (carved marble, Hellenistic, Turkey, first century B.C.)

both varieties of the Indo-European complex. At the same time, the Persians were pressing in on the east.

The extent of the Roman Empire is almost impossible to imagine: it was enormous, encompassing the whole of North Africa, Europe, and the Near East, to the very borders of Persia. There were Roman roads right across Persia, and there was a Roman trading station on the border of China. We have a text called *The Periplus of the Erythraean Sea*, which is the logbook of a Greek mariner sailing Roman ships in the Indian Ocean. His principal trade route was from Egypt through the Red Sea down the whole coast of Africa to Mozambique and westward and eastward, south of Arabia to India. There was a Roman trading station south of Madras on the east coast of India at a place called Arikamedu, dating from around the same time as the invasion of Britain, and Roman coins have been found in Vietnam and in the Philippines. It's incredible, the power and majesty of the empire at its height.

This whole empire became Christian in the fourth century A.D., with the emperors Theodosius I and II. Theodosius I (r. 379–395) declared Christianity to be the only permitted religion, thus beginning persecutions throughout the empire.

For us, the important thing is the missionization taking place in that early period of the British Isles. Great Britain became Christian, along with the rest of the empire, and with the legendary Saint Patrick, Ireland became Christian in the fifth century. One of the paradoxical calamities of Christianity was that after Rome was Christianized, it fell. The whole point, really, of Saint Augustine's *City of God* is, yes, the city of man has fallen, but the City of God had triumphed. Well, that was small comfort! The fact was that the place collapsed. The Christians were comparable, I would say, to the Communists in our part of the world today: they were eating it out from the inside, like maggots.

At the same time, the Germans were pressing down from the north, and this pressure became emphatic when Attila the Hun came smashing in from the east and one German tribe after another was pushed westward, and just out of terror, you might say, broke down through the Roman Empire. With that happening in the fifth century, the Romans had to retrench and shorten their lines. The whole Roman defense line up the Danube to Britain was pulled back, and they pulled their troops out of England. That left England, after five hundred years of Roman occupation, like an oyster with the shell taken off, and what begins to happen is that the Picts from the north began pushing down, while the Celts from the west began pushing in, and the Germans came into England from Jutland. There's a long story here of the collapse of British rule in what then became England, but it is that moment—with the collapse of the Roman Empire, the invasions up and down the line by the Germanic tribes, and the inadequate defenses of the Celtic people in Britain—that is the background of the Arthurian legend.

FIGURE 3. The Book of Kells Tunc page (ink and gold on parchment, Ireland, c. 800 A.D.)

CHAPTER 2

Irish Christianity:
Saints Brendan and Patrick

FOR SOMETHING LIKE THREE DECADES, as a leading member of the New York chapters of both the Ancient Order of Hibernians and the Friendly Sons of St. Patrick, my maternal grandfather annually rode up Fifth Avenue in the first rank of our spectacular Saint Patrick Day parades. My paternal grandfather, Campbell, came from County Mayo, and my Scottish grandmother, MacFawn, from Dundee. With such a galaxy of Celts behind me, I am sure that in a remoter past there must have been more than a few of my forebears who knew Saint Patrick, and possibly even one or two, who, centuries ago, arrived in Canada with that great and blessed discoverer of North America, Saint Brendan.

The story of that navigator's ordeal is most remarkable, circulating as he did for no less than forty years, among the islands that in those days dotted the Atlantic. He sailed in his coracle eastward, with a company of twelve companions chosen from his monastery of a thousand. The first island they came to was so rocky that they floated around it for three days before discovering a landing. Ashore, they were greeted by a very comely hound that fell down before the saint and in its own way bade him welcome; then the hound led the company into a noble hall, where a table covered with a cloth of gold was set with a meal of bread and fish. Such magically provided feasts are common features of Celtic traditional tales, whether of the pagan or the Christian eras, and in the present medieval example the food provided suggests Christ's miracle of the loaves and fishes feeding the multitude. And the little scene of Brendan with his twelve at table is in a playful way a reflection of the great scene of the Last Supper: Christ's celebration of Passover, immediately following which he was to endure the ordeal of Gethsemane and the Via Crucis. The original Passover of the Jews was followed by their crossing of the Red Sea and the ordeal of forty years in the wilderness. Brendan, too, with his monks, after their meal on the Island of Rocks, was to spend forty years tossing on the briny deep, likewise en route to the Promised Land—though one far from Canaan.

Where, then, or what, is that land? Where is Eden with its two trees—of the Knowledge of Good and Evil, and of Life?

It is one of the prime mistakes of many interpreters of mythological symbols to read them as references, not to mysteries of the human spirit, but to earthly or unearthly scenes and to actual or imagined historical events—the Promised Land as Canaan, for example, and heaven as a district of the sky—or to see the Israelites' passage of the Red Sea as an event such as a newspaper reporter might have witnessed. It is one of the glories, on the other hand, of the Celtic tradition that in its handling even of religious themes it retranslates them from the languages of imagined fact into a mythological idiom, so that they may be experienced not as time-conditioned but as timeless, telling not of miracles long past but of miracles potential within ourselves, here, now, and forever. This aim is basic to the Grail tradition, basic to Arthurian romance, as it was basic, also, to the earlier Celtic way of storytelling, whether of pagan heroes or of Christian knights and saints.

When Brendan's monks had eaten their fill, they found beds prepared for them and, in the morning, set off to sea again, refreshed. Their second landfall was an island, very green, where they found sheep on every side, the whitest ever seen, every one the size of an ox. And a very good-looking old man approached, who gave welcome and introduction. "This is the Land of Sheep," he told them. "It is never winter here, but a summer everlasting." Then he spoke of the island next to come, the Paradise of Birds, to which his own was but a station on the way.

An extraordinary adventure befell the voyagers halfway along, which is the most famous of the legend's marvels. On what appeared to be an island, level and without trees, they landed and, building a fire, set a cauldron full of fish to boil. However, no sooner was their fire alight than the island began to quake, and when, in terror, they had tumbled back into their boat, they saw the island swim away with their cauldron. It was a whale, a great fish, the biggest of the fishes of the world, and it was ever trying to put its tail into its mouth but could not do so, because of its great bulk.

One sees in the Book of Kells a representation of such a tail-biting monster. It appears on the so-called Tunc page, which is devoted to the Crucifixion. (*Tunc crucifixerant cum eo duos latrones*, reads the text: "Then there were crucified with him two thieves.")

FIGURE 4. The Book of Kells: the whale (ink and gold on parchment, Ireland, c. 800 A.D.)

What the tail-biting monster represents is the world-surrounding Cosmic Ocean, a motif known to all the major mythologies of the world: Okeanos of the Greeks, for example, beyond which lie the Hesperides; the blessed Isles of the Golden Apples and immortal life, which correspond precisely to the Avalon ("Apple Land") of the Arthurian legend; and to the mysterious site as well of the Castle of the Grail.

In Brendan's case, whereas up to this point he had been sailing eastward to the sunrise, he would now, without reversing course, be sailing westward, to the setting sun. He and his shipmates have passed, that is to say, the point where the pairs of opposites come together and where the consciousness transcends them: East and West, life and death, good and evil, even being and nonbeing. Their next adventure, accordingly, led them to an island full of flowers and trees, the Paradise of Birds, where there was a tall tree beside a well, and on every branch of it, so many beautiful white birds happily singing that scarcely a leaf of the tree could be seen. This is a characteristically Irish vision of the mythological Cosmic Tree, the axial tree about which the universe turns, the Tree of Life in the middle of the Garden. And a little bird flew toward Brendan from that tree, with the flickering of his wings making a merry noise, like a fiddle; and Brendan asked: "If you are a messenger, then tell me why it is you sing so happily."

To which the bird replied: "We were every one of us angels, and when Lucifer fell, we fell with him. But because our offense was but a little one, our Lord put us here, without pain but in great joy and merriment, to serve what way we can upon this tree."

Most remarkable! We have just passed beyond the bounding rim to the world of knowledge of the pairs of opposites, and immediately we have come to a tree of only somewhat fallen angels, merrily singing. In *Parzival*, the version of the Grail legend to which I shall be calling attention shortly, the miraculous vessel itself is declared to have been brought from heaven to earth by the "neutral angels," who, during the War in Heaven, sided neither with Lucifer nor with God. That is, between the claims of the ultimate pairs of opposites they have held steady, and so, in a mystical sense, represent what has been called the Middle Way between all pairs of opposites, which leads to the realization of transcendence. For any deity, defined, personified, and with qualities—good, not evil; true, not false; merciful and just, not merciless and unjust; and so forth—is by such definition bounded. God's opposite, Satan, is thus inevitably his fellow. When, however, the Middle Way has been found—as taught, for example, by the Buddha—a place unknown to the Land of Sheep, the merry song of the white birds of the axial tree tells of the rapture named in the Sanskrit of the Indian mystics, *nirvikalpa samādhi* ("rapture without qualification"), in contrast to the "rapture *with* qualification" of *savikalpa samādhi*. And in the legend of the Grail the sign of such realization is the Grail itself.

Beyond the Paradise of Birds there was but one island more to be passed before the Land of Promise should be gained, and that was not of song but of silence; nor was it to be reached before the end of a stormy trial of four months and another forty days: the little craft so hurled between earth and sky that the company were tired of their lives. It was the island of a great abbey of twenty-four monks and their abbot, who for eighty years had kept silence so well that not one of them had ever spoken to the others. Here one recognizes something like the holy fellowship of the Grail. Clothed in royal cloaks woven of threads of gold, with a royal crown before them and candles on every side, the crew was fed miraculously with loaves and drink brought daily by an angel in the form of a strong man, of whom nothing was known. And at prayers in the chapel each evening, Brendan saw an angel that came in by the window and lighted all the candles and went out by the window again, to heaven, and the saint marveled. "There is a wonder on me," he told the abbot, "those candles to burn the way they do, and never to waste." The abbot and his monks were at the interface of Eternity and Time—Eternity *in* Time, which is where we all are, actually, if we but knew. For is not the natural world renewing itself all around us continuously? It is only in holding on to the idea of ourselves as mortal that we are blinded to this truth. Brendan's monks had all but died to themselves in their passage of the terrible sea, and it was bliss, now, of an undisturbed meditation on the everlasting mystery of Being itself, that held them here in a state of rapture.

Early Christian Ireland was known as the Isle of Saints; and in many parts of the island today, one is shown the little stone one-room huts (beautifully built) that are said to have been the retreats of the early sixth- to tenth-century hermits. For early Irish Christianity, something very different from the medieval Roman form of the religion, was brought in to Norman England at the time of the conquest by Henry II, 1171 A.D.

The date of Saint Patrick's mission is generally given as 432 A.D. This was, almost certainly, not the actual date. Four hundred and thirty-two is a mythological number. For example, in the Purāṇas, the old Indian epics, it is declared that the number of years in a *mahāyuga*—a "Great Cycle" of the world creation, flowering, and dissolution—is 4,320,000 years. This is known as a "Day of Brahma," and it is followed by a "Night of Brahma" of the same duration, the sum of the two being 8,640,000. In one of the verses of the Icelandic *Poetic Edda* (*Grimnismol* 23) we are told that in Valhall, Othin's warrior hall, there are 540 doors, through each of which, at the end of every cycle of time, there go 800 warriors, to give battle to the antigods in a war of mutual annihilation; 540 times 800 is 43,200. And in Chaldean Babylon, from about the sixth century B.C., it was held that between the imagined time of the first city of the world, Kish, and the coming of the mythological deluge of Utu-napishtim (Noah's predecessor and prototype) there were 432,000 years. To my surprise, one day I discovered the following statement in a popular book on physical culture called *Aerobics*: "A conditioned man, who exercises regularly, will have a resting heart rate of about 60 beats per minute or less...Sixty per minute, times 60 minutes equals 3,600 beats per hour. Times 24 hours, equals 86,400 beats a day."[1]

So our little human days and nights are miniatures of the Great Days and Nights of Brahma, the opening and closing of whose eyes bring forth and dissolve, again and again, all the forms of the universe; the beating of our hearts, meanwhile, remains in accord with the pulse of creation. There is much more to be told of this number, but one more point will suffice; namely, that astronomically, the number of years in one complete cycle of the precession of the equinoxes is 25,920 (one Great, or Platonic, Year), and that this sum, divided by sixty, is 432—sixty being the basic multiple (the so-called *soss*) of the most ancient Mesopotamian mathematical system.

The dating of Patrick's mission suggests, then, that one world era, the pagan, ended, and that a new one, the Christian, began. However, the dating itself suggests that something of the old vision of the universe was taken over: the idea of a single accord informing not only the great universe of the heavens and earth but also the little universe of the individual. This accord was seen as the inspiration of the forms of religious art and rite, so that by contemplating and participating in these, one is put in accord both with the order of the universe and with the ground of one's being. A good deal of evidence suggests that many of the earliest Irish monks had been Druids and *filid*, or bards, before their conversions, and that they brought to their Christianity something of their earlier sense of a common spiritual ground to be recognized, in silent wonder, in themselves and in the natural world all about.

It was something like this that Brendan experienced during his Silent Brotherhood. And when the time came for departure, the angel of the isle provisioned the coracle, and Brendan with his company of twelve sailed back to the Land of Sheep, then back to the Paradise of Birds, and back again to the abbey, and so on, around and around, for the length of forty years. Annually they celebrated Easter on the back of the great fish that remained still for them, till at last the moment came for them to go sailing in their coracle past the very border of hell, where the shadow of Judas sat miserably, and past a very blessed island, where a certain Paul the Hermit dwelt alone in piety, and on then to the Land of Promise itself—which was the loveliest country anyone had seen, with trees full of fruit on every bough and apples ripe all the year.[2]

The mention especially of apples suggests both the classical Hesperides, the western Isles of the Golden Apples, beyond the earthbounding Ocean, and the Celtic Avalon of King Arthur's enduring repose. It is actually everywhere and nowhere, the Earthly Paradise, that place—or, rather, that condition of the experienced world—where the transcendent radiance of that which is beyond form is made visible through, and from within, the forms of all things. This is not a revelation for which one has to wait until the end of time.

In the Gospel according to Mark (in chapter 13, which describes the terrors that should occur in the last days: the sun darkening, the moon failing of its light, stars falling from heaven, the Son of Man coming in clouds, and so on), Jesus is reported to have said, "Truly, I say to you, this generation will not pass away before all these things take place." But actually, that generation did pass away, and many more have passed away, and those things have not taken place. Some theologians speak, therefore, of the "great nonevent." Others—the majority—have reinterpreted the word *generation* of Jesus's prophecy as referring not to Jesus's contemporaries but to the generation of man, meaning that the generation of humankind and the world will pass away with the coming of all these things. That is to say, by taking the mythological symbol of the End of the World concretely and interpreting it as referring to an actual historical event to come, our commentators have postponed it to some undefined future, and we are warned, meanwhile, simply to go to church, receive the sacraments with faith, and await the day.

There is another way, however, an altogether different way, to interpret the End of the World. Some scholars believe Mark 13 to be an interpolated late chapter, misrepresenting whatever words might have been spoken by interpreting them in the sense of the current Jewish apocalyptic hysteria represented in the texts of the Dead Sea Scrolls. And this view of Mark 13 has been now strongly reinforced by the discovery in 1945—in a jar found buried in the Egyptian desert, near the village of Nag Hammadi, on the first sharp bend of the Nile—of a Coptic translation from the Greek of the long-lost Gospel according to Thomas.[3] Here we read in the last saying (*Logos* 113) of Jesus, the following: "His disciples said to Him: When will the Kingdom come? Jesus said: It will not come by expectation; they will not say: 'See, here,' or 'See, there.' But the Kingdom of the Father is spread upon the earth and men do not see it."

The function of art, we might say, is to render a sense of this hidden radiance of the Kingdom, right here and now, among us. And all that is required for the vision is a slight but radical shift in perspective of the eye to bring us to a realization transcendent of the pairs of opposites: *I* and *Thou, right* and *wrong, this* and *that.*

We may read Brendan's voyage, if we like, historically interpreted, as a legend inspired in part by actual Celtic voyages to America. For when the Norse arrived in Iceland in the ninth century A.D., they found there a community of Irish Culdees, or meditating anchorites, already long established, who then moved out, no one knows wither, but not impossibly to Greenland and thence to Canada. There was a climate of relative warmth in those northern regions at that time, as in the centuries also of the Norse settlements. In any case, the abbey of the monks of Brendan's Silent Brotherhood must have been inspired by the model of the Irish Culdees communities, in flight from the noise of the world.

Years ago, when I was involved in the study of North American Indian mythologies, I came upon a number of tales of inexhaustible vessels, and it seemed to me that these were particularly numerous among the Algonquin tribes, and especially the Micmac of Nova Scotia.[4] At the time, I recall, this suggested to me the possibility of some kind of influence from the Celts of Scotia proper, namely

Ireland; and discovering, then, on the map of Nova Scotia, not only the name Cape Breton Island but also, off nearby Newfoundland, a peninsula named Avalon, I found myself, as an Arthurian scholar, very much at home. My reason for mentioning the matter here, however, is not to propose a theory of Saint Brendan's influence on the Micmacs, or of the Algonquin as possible Celts, but to point out that, like the Europeans of this Canada, the Indians, too, have in their background a knowledge of the vessel inexhaustible. Hence, they participate in that knowledge of the mystical ground of consciousness that I have been celebrating as characteristic of the Celts.

FIGURE 5. Troubadour entertaining the court of Alfonso the Wise
(ink on vellum, Spain, thirteenth century)

CHAPTER 3

———————•———————

Theology, Love, Troubadours, and Minnesingers

I'M GOING TO BE TALKING ABOUT THE GRAIL LEGEND, particularly as it appears in Wolfram von Eschenbach's great epic poem, *Parzival* (written c. 1210). To me it is the great mythos of the modern European world. The dates for the emergence of the European spirit in its own terms in this secular literature and mythology are between 1150 and 1250. That's the crucial century here. It's the century, as I've said, of the building of the great cathedrals and also of the flowering of Arthurian romance. Before that date we do not have it; after that date we do not have it. It's a recollection and vestige from that date on.

In this period the European world was reemerging from almost five hundred years of abyssal darkness. The Roman Empire had extended its domain all the way up to Scotland in the period shortly after Caesar's conquest of Gaul. And so Roman civilization had been present and very well developed. All you have to do is visit the city of Bath in England and see the Roman remains there, and those in Spain, in France, and along the Rhine in Germany. Into the Roman world at this time came the great influences of the mystery cults, which were flourishing in the late Alexandrian world of the Near East: the Orphic mysteries, the Mithraic mysteries, the Dionysian mysteries, and others. We've found an enormous number of altars to Mithras all the way from along the Danube and into France and on into England, as well as remains of the Orphic cults throughout Europe at this time.

As we know, in the early days Christianity was generally associated by the classical world with these mystery cults; its mythology—its *miracle*—was essentially equivalent to that of the mysteries. When

Constantine became emperor in the early fourth century, he recognized Christianity as one of the religions of the Roman world, but then shortly thereafter Theodosius I declared that Christianity was the only religion permitted. The great classical temples were torn down. These vestiges of pagan temples that we see all over the Near East and Europe did not come to be ruins by accident. The burning of the library in Alexandria, the closing of the classical philosophical schools in Athens: all these things followed.

Meanwhile, Christian doctrine presented great theological problems, and these were resolved in that series of fourth-, fifth-, and early-sixth-century councils of Chalcedon, Ephesus, Constantinople, and so on. I am referring to the problems of the relationship of the Son to the Father, and the Holy Ghost to his Father and Son, the problem of the birth of God—was Mary the Mother of God, or was she the mother merely of Jesus? Did Jesus become the vehicle at the time of baptism or at conception?—and whatnot. All these difficult and intricate problems were decided by councils of Levantine bishops. There were hardly any European participants in these debates.

The center of gravity of the Roman Empire shifted to Constantinople. Constantinople was an Asian city, not a European one, and the European world fell into a very miserable second place. Of course, the European Roman Empire fell only a generation and a half after its conversion to Christianity, and it was Augustine's problem in *The City of God* to rationalize this disaster. Augustine was a North African, so again we have a non-European perspective.

Meanwhile, a number of heresies were flourishing, two of which are most important for our present point. One is the Pelagian heresy. Pelagius was an Irish monk (here we are in Europe), and the crux of the Pelagian heresy was this: that no one can inherit the sin of another. Consequently, humankind had not inherited the sin of Adam, there is therefore no value in the doctrine of original sin, and therefore man does not have to be saved from original sin. Man can save himself; he does not need the sacraments.

Pelagius believed that having Christ as a model was of great benefit to the Christian world because through that model, the individual could be inspired to that act of will that enables one to release oneself from the darkness of ignorance. But it is not through vicarious grace gained by the Crucifixion of Christ that the individual is to be saved: it is through that person's own will.

This, then, was the first great heresy that Augustine launched himself against. Without original sin, without the inheritance of original sin, the whole doctrine of the necessity for the incarnation is in trouble. But from that individualistic standpoint, with which I have identified Europe, it's impossible to think of this racial heritage of sin, and so we're in a situation there. That's the first point.

The second great heresy was known as the Donatist heresy, which, although it accepted the necessity of the sacraments, argued that sacraments administrated by an unworthy priest do not work. This brought up a terribly difficult problem because it rendered the administration of sacraments questionable all the time: Who knew what the moral condition of the priest was? And again Augustine let go at Donatist heresy with the doctrine of the incorruptibility of the sacraments: that regardless of the priest's character, the sacrament works.

So here we have as the official doctrine the absolute necessity of the sacraments for salvation, since man cannot save himself, because we have inherited original sin and that is only overcome by Christ and Christ's virtue, which is communicated to man only through the sacraments. This doctrine stipulates the absolute necessity of man accepting the sacraments from the Church, which is the only authorized organization to administer them, and stipulates as well the absolute freedom of the clergy to behave any way it wanted in administering the sacraments. That may have been all right in the fifth century and sixth centuries, but by the twelfth century the clergy had become notoriously immoral. Pope Innocent III himself called his clergy a sty of swine. Their behavior was disgraceful, and yet these men held the keys to heaven, and everyone had to submit to them.

Now, this question of a clergy misbehaving and forcing beliefs on people brought about a condition that was spiritually terrible, and this is the condition represented in the mythological image of the Waste Land, which is the basic motif of the Grail romances.

The basic theme of the Grail romance is of a king, a Fisher King. Christ had said, "I will make you fishers of men." The pope's ring is called the fisherman's ring, and it bears a picture of a great draft of fishes. The Fisher King has been very seriously wounded, and as a result of the wound, the land is laid waste. The central problem of the

Grail romance is to heal the Fisher King. The goal of the Grail hero is to heal that wound, but he is to do so without knowing *how* he is to do so. He is to be a perfect innocent, not to know the rules of the quest, and he is to ask spontaneously, "What is the matter?"

With respect to life in the domestic sphere, marriages in the Middle Ages were marriages of convenience, made sacred by those clergymen in the sacrament of marriage. Love posed a danger to that. Woman was called the Gate of Hell because of her seductive beauty and the danger of love. This situation of a sacramentalized marriage without love being the norm brought about a powerful reaction in the aristocratic circles, and this is the reaction represented in troubadour poetry and its ideal of love.

I want to say a word about these ideals of love that were in the air at that time. There were in the Christian tradition two loves in opposition: love that was known as *eros* or erotic passion, and love known as *agapē*, which was spiritual love, of the love-thy-neighbor sort. Both these loves are impersonal. "Love thy neighbor as thyself" means that no matter who your neighbor is, you must love him or her as yourself. Also, it is the basic nature of *agapē* that you don't select whom you're going to love; the love of Christ is for all.

Eros, the antipode to this, is also basically impersonal; it is the zeal of the organs for each other. It is purely a biological situation, not always a personal one. And during the great festivals, orgies were the typical manifestation of this, where it didn't matter whom you found as long as the person was of the opposite sex, and there were actually cult situations in which this pattern was developed. So we have these basically impersonal loves.

The love idea of the troubadours was completely different from either of these; it's a third idea; it is not love in the dark, you might say. The Provençal troubadour Girhault de Borneilh, who flourished in the middle and end of the twelfth century, epitomized the troubadour ideal. There were many, many arguments, debates in verse, as to whether the eyes or the heart were the prime factor in love.

Borneilh synthesized the two traditions in the following way. Love, he declared, is born of the eyes *and* the heart. The eyes are the scouts of the heart. They are looking for an appropriate object of beauty; that is to say, they are selective. This is discriminative, this is elite, this is personal choice, and having found their image, the eyes recommend that image to the heart—not to just any heart but to the noble heart, the gentle heart, the heart capable of love; this is not a case of sheer lust. When these three, the two eyes and the heart, are in accord, love is born. Love is born of the eyes and the heart; it is an individual experience. The eyes quest in the outer world for the object of inspiration, and the heart receives the image, and this image then becomes the idol of individual devotion.[1]

Exactly at this time in Spain, just over the border from the Provençal courts, as well as in Sicily and in the Near East, there flourished the great Sufi movement, the mystical tradition of Islam, very powerfully influenced by that of India. Exactly at this period in India we see the flowering of the great erotic mystical cults. The great poem in celebration of this is the *Gītā Govinda* of Jayadeva, *The Song of the Cow Herd*, celebrating the love of Kṛṣṇa for Radha. That poem was written about 1172, almost the same date as the Tristan stories. Meanwhile, in the Fujiwara courts of Kyoto, Lady Murasaki wrote *The Tale of Genji*; the love theme (*aware*) in Japanese aristocratic circles was associated with cosmic love.

In Oriental love, the woman becomes the vessel of a supernatural power of a transcendent energy, whereas in the European cult she is adored for herself, not as a symbol of anything. Furthermore, in the Orient the woman was very often of inferior caste—not in Japan, but in India, and in the Sufi world—and it was exactly that loss of contact with the social order that represented the plunge into the divine, sacred sphere that is beyond social norms. Not so in the European sphere, where the woman was honored for herself, and she was usually of at least as high a station as the poet or the worshipper.

All these loves were adulterous. It is absolutely basic to courtly love, as it was to the love in India and Sufism and Japan, that it *should* be adulterous. In the little courts that grew, called the courts of love, noble ladies made decisions in cases that had been brought to them. For example, there's one account of a young man who declared that the lady whom he addressed was bound to accept him because she had told him formally that she already had a lover, but that when this other man was no longer her lover, he would be next on her list. *Well*, he said, *she has now* married *that man, so here I am!* And the court decided absolutely that since love is incompatible with marriage, the lady could not be said to be in love with her husband, and that therefore this lover is eligible. Here you get the challenge of personal love to the impersonal sacrament. Marriage was regarded as a violation of love, and when you think of the Provençal and the Latin word for love, *amor*, and spell it backward, you get *Roma*. Rome was regarded as representing the exact opposite principle to love—and love was held to be the higher principle.

It is against this background that German knight and poet Wolfram von Eschenbach appeared. The troubadours' solution to the problem seemed inadequate to him. The tension between the socially accepted and the actual experience of love was not to be endured. And so in *Parzival*, his telling of the Grail romance, his hero and heroine represent the refutation, you might say, both of the ecclesiastical *and* of the troubadour approaches.

The minnesingers of Germany received the tradition of love from the troubadours. They are of a slightly later generation, but as always in the German sphere they found a depth in these themes that the French had failed to recognize. They recognized that this power of *amor* was indeed divine. It wasn't simply a secular thing but contained the compulsion of the goddess Venus. The word *Minne* in German is a reference to this kind of love, and *minnesinger* means "singer of love." The greatest of all these poets was Walter von der Vogelweide, a delightful figure whose poetry is simply delicious. Walter speaks of the goddess Minne in her power, in her majesty, and so here you're on the brink of a religion of love.

This religion of love was actually rendered most powerfully, I would say, in the *Tristan* of Gottfried von Strassburg. Gottfried's poem was left incomplete when he died in 1210. In this story (which I will discuss in depth in chapter 5), the potion that Tristan and Iseult drink represents the breakthrough of compulsive love. The *Tristan* story—the story of how Tristan was wounded by the uncle of Iseult, whose sword was poisoned by a poison fabricated by Iseult's mother, and how the cure for this poisoned wound could be derived only from the woman who had fashioned the poison—was one of the great stories of the Arthurian tradition. Tristan by device finds himself in the court of Iseult's mother, whose name also is Iseult, in Ireland, and she cures him. And he becomes the younger Iseult's harp teacher and is so fascinated by her that when he goes back home he does nothing but sing the praise of Iseult. He recommends her to his uncle King

Mark, the bachelor king, as a proper queen. So what you have here is a person utterly in love who hasn't recognized love—this is the real fault of Tristan. Iseult was also in love, only she didn't know it either. Then Tristan's sent back to get Iseult, and on the way to King Mark they drink by accident what they think is wine, and the compulsive takeover of love occurs. Then they are torn between colliding virtues: the virtue of love and the virtue of honor.

That's the situation when Wolfram turns to the Grail romance. As we've seen, all these Arthurian romances are based on old Celtic myths. The knights and ladies, wizards and witches, of these tales are the gods and heroes and heroines and goddesses of Celtic mythology. We can identify them, the themes, the incidents, and all; there's no doubt about it. The Arthurian characters are really gods—as we all are, according to this view—and the relationships of these people to one another are the relationships of the myths. Our problem is simply recognizing this identity. We are all undergoing the mythological adventure without even knowing it, just as Tristan and Iseult didn't realize that the goddess Minne had come to their shrine.

Gottfried goes so far in his celebration of Minne that when he takes his couple away from the court and brings them to the forest, he brings them to a cave that was fashioned by pagans in ancient times. The cave was created in the style of a chapel; it is the chapel of love, and where the altar should be is this crystalline bed of love. He actually uses the words of the Mass and the words of Bernard of Clairvaux, the great mystic celebrant of the love of the Virgin, to deify his couple and to sanctify their love. The bed is the altar; the altar is a bed. Augustine himself brought forth that image. It is on the altar that Christ is brought into the bread and wine by the miraculous words of the priest: *Hoc est enim corpus meum,* "this is my body." Christ comes to life there on the altar, so the altar is the bed of Christ's birth, and Christ is sacrificed on the altar, so the altar is the Calvary cross of the sacrifice: it is birth and death, which are the same.

There are beautiful fourteenth-century paintings of the Annunciation in which the angel Gabriel is carrying the caduceus of Hermes, the guide of souls to rebirth, and he is announcing to the blessed Virgin that she is to be the mother of God. And on a beam of light from the sky comes the little child Christ to his mother, this tiny little manikin, and on his shoulder he's bearing the cross. The idea is that

FIGURE 6. Galahad, Bors, and Percival seeing the Grail
(print, England, 1911)

Christ's coming already contained the acceptance of the agony, the
terror-joy of life, which is itself the Crucifixion. These are the themes
that inhabit this mythology.

One might ask why anyone should quest for the Grail in the
twelfth century when anywhere you turned was a little church where
the Mass was celebrated every morning, with Christ himself on the
altar and with you there to receive communion. The answer is that
the priest was ordained by a sacrament and that anybody who simply
follows the routine rituals is eligible to receive the host and made eligible for heaven by making good confession and proper contrition and
all that. What has this got to do with the development of character?
What has this got to do with the integrity of your life? What has this
got to do with bringing forth the potentialities and rendering them
glorious in the world? Nothing.

The Grail hero must achieve his result through character, through
the integrity of character, and the clergy plays no role whatsoever. The

Grail is not in a church; it's in a castle. The keeper of the Grail is a king, not a clergyman. The carrier of the Grail is a woman, the Grail Maiden, and she is accompanied by maidens, and it is required of these maidens that they should be absolutely pure in virtue. In other words, this is a direct challenge to the Church in the twelfth century, and it was understood to be such, so that when the Inquisition was instituted in the beginning of the thirteenth century, we hear no more of the Arthurian romances for a while.

PART TWO

KNIGHTS IN QUEST

FIGURE 7. Wolfram von Eschenbach (artist's representation of ink on vellum, Germany, thirteenth century)

CHAPTER 4

Wolfram von Eschenbach's
Parzival

PARZIVAL BY WOLFRAM VON ESCHENBACH is a truly magnificent work—in my opinion, the greatest of the Middle Ages, surpassing even that of Dante.[1] I think of it as a cathedral of love, celebrating the mystery in its many facets. This was the legend that inspired Wagner, though he greatly changed its character and meaning by turning Parzival into a Galahad and eliminating the Grail Queen and Grail Maidens. Nor does he open his stage to the great scenes of Oriental crusade that in Wolfram's poem are of the essence. For whereas the legend in Chrétien de Troyes's *Perceval, le Conte del Graal* unfolds in the usual never-never land of Arthurian romance, Wolfram has his heroes participate in the actual historical events of his time. And this was the high period of the Crusades. The poet himself was a Bavarian knight—Bavaria, it is worth noting, being the area from which the Celts originally sprang.

Sometime around 1000 B.C., the people of what is known to historians as the Hallstatt culture began spreading both eastward and westward, out of the lands that are now part of Austria and southern Germany. By 500 B.C., those of the westward migration had developed in France and northern Switzerland a new and brilliant culture, known as La Tène. It was these Celts who, in that period, invaded Rome. They entered the British Isles about the second century B.C. with their priests and magicians, the Druids. There they became assimilated with the earlier inhabitants, the people of that wonderful cosmic image of the great heartbeat of the universe, which—as I have already shown, was known as well to India as to Europe—its cycles

35

of 432,000 years being a feature of both the Indian Purāṇas and the Icelandic *Grimmismol.*

Wolfram had the gift of recognizing in the materials of his legend the numerous analogies with the various Oriental mystical traditions that were becoming known to the crusaders of his day. Indeed, one of the great aims of his thinking was to span the breach of the two worlds. He seems not to have gone on crusade himself, but there were reports coming back into Europe, not only from returning crusaders but also from the Genoese and other returning merchants of the time, whose trade connections extended far into the great East, beyond Palestine, Syria and Egypt, into Iraq, Iran, India, and even Central Asia. We have to remember, furthermore, that throughout that period the forces of Islam were engaged in serious warfare, not only with the peoples of Europe, in Spain, and of the Near East, but also with those of Hindu and Buddhist India. Their conquest of India had begun in earnest about the year 1001, and by 1200 they had reached Bengal. Indian and Muslim ideas as well as merchandise were in widespread circulation. Indeed, already in the year 1085, with the conquest of Toledo by Alfonso VI of León and Castile, the gates of Oriental poetry and song, mysticism and learning, had been opened to the courts and monasteries of Europe. And the mystics of Islam, meanwhile, the Shi'ites and the Sufis, had been absorbing influences from India. In southern France the neo-Manichaean Albigensian heresy was rife, inspired by the teachings of the third-century Persian prophet Manes, who had combined in one harmonious system Zoroastrian, Buddhist, and Christian ideas. It required a full-size crusade within Europe itself to eradicate that heresy: the infamous Albigensian Crusade, instituted by Pope Innocent III in the very years of Wolfram's writing of *Parzival.* And if Innocent was not his model for the malignant, castrated magician of the Waste Land, Clinschor (Wagner's Klingsor), I have missed my guess.

GAHMURET

Parzival begins with Parzival's father, whose name is Gahmuret, a very forthright and courageous son of a king. His older brother inherits the throne and invites Gahmuret to share it with him, but Gahmuret says, "No, I want to earn my own life. I do not simply accept my life from

others. I will go forth on adventure myself." This is point number
one: Gahmuret consciously sets out on his own adventure, not the
one prescribed for him.

FIGURE 8. Gahmuret
(print, United States, 1912)

He does go forth and arrives in Baghdad, where he becomes a
champion of the caliph, who was very famous at that time, and a very
saintly man as well. Gahmuret's fame spreads throughout the Islamic
world, and then he leaves the caliph and goes on a voyage farther into
its depths, until he arrives in a sort of mythological echo of India, in
the land of Zazamanc, where the people are black. And he marries,
saving Belkane, the besieged queen of Zazamanc, and becomes her
king.

Belkane turns out to be quite the matriarch, marvelously described:
she comes in wearing all the jewels of the East and a fabulous crown
made of a ruby that's like a big bubble placed over her head, with her
dark face shining through. And when these two greet each other, the
light of their eyes meet, and their hearts are graced with love, so he
becomes her husband. But she does not allow him to fight anymore;
she isn't going to have her husband, her king, getting killed in battle.
But he prefers battle to anything else, and so one dark night he takes
ship and sails away. The queen is left abandoned and gives birth to
her child, whose name is Feirefiz. He is black and white, piebald like a

magpie, and, in lament for her husband and in nostalgic love for him, when she sees her little child, she kisses him over and over again on all the white spots.

Wolfram had opened his story with this statement: life is both black and white; it cannot be all one or the other. Living your life irresolutely tends to increase the black. Living with resolution and determination moves you toward the white. But no matter what you do, it's going to be both black and white, and the world is going to criticize you—but be resolute! So the primary virtue of Wolfram's heroes is resolution. The black queen of Zazamanc is in mourning, thinking that her lover has died as a result of her irresolution in accepting his love. She doesn't know that Gahmuret, desperate to show what a wonderful hero he is, has ridden into battle without armor.

Gahmuret survives and returns to Europe, where the white queen of Wales—a virgin queen without a husband—seems to have gotten sick and tired of waiting for somebody to propose to her, so she has arranged a tournament, of which she (and her kingdom) would be the prize. All the princes of all the lands of Europe have come to compete. They're all there, all the Arthurian heroes. It's a grand, grand affair. And the queen is sitting in her window looking out at the knights as they're assembling on the field, pitching their pavilions, and her page says to her, "Look at that pavilion over there, your whole realm isn't worth that much. It had required forty horses to transport it." It was the pavilion of the king of Zazamanc, namely Gahmuret, who becomes the winner of the event.

When he returned to Europe, Gahmuret learned of the deaths of his brother and mother, so he is rather melancholy. Even so, he wins the tournament even before it begins, in what were called the vesper games. The knights started warming up on the field before the official start, and they warmed up so wonderfully that the whole thing developed into a battle, and spears were splintering, like snow on the field, all over the place, and Gahmuret comes off the victor before the official battle even begins. There he is, sitting in his pavilion, when he receives a letter from the queen of France saying, "You really are supposed to come to me," when in comes beaming Herzeloyde, the queen of Wales, and says, "You've won. I'm yours."

And he says, "Just a minute now, this wasn't an official fight, and besides, I'm married. I have an Islamic wife."

Herzeloyde says, "You'll have to get rid of that pagan wife and be married according to Christian custom."

Finally, by argument and legal address, she wins him over, and the text says that she takes him by the hand, and he dismisses his sorrow, and she her maidenhead. However, as Wolfram put it, the blade of her happiness breaks at the hilt. Gahmuret receives word that the caliph of Baghdad is in dire straits, so he goes to give battle in the caliph's cause and is killed. In great sorrow, Herzeloyde departs.

PARZIVAL

After Gahmuret's death, Queen Herzeloyde dismisses her court, goes into the forest, and brings her child up ignorant of who he is, ignorant of his noble heritage, ignorant of war, ignorant of the court, ignorant even of his name. She calls him *bon fils, cher fils, beau fils* ("good son, dear son, beautiful son"), and that's all he ever hears of himself. He grows up in the forest in the beginning of this great adventure, a child of nature: sheer nature, no culture. When he hears the birds sing, they fill his breast with such joy that he makes himself a little bow

FIGURE 9. Parzival sees three knights (print, United States, 1912)

and arrow and shoots them, and then, when he sees them dead, he can only weep. But their song excites him, so he shoots them some more. This is the way human beings are! And his mother has told him nothing of his background but only about God, how God is good and loyal and must be worshipped, while the Devil is bad and must be despised.

When Parzival reaches the age of sixteen or so, he is wandering the hills when he hears hoofbeats. These are the first hoofbeats he's ever heard, and he thinks there must be devils coming. And there appear three knights in flashing armor, and he thinks these must be angels, so he gets down on his knees to pray to them, when their lord, a great prince, arrives with bells ringing from his armor. He's absolutely glorious, with feathers and such adorning him, and here's this country bumpkin praying on his knees, "Oh, Lord, give me help!"

So the knight courteously says, "We're not angels and divinities, young man, we're knights."

"What are knights?" he asks. His heart is rising in excitement because he is knightly in his character, and his father was a great knight. He learns what knights are. He learns what swords are for. He learns about lances. And he learns about Arthur's court, where knights are made.

When he tells his mother that he intends to join Arthur's knights, she faints. Once she recovers, she thinks, *Well, I'll fix it up so he'll disgrace himself and be sent back to me.* So she dresses him in a fool's costume, with a long cloak of raw hemp pants that come halfway down his legs, tied to the shirt, and big, bulky, raw leather shoes. She finds the stupidest horse in the neighborhood and sits him on it. She also gives him certain instructions. She says, "When you come to streams, cross at the shallowest point." Now, the characteristic of this young man is that he does what he's told—this is his first fault.

He takes his javelins and goes riding off to King Arthur's court. When he comes to a stream that Wolfram says a rooster could have crossed, he rides along beside it until he comes to the shallowest point, and then he goes across. His mother also told him, "When you see a fair lady obtain a ring from her, and a kiss. When you see people with gray hair ask them for advice. And when you meet people on the road greet them by saying, 'God be with you.'"

FIGURE 10. Parzival rides forth (print, United States, 1912)

So this lout crosses the stream, and there on a plain before him he sees a beautiful pavilion. Entering the pavilion he finds a young wife named Jeschute (French, *je chute:* "I fall"). She is alone, sleeping on a bed with her bedclothes down, and, as Wolfram says, God had fashioned that body. This youth sees that she has a ring, so he pounces on the bed to get the ring and a kiss also, and this poor woman wakes up with this thing bouncing around on the bed trying to get her ring off and grab a kiss. He's a husky boy! So he succeeds. And then he sees a sandwich on a shelf and he makes a meal of what she has. Then he jumps on her for another kiss, and sees that she has a brooch, so he takes the brooch and rides off.

Her husband, Prince Orilus, returns in enormous indignation and does not believe that she hasn't been violated by this fellow. So he tears her clothes to pieces, and when he's done, he smashes up her saddle. Then he says, "You get on this horse!" and she has to ride off on this poor nag, with him before her, racing after this youth who's ridden off.

That's the first act of this ignorant boy—naive, destructive, and violent. He's a brute. He is riding along and comes upon a woman seated with a dead knight on her lap, lamenting. Parzival rides up to her, and she says, "Who are you?"

He says, "My name is *bon fils, cher fils, beau fils.*"

She recognizes that formula: she is his aunt Sigune, his mother's sister, and the knight who's dead on her lap has been killed defending Wales, the land that Parzival himself should have been defending. She tells him who he is and what his name is: Parzival. And she renders it in terms of a French translation that Wolfram invents: *perce le val,* through the middle, between the pair of opposites, between black and white. Wolfram's own coat of arms was a coat of two flags flying in opposite directions, and his helmet and shield had these two prongs. The theme of his whole story is about going right through the middle, between black and white, incorporating both, without going to this side or that.

Parzival tells his aunt that he's looking for Arthur's court, and she's afraid of what will happen to him there, so she misdirects him, and he goes down the road, greeting everybody with a "God be with you," until at nightfall he finally arrives at a fisherman's hut. Now, this fisherman is a very interesting figure: Anfortas the Fisher King, the Grail King whom Parzival is going to encounter later. But right now Parzival is just biologically motivated, a little animal, you might say, looking for fame and success. So when the boy comes in and asks, "Will you put me up for the night?" the fisherman says, "No, I won't; I don't want anything to do with you."

"Well," Parzival says, "how about this brooch?"—the wonderful brooch that the boy stole from the young woman. The fisherman accepts it and offers him great hospitality that night and then conducts him to Arthur's court.

As Parzival approaches the castle, he sees riding out of its portal a knight in bright red armor with a golden goblet in his hand. This is a great and famous champion, King Ither of Kukumerlant, who has just seized the cup from Arthur's table in token of his claim to a portion of Arthur's kingdom, and with a challenge to the court to avenge the insult he's just given by sending a champion to meet him in the jousting yard.

Parzival rides into the castle, led by a young page.

There's a woman in Arthur's court named Cunneware de Lalant who has never laughed. A prophecy decrees that when she sees the greatest knight in the world, she will laugh, and indeed, as Parzival enters, she breaks out laughing hysterically. This irritates Keie, Arthur's foster brother, so much that he flogs her, and when Parzival sees this happen, he says, "I'm going to avenge that." And out he goes.

He sees Ither, the Red Knight, so he gets on his nag and trots toward him. When the knight sees this kid coming as the champion of Arthur's court (a true knight, you know, wouldn't soil the front part of his lance on the lout), he just turns his lance backside to and gives Parzival a *biff* that knocks both Parzival and the horse over. But Parzival takes his javelin, and *zing*, sends it through the eyepiece of the knight, killing him right there on his horse, just like that. That's his first great deed, but this is not a knightly act.

The little page who had brought Parzival into the court comes rushing out and sees him dragging this knight around, trying to take off the armor. Parzival doesn't know how to get it off. The page helps him get the armor off and puts it on him. But Parzival won't take off the clothes that his mother gave him. Here he is clothed as a knight, yet underneath is this fool's costume. He's then taught by the page how to hold the lance and sword, but the page says, "You can't take those javelins with you; that's not a knightly weapon."

So Parzival gets on Ither's horse, a big Castilian, which goes galloping, galloping, galloping all day, out of the castle and across the countryside, because young Parzival hasn't learned how to stop it. The horse just rides off with him. This theme of the horse leading the way will return.

The horse then brings him to the beautiful little castle of a knight named Gurnemanz. Wagner's Gurnemanz opens the opera by introducing Parzival to the Grail Castle, but in Wolfram's text—and this is important—this knight has nothing to do with the Grail.

The boy's horse finally stops before the knight, who has a little hawk on his hand, and when Parzival sees that the knight has gray hair, he says, "I come to ask you for advice."

"Well," the knight says, "if you're going to ask for advice, I must have your assurance that you're not going to try to take this castle."

FIGURE 11. Gurnemanz and his daughter (print, United States, 1912)

Parzival says, "You have it."

The knight brings him inside, and when Gurnemanz and his daughter take the red armor off, what they find inside simply mortifies everybody in the castle. But Parzival is such a beautiful youth that they accept him, and Gurnemanz gives him lessons in knightly conduct. He coaches Parzival in handling himself on a horse and in jousting and in all the knightly forms of combat, so that in a few weeks this extremely gifted youth becomes a full knight under the surveillance and supervision of this knight-coach. Gurnemanz instructs him in knightly rules, which will unfortunately lead to a few more mistakes on Parzival's part: "Don't do this, don't do that, and above all, *don't ask too many questions.*" That's the rule that proves to be Parzival's downfall later.

Gurnemanz then offers his daughter's hand to Parzival. His three sons have been killed in combat, so he sees in Parzival a fourth son. But Parzival—and here is the point—feels that he must not simply accept a marriage, not simply accept a castle, simply accept a life: like his father before him, he must *earn* it. Here we come to the first critical test of this unintentional savior to be. Throughout the Orient, throughout all antiquity, and throughout the Middle Ages, families arranged marriages; brides were given to grooms. This young man thought, however, that before receiving a wife and enjoying her love, he should fashion himself into something and gain her through an act of his own will. In the poet's words: "He sensed in noble striving a lofty aim for both this life and beyond."[2] And there follows a gentle, gracious scene, in which the old knight bids the magnificent youth adieu and watches him ride away.

Now we come to the next stage of the story. Parzival is now not only a competent but a superb knight, a youth of great battle prowess and nobility who has been trained by a first-rate mentor in the arts and courtesies of knighthood. Thus he rides forth, letting his horse take him where it will, with the reins loose. If we take the horse and rider as symbolic, respectively, of instinctive nature and controlling mind, this suggests a trust, on Parzival's part, in the life force itself as an adequate guide. His horse takes him down a great slope, following a stream to the water's edge, where there is a rickety wicker bridge, and across from it is a castle. The castle is under siege, and it's the castle of a young queen, Condwiramurs (French: *conduire amour,* "lead to love"), who, like the fairy queens of the Celtic Sidhe, is in trouble.

Parzival is given entry, relieved of his armor, and dressed in a wonderful mantle, of the kind of greeting clothing given in castles. But since he was told by Gurnemanz not to speak unless spoken to, he sits there like a lout.

Condwiramurs thinks, *Well, I guess as hostess it would be all right for me to talk,* so she asks him a couple of questions, and he replies.

When he goes to bed and falls asleep, he is awakened by Condwiramurs kneeling at his bedside, and he says, "Lady, are you mocking me? One kneels only to God."

She says, "Well, if you'll promise not to wrestle with me I'll get into bed with you."

And he says, "All right, that would be fine."

And neither he nor she, states the poet, has any notion of joining in love. Parzival lacks, in fact, all knowledge of the art, and she, desperate and ashamed, came in misery. In tears, she tells him of her plight: A neighboring king, Clamide, sent an army under his seneschal, Kingrun, to appropriate her land, when he would himself arrive and, in the good old way, make her his wife. "But I am ready," she

FIGURE 12. Condwiramurs
(print, United States, 1912)

says, "to kill myself before surrendering my body to Clamide. You
have seen the towers of my palace. I would cast myself into the moat."

This is the medieval marriage problem. The point is that she has
resisted the system and demands to marry for love only. She desires
marriage for love—not marriage and then adulterous love. This is the
beginning of Wolfram's solution to the problem of reconciling the
troubadour tradition with that of the minnesinger.

Parzival readily promises to get rid of Kingrun in the morning,
and when dawn comes, he rides as the Red Knight from the castle
gate for his first battle. And before another half hour passes, Kingrun,
whose fame in the world is great, lies on his back, with Parzival's knee
on his chest.

Now, Gurnemanz instructed him that when an enemy has been
knocked down and pleads for mercy, a proper knight would not kill
him but take his vow of service. So when this great knight is knocked
down and pleads for *merçi*, Parzival sends him to Arthur's court to be
in the service of Cunneware, the woman who was beaten by Keie—
Parzival said he was going to avenge the wrong done to her, and now

he has. He will do this with every knight he defeats, and there are many.

So now all these great knights of world fame are coming to Camelot, all beaten up by the Red Knight, who was the laughingstock of their community when he was there. The news keeps coming that this chap Parzival is a force to be reckoned with, and Arthur's beginning to think that this is somebody for the Round Table.

When Condwiramurs's hero returns from his victory, he sees that Condwiramurs has put her hair up in the way of a married matron. She embraces him before all; her citizens pay him homage, and she declares him to be her lord and theirs.

That night they are again in bed together, but, as Wolfram says, "He lay with her so decently that not many a lady nowadays would have been satisfied with such a night." Yet she thinks of herself as his wife.

Two days and two nights more they are together in this way, until, on the third night, he remembers that his mother said to take a kiss from a girl, and so they touch, and as Wolfram is very gentle and discreet, he says, "They found it sweet and from then on that was their custom."

The point is that the marriage took place in the psyche first, and the physical realization of their love was the fulfillment of a spiritual marriage; it did not work the other way around. No priest confirmed the marriage. It was confirmed in love and was itself the sacrament of love. And neither lust nor fear, but courage and compassion, were its motivations, indifference to social opinion having been a prerequisite to its occurrence. What their world would have called "good marriages" both rejected; and thus Parzival's first great step away from the Waste Land of the way of the world has been accomplished.

The two remain together for fifteen months. Condwiramurs bears a son and is pregnant with a second when her husband asks permission to leave to see how things are going with his mother, not knowing that she died soon after he took his leave of her. His wife cannot deny him, and it is thus that his next adventure begins: the Quest of the Castle of the Grail.

In contrast to the version of the Cistercian *Queste*, in which the hero is the virgin Galahad, in Wolfram's romance, the Grail hero is a married man and father whose adventure is to be the fulfillment of a

FIGURE 13. The Grail
Castle (print, United
States, 1912)

life already lived well in the world rather than of one consecrated to renunciation.

With that power of life in full flower, Parzival goes riding in quest for his mother, when he comes to a lake, and floating on the lake is a boat, and in the boat are two men fishing. One is the Fisher King, with peacock plumes flowing from his helmet. (The peacock sheds its feathers in the wintertime and then grows them back again and thus reflects the round of the seasons. The peacock's tail, with those eyes, is symbolic of the nighttime heavens. Also, the single eye in the feather symbolizes the interior, third eye of the passage to the spiritual realm.)

Parzival calls out, asking where he might find lodging for the night, and the one richly clad replies that he knows of no habitation but one within thirty miles. He then directs the rider: "If you'll go up that path, turn left, then ride up the hill and don't have a misadventure and lose your way, you'll find a castle. But have a care," he adds. "The roads here lead astray; no one knows whereto. If you arrive, I shall be your host."

FIGURE 14. The Fisher King
(print, England, 1911)

For this is Anfortas, the Grail King, known also as the Fisher King
and the Maimed King (Old French, *entfertez, enfermetez*: "infirmity").
This whole place is an apparition that has appeared to Parzival because
he's ready for it. People have ridden through that wilderness time and
time again and never encountered the castle. Parzival sees the castle; it
is *his* castle, his destiny. He is in readiness, and he enters.

He is received, and a great procession takes place, with the king
lying there wounded. In an immense hall, Parzival witnesses the ceremonial of the Grail. There are many knights on couches, all about.
Anfortas is borne in on a litter.

Why is the king wounded? Here's a critical point: this king's name
is Anfortas, from an old French word *enfertez*, which means "infirmity." He received his position by inheritance; he had not earned it.
Here again we have this business of receiving by anointment. As a
young man, like all young men, he was moved to love, and he rode
forth with the war cry *amor*. That is not proper for the Grail King.
The Grail King should have got past that.

So Anfortas was riding forth, and he encountered a heathen who had ridden from the gates of paradise in quest of the Grail; he had the words *The Grail* written on his spear. And the heathen knight wounded Anfortas, piercing him through the genitals, emasculating him with that spear. Anfortas lost his biological virility, yet he killed the heathen. So here is the pair of opposites, nature and the spirit in collision with each other, as they were in the Middle Ages in Europe, a condition that brought about the Waste Land. The king's whole land was laid waste by this terrific blow. Yet he manages to get back to his castle and is brought to behold the Grail, which keeps people alive.

Wolfram's Grail is a stone; it is not a cup. In the Grail romance of Chrétien de Troyes, a slightly earlier one than Wolfram's, the Grail is a kind of bowl. Interpreting the Grail as the chalice of the Last Supper is a deviant tradition that stems from a slightly later Cistercian monastic version of the Grail story. And in that tradition, too, the lance in the castle is equated with the lance that pierced Christ's side. This story of the Grail of the Last Supper and the lance of the Crucifixion having been brought to England by Joseph of Arimathea, in whose tomb Christ was buried, is a monastic legend, and the hero of the Grail of the monastic tradition is another hero entirely, namely, Galahad. *Galahad* is a word from the Old Testament meaning "mountain of witness," and it is understood to mean a mountain of witness to Christ. The whole tradition of the Grail Knight as a virgin knight belongs to a Cistercian monastic line, whereas Wolfram's version is a secular one of a knight who is married, and, as we're going to see, it's because of his loyalty to his marriage under all circumstances; his courage, fearlessness, and resolution in combat; and his integrity in love that he finally becomes the Grail King and heals Anfortas and the land.

The problem of Parzival at the castle is this: Here's this great procession of maidens, bearing candles and clothed in elaborately symbolic colors. They present the king with various tokens, of which the last is the Grail itself, the Joy of Paradise. The Grail is carried in on cloth-of-gold by a radiant Grail Queen, clothed in Arabian silk, and her name is Repanse de Schoye (French, *Réponse de Joie:* "Joyous Answer"). A hundred tables are carried in to be set before all the couches. "And I have been told," states Wolfram, "and I pass it on to you, that whatever one reached one's hand to take, it was found there before the Grail."

FIGURE 15. Parzival holding his peace (print, United States, 1912)

Parzival remarks upon all this and the anguish of his host, and is moved by compassion to ask about the king's sorrow. If he were to ask that question, the land would be healed, the king would be healed, and joy would abound—but he doesn't, because Gurnemanz counseled him not to ask too many questions. So he holds his peace.

"For that I pity him," states Wolfram, "and I pity, too, his sweet host, whom divine displeasure does not spare, when a mere question would have set him free."

Nevertheless, very politely, at the end the king says, "I think it's bedtime." The queen, along with twenty-four attendant maidens, advances, bows to Parzival and his host, takes up the Grail, and leaves the hall. The ceremony has ended. The room clears, and the guest is courteously conducted by four maidens to his room, where he is seen to bed with wine and fruits of the kind that grow in Paradise.

And he sleeps long but has threatening, terrible dreams. The quest has failed. For the first time in his life Parzival has suppressed the impulse of his heart in deference to an alien social ideal: his public image as a proper knight. The baleful impulse of the motivating principle responsible for the wasting of the Waste Land itself has cut off in Parzival an impulse of his nature. *Dharma,* "duty," the last temptation of the Buddha, the force of social opinion, has turned him from his noble course, and thereby has compromised the authenticity of his life.

When Parzival wakes up in the morning, the castle is completely silent. There's nobody around. His armor is beside the bed, but he has to put it on alone. He goes out to find that his horse has been tethered to a post. He mounts his horse and, as he crosses the drawbridge, it is raised up so fast that the horse has to jump over, and a voice from the battlements calls out, "Ride on, you goose!" In Wagner's opera, at the end of one of the scenes when Parzival fails to answer the question, Gurnemanz says to him, "Go on you gander, find a goose!"[3] That is exactly the opposite mood to Wolfram's. Wolfram's theme is the integrity of love in marriage—not *agapē,* but *amor.*

What has happened so far? Our lout has become a knight of great honor; he has found the proper woman for him and recognized her immediately. They have accepted each other in virtue and in permanent marriage, and then he has ridden forth. He has accomplished the worldly adventure of fame and marriage and now has come to the spiritual adventure, the one of asking the question, one that involves the Bodhisattva realization of compassion for all suffering beings.

This spiritual adventure begins when Parzival is dismissed in this very telling way from the Grail Castle. Riding once more into the forest, he comes across that woman again, his aunt Sigune, with the dead knight on her knees. Her hair is now gone; she's bald. And when he approaches her, she curses him, asking why he hadn't the heart to ask the question that would heal the king and redeem the Waste Land. His nature prompted him many times to ask the question, but he thought of his knightly honor. He thought of his reputation instead

FIGURE 16. Leaving the Grail Castle (watercolor, United States, 1912)

of his true nature. The social ideal interfered with his nature, and the result is desolation.

The bald woman says, "You are a curse on the face of the earth, and you have cursed the earth; it has lost its fertility and the whole world is desolate; the castle has disappeared, and you will not find it again!"

He says, "I will repair this."

But she says, "You can't. No one can ever visit the castle a second time."

So with this Parzival turns away in anger from her. He sees hoofprints and looks down the road, and there's a woman all in tatters riding on a nag. She is Jeschute, the young woman from whom Parzival took the brooch, and behind her rides her jealous husband, Orilus. She looks at him and says, "I've seen you before and I hope the world has treated you better than you've treated me." This is the woman of the tent, along with her husband, who is in quest of this fellow who stole his wife's brooch and her kisses, and, he believes, even more. And when Parzival's horse sees the mare on which the woman is riding, he whinnies, and the knight turns around and without a word comes charging at Parzival. And the two go at each other, while Jeschute wrings her hands, hoping that nobody will get hurt.

Parzival, of course, ends up on top and takes the knight in service, swearing to him on a relic that they find nearby in a little hermitage that he was just a fool at the time, didn't know what he was doing, had done nothing to dishonor the woman except take her brooch.

Jeschute is in great fear of what her husband will do to her, now that he has been beaten in her name. But Orilus, with his head all bloody, says, "Come kiss me, darling," so she jumps up and runs to kiss him, and Wolfram tells us that lips are sweet when there are tears—a lovely scene! And so they're reconciled. Parzival, of course, tells the defeated husband to go to Arthur's court and to tell everyone there who's beaten him.

Parzival continues on his sad journey and by chance arrives in the vicinity of Arthur's court, which has set forth in pursuit of the Red Knight, who has been sending all these captives back to offer their service to Cunneware, the woman who laughed when Parzival first arrived. With all these famous defeated knights coming, Arthur finally says, "We've got to go find that fellow." So the whole court of Camelot packs up and leaves. In those days a thing like this was a kind of first-rate picnic, with all the pavilions, ladies, and horses. And the whole court of Camelot is encamped with all these people who've come in service to Cunneware, the girl whom Keie beat for laughing—for recognizing Parzival as the world's greatest knight, which he has, in fact, become.

Parzival is riding through the forest, trying to find his way back to the Grail Castle. It happens that the king's falconers lose a hawk; it flies away and won't come back. They try to tempt it back by putting food out, and Wolfram, a poet who is something of an aristocrat himself, says this is what comes from overfeeding your hawks. So here's this poor hawk flying around in the woods. It's a young hawk, and it's a little frightened. It senses a campfire somewhere and flies to it, and guess whose it is? It's Parzival's.

So there's Parzival in the woods, and the hawk in the woods, and Arthur's court looking for both. That night marks the end of winter; there's a light snow on the ground. Parzival rides his horse out in the morning, and the hawk follows him. A whole flock of geese flies up, and the hawk goes at them, hits one of them, and draws blood.

The blood drops on the snow. And when Parzival sees that blood on the snow—three red drops on the pure, white snow—he thinks of his wife, Condwiramurs, with her two pink cheeks and her red lips. Lost in his dream of Condwiramurs, he sits there on his horse, mesmerized, looking at the snow. It is dawn now, and one of the pages in King Arthur's camp looks out and sees this knight on a horse there, gazing at the snow, and he comes rushing into the camp saying that the Round Table is disgraced; there's an enemy out there trampling down its tent ropes. So the whole camp wakes up in a commotion, and one young man, one of the nephews of King Arthur and Queen Guinevere, goes rushing into their tent, pulls the bedclothes off the king and queen, who are lying there in bed, and says, "Let me be first." Arthur laughs and lets him go. And this youth rides out full tilt at the knight who is gazing at the snow.

Parzival's horse—this wonderful Castilian—knows what to do. He turns to charge this young knight, breaking Parzival's trance. Parzival raises his lance and knocks the young knight to the ground. The Castilian turns back, and Parzival returns to brooding on the three drops of blood in the snow.

FIGURE 17. Parzival gazing at the snow (print, United States, 1905)

The next one who comes is Sir Keie, the seneschal who beat up Cunneware, and he comes charging. Exactly as before, Parzival's horse automatically turns, and as Wolfram put it, Cunneware is well avenged. Keie ends up with a leg broken between his saddle and a rock, and his horse beside him dead—and Parzival returns to gazing at the drops of blood on the snow.

Then Gawain—the ladies' knight, the gentle knight—arrives without a weapon, and when he sees Parzival looking at the blood on the snow, he thinks, *What if it should be a love dream? I've had many myself.* So he just takes a light silken scarf and tosses it gently on the snow, covering the bloody drops, breaking Parzival's vision of Condwiramurs.

Parzival finally comes out of his trance and asks, "Where is she? And where is my lance?" His lance was broken on Keie, but Parzival does not remember. Gawain tells Parzival what has happened, calms him down, and invites him back to King Arthur's camp.

Now, Gawain (who does not appear in Wagner's opera at all) is a very important character in this story. Gawain is a ladies' knight; he is the counterpart to Parzival. Parzival is young; Gawain is an older, more sophisticated, gracious man—a man of the world. And Gawain's adventure is in balance with Parzival's, which is that of the youth who meets just the right girl at just the right moment. Gawain has not yet done so. He escorts this brilliant youth, Parzival, to Arthur's court, where he's received in great glory, and the king decides to celebrate this arrival with a Round Table party. They set a big silken cloth of Oriental manufacture in a circle, and all the knights and ladies sit around it, ready for the feast. But it's a custom of King Arthur never to commence a feast unless an adventure occurs. So they're sitting around this round cloth, waiting for an adventure, when what do you know, an adventure takes place.

A maiden arrives, riding a tall mule, yellow-red with nostrils slit and sides terribly branded. She wears a cape, very blue, tailored in the French style, with a fine hat from London hanging down her back, and in her hand a whip with a ruby grip, but with fingernails like lion's claws and hands charming as a monkey's. She has a switch of long black hair, as coarse as the bristles of a pig. She takes off her veil, and what do we see? She has a great nose like a dog, two protruding boar's tusks, eyebrows braided to the ribbon of her hair, a hairy face.

She's a horrible creature, yet she is the Grail messenger. She comes from the Orient, from the land of Zazamanc, in fact, and her name is Cundrie.

FIGURE 18. Cundrie (watercolor, United States, 1912)

Cundrie rides directly to King Arthur. "What have you done today," she says, "in welcoming this one who looks like a knight but is no such thing, has brought shame to you and destruction to the Round Table?"

Then she approaches Parzival. "Cursed be the beauty of your face! I am less a monster than you. Speak up! Tell them why, when the sorrowful Fisherman lay before you, you did not relieve him of his sighs. May your tongue now become as empty as your heart is empty of right feeling. By heaven you are condemned to hell, as you will be by all the noble of this earth when people come to their senses. Your noble brother, Feirefiz, son of the queen of Zazamanc, is black and white, yet in him the manhood of your father has never failed. He has won, through chivalrous service, Queen Secondille of the city of Thabronit, where all earthly desires are fulfilled; yet had you asked the question at Munsalvaesche (French, *mon salvage*: "my salvation"), the Castle of the Grail, riches far beyond his would here and now have been yours."

She wrings her hands, bursts into tears, shames him further, and then asks, "And what, knight; wilt thou go on adventure to release four hundred maidens and four queens from enchantment in the Castle of Marvels?" That last part is going to be Gawain's adventure.

Parzival has been disgraced before the world. He has been a knight of that world, and yet because of his failure in an adventure that was superior to that of becoming a member of the court, he's disgraced before that court. He resolves to find the Castle of the Grail again and heal the king. At the same time, Gawain is about to depart on his quest to free the maidens at the Castle of Marvels, so he and Parzival bid each other good-bye as they ride forth on adventure. Gawain says, "I commit you to God."

Parzival responds, "I despise and hate God." He adds, "I have served God and he has not been loyal." In other words, Parzival is applying the human, courtly values—the highest values of his time—to God, and this is improper. But now he rides forth, having renounced the God of his mother, the God of his culture, on adventure, and he's going to spend five years in the desert of his soul. The world's become a desert through him, and he himself has become a desert in quest of regeneration.

This is the true beginning of the Grail Quest. Everything up to this point has taken place in the way of our hero's nature; Parzival's character has carried him through, but his desire to achieve fame in the world has cut him down at the high point, and he's lost both his spiritual and his earthly career. It's in this condition that he sets forth on his great adventure, while Gawain rides forth on his.

For Parzival it is to be an ordeal of five lonely years, as he searches through the forests. For, like the fairy hills of Ireland, the lake with its two fishermen and the castle of sorrowful knights and ladies lie hidden, though everywhere there is a haunting sense of their presence. This is the Forest Adventurous, where we meet our adventures when we are ready for them. The forest brings forth our own world, and here, in this attitude of hatred, rejection, ego, and pride, Parzival rides. And something becomes ready in him during this time.

One day he notices a little hermit hut in the forest that he hadn't noticed before, and he rides up and calls out, "Is there anybody in?" and a woman's voice answers. When Parzival hears that it's a woman's voice he turns away quickly, tethers his horse, and gives her a chance to come out. She is in hermit's garb. When she sits down beside him, he notices there's a ring on her finger, and he says, "That's strange."

FIGURE 19. The Forest Adventurous (print, United States, 1912)

She says, "This ring is for one who died for love of me. And though we were not married, I am married to this ring. Our love was never fulfilled, but I will go to God with this ring as married."

Parzival realizes this is his aunt Sigune again. In the hermitage lies the coffin of her beloved, where she has been kneeling in prayer. A chill goes through him, and he removes his helmet. When she sees who it is, she stares at him in a hard way and says, "Oh, it's you. Have you found the Grail Castle yet?"

He says, "Don't be hard on me; after all, we're related, and you know that I've been riding five years in terrible suffering, pain, and deprivation."

"Well," she says, "Cundrie the Sorceress left here only a little while ago. You might follow her path. That's where her mule went. She might be there now."

Thanking her, he mounts his horse and follows the path, but loses it in the woods. He's close, but he's not there. Shortly after leaving

Sigune to follow the path of the sorceress, he sees a knight riding at him, and this knight is a Temple Knight—one of the knights of the Temple of the Grail. That's how close Parzival is. And this knight says, "Get out of here unless you want to face death."

Well, Parzival isn't afraid of anybody, so he rides at the knight and overthrows him. But both the knight and Parzival's horse go over a chasm and fall into the abyss. Parzival grabs a tree and lets himself down into it, too. His horse has died, but here's the Temple Knight's horse, without a rider, whom Parzival sees climbing up the chasm on the other side. So now Parzival is riding a horse that is branded with turtledoves, the insignia of the Grail Castle.

Then he sees a curious procession of pilgrims, with an old noble-man and his wife at the head and their two daughters and a whole company of people following. They are out on pilgrimage, barefoot in the snow. It's Good Friday, and this is what we could call a secular charade, a kind of make-believe pilgrimage. They go out for the day of Good Friday in bare feet and feel that they're very pious, with this sacrifice and this celebration of an important festival, and they come upon this knight who has endured five long years of penance. He makes way for them. I might also add that the ladies have their little dogs trotting along by their sides. And the old gentleman out in front looks at this knight and says, "How dare you be riding in knightly armor on this day of the death of our Savior?"

And the knight says, "I don't know what day it is. I don't know what year it is."

The old man starts abusing Parzival for his lack of piety, but the daughters say, "Oh, come on, Daddy, the man must be very cold in that ice-cold suit of armor, and here we are with a whole camp full of blankets and food and everything else. Why don't you invite him to share our hospitality?" Then the girls fall quiet.

Looking at them, Parzival thinks, *They love him whom I hate. I will be polite and just make my departure.* So he bids them farewell and prepares to go his way. They have learned from him that he hates God, and the old man looks at him and says, "Perhaps when your heart turns you will wish to confess your sins. There's a hermit down the way."

So here's the amusing thing: this little charade—the make-believe austerity of this family—the image of it actually works on Parzival. At

that very moment he begins to think, *Perhaps God will guide me.* Once
more he lets his horse go, dropping the reins. The horse goes down the
path and sure enough comes to a hermitage. This is the hermitage of
the Grail King's brother, Trevrizent, who has abandoned the world.

Wolfram's period, the early thirteenth century, is a great period
of hermits. This is the time of Saint Francis, of Saint Dominic; this
is the period also, and most important, of Joachim of Floris, who
wrote a very significant work having to do with the three ages of the
manifestation of God. The first age he called the Age of the Father,
and that's the age of the Old Testament, the age of the people of
Israel and the preparation of the world for the coming of the Son.
The second is the Age of the Son and of the Church. And the third
is to be the Age of the Holy Spirit, which will be an age when the
Church will dissolve; the institution will be unnecessary because the
spirit will speak directly to individuals. Here, in monastic guise, is the
same story of the recognition of the individual as the one to receive
the message.

It is important to note that these hermits, Sigune and Trevrizent,
are not ordained clergy. Trevrizent is a noble layman. Sigune never
attends Mass. She never receives the sacraments. Yet, says Wolfram,

FIGURE 20.
Trevrizent (print,
United States, 1910)

her whole life has been spent in kneeling, and her devotion was to the love that she had for this knight who died in battle for her. And as we'll see a little later, her love has kept his body as fresh as though he were still young. This entire poem can be seen, as I have said, as a kind of cathedral, with stained-glass windows showing loving people, people engaged in different forms of loving relationships.

Parzival arrives at Trevrizent's hermitage, and when this noble hermit comes out to greet him, Parzival asks, "Aren't you afraid of a knight riding up at you like this?"

The hermit says, "I've been here many years. I'm afraid sometimes of bears, but never of men. Here, give me your horse." He takes the horse and puts it in a little stable he has under a ledge and takes the knight in.

First thing, Parzival says, "I hate God!"

"Well," the hermit says, "that's interesting. Tell me about it."

Parzival says, "I am a sinner and I will confess my sins."

Notice that he's making a confession to a man who is not ordained. This is once more the secular line in the story. There are no priests here, though we're going to get a comic priest a little later on.

"Now, before you tell me about your hate for God," the hermit continues, "let me tell you some stories."

And he reviews the story of the creation, and of man formed from Mother Earth, the virgin earth giving birth to man, and then the Virgin Mary giving birth to the Savior. (This is something I love: reading these old stories in a new way.) "Now," says the hermit, "you hate God, but God has an abundance of hate for those who hate him and of love for those who love him." This is a very important point: God is seen as a reflex of the spirit of the devotee. If you hate, hate is going to come to you. If you love, love is going to come to you. And so Trevrizent says, "Whom do you think is being hurt by this hatred of yours to talk that way? You speak like a fool."

Parzival asks, "Who are you?"

And the hermit tells him that he's the brother of Anfortas, the Grail King. Then Trevrizent looks at Parzival and says, "There's a horse in my stable from the Grail Castle. Who are you? Some years ago a fool came to the Grail Castle and made a terrible mistake. This man is cursed of God." (He knows he's talking to Parzival.)

It takes a long time for Parzival to say who he is, for he undergoes a conversion here. He is now moved to trust in God—but not the God of his mother. It's the same name, but not the same God. (This is a vital point. We all say, "I believe in God." But when you talk to various people, you find totally different capacities for belief, for conceptions of God. Although different people use the same word for God, it's not the same God. This is one of the ironies of monotheism. It isn't monotheism at all because everybody believes in God in a different way. If you're a Christian, for example, some Muslims may have beliefs that are more like yours than your neighboring Christian.)

So Parzival undergoes this conversion and learns that he can never return to the Grail Castle, never see it again. He learns that the one who has not asked the question spontaneously on first coming can never arrive again. But he says, "I'm going to arrive, I'm going to do it, no matter what the divine rule is."

"Well," says Trevrizent, "boys will be boys."

And so it will come about that, at the end of this five-year ordeal in the dark woods of the soul, Parzival will finally return to the Grail Castle and be reunited with Gawain, with Arthur's entire court, with his half-brother from the Orient, and, most important, with his wife and children. But before that happens, we must turn to the parallel adventures of Gawain.

GAWAIN

In *Parzival* we have, in fact, two heroes: Parzival and Gawain. Gawain is a charming character in Wolfram's work. In fact, he's a delightful character wherever he appears. In the English medieval poem, *Sir Gawain and the Green Knight*, for example, he is a forthright, lovely person, graceful and sensitive, with a wonderful—how to put it?—*responsiveness* to feminine beauty.

Wolfram's story carries Gawain forth on adventure now, and the first thing we hear of Gawain is that after he starts out, he sees an enormous army, with banners, coming past, and he asks one of the passing knights, "What army is this?" He hears there's this young King Meljanz (French, *mal chance*: "bad luck") who was brought up by an old knight, who's over there, and that old knight's daughter refused this young king in marriage, and so now he's coming to take the castle and the girl by force—the exact thing we saw with Clamide

FIGURE 21. Gawain approaches the castle (print, United States, 1911)

and Condwiramurs. And here are three armies that Maljanz has assembled on his own, all going against this castle.

Gawain has a big adventure ahead, and he's trying to save his strength for that, so he doesn't want to get into this mess, but he's terribly curious. So he rides along with them. Knights ride with squires and equipment, and Gawain has his tent pitched right under the castle that's going to be under siege.

And in the castle window sits the wife of the old knight and her two daughters: one the daughter who refused this young king, and the other her little daughter of five years or so, Obilot. The mother asks, "Who's that handsome knight down there?"

The saucy older daughter says, "That's no knight; that's just a merchant!"

"But oh," says the mother, "he has all those shields and all those weapons. Merchants carry things like that sometime."

"Well," little Obilot says, "that's no merchant. That's a knight, that's a beautiful knight, that's a gentlemanly knight, and he's *my* knight. I love him and he's my knight, and you can't talk about him that way."

At the same time, the father goes out to talk to Gawain, who's a famous champion, and tells him about the situation: "Here are all these armies coming against me. Would you, you know, go into battle for me?"

Gawain says, "I'm saving myself for an important engagement, and I just can't do that."

So the father very unhappily returns to his castle, and there's his little daughter Obilot. He says to her, "What are you doing here, dear?"

"Waiting for the pretty knight to come and help us."

"Alas," says the father, "he has refused my plea to do so."

And she says, "He'd do it for me."

So the father lets his little girl trot out with her attendant, the burgomaster's daughter, and they arrive at Gawain's tent.

When Gawain stands up to greet the young ladies, Obilot, says, "I hope you will believe me. This is the first time I've ever addressed a gentleman alone. My nurse has told me that by one's speech one betrays one's character and upbringing. I hope that mine stands by me and gives you a good impression." Then she says, "I'll tell you why I've come. I have come because you are me and I am you, and when you are fighting in the field, it will be me who is fighting, and my strength supports you."

This is proper knightly protocol. Gawain says, "I am engaged. I am your knight."

And then, as the act of fealty was rendered in the Middle Ages, the knight kneels down and puts his hands up, and the little lady takes the huge, gauntleted hands in her tiny ones.

And then she says, "Excuse me, I have something to do now," and she goes running back home with the little servant girl. Why is she in such a hurry? Because she has to get a sleeve for Gawain to wear on his shield, of course.

Once Obilot explains what has happened, her mother says what a lovely man Gawain is and has a very beautiful dress made for the girl, of the most ravishing silk. They take off one sleeve, and the other little servant girl carries it out to Gawain, and he accepts it with thanks and nails it to one of his shields.

The next day he rides to battle as Obilot's champion, and a grandiose battle it is. Gawain comes off victorious, so little Obilot's great knight is the victor of the day. And now he has power over the king who came to claim the sister, so Gawain sends him in service to Obilot. This king finds himself in service to a five-year-old girl. And then, of course, love takes over: he marries the older sister, who caused the siege by rejecting him in the first place but who accepts him now.

When Gawain returns to say he's going off on his adventure, there's a darling scene. The little girl, Obilot, says, "You may kiss me, you know, and I give you my *merçi.*" So he takes her in his arms like a little doll and kisses her. But then she won't let go of his hand, and the family has to detach her from Gawain so that he can ride forth—and that is the end of this adventure.

The next adventure will bring Gawain his illumination, and his own version of the Grail experience, in the Château Merveille—the Castle of Marvels. He's trotting along and sees leaning up against a tree a shield that is pierced through and a horse standing there with a woman's saddle on it. *Oh,* he thinks, *this is going to be interesting.*

FIGURE 22. Gawain and Orgeluse (print, United States, 1903)

Perhaps I'll have a wrestling match. He peers around the tree, and what he sees is a woman sitting there with a knight on her lap who has had his chest pierced and is bleeding. Since Gawain is rather clever with wounds, as many knights were, he helps the woman heal this knight.

And the knight says, "Don't go down the road the way I came, or you'll run into an adventure you won't like. I'm warning you against this." In folklore, we call this "the one forbidden thing"; of course Gawain is going to go down the road.

Now we're entering the field of an adventure, and again you have that pietà scene of the woman with the almost-dead knight on her lap— like Parzival's encounter with Sigune. These are parallel spheres now.

Nothing's going to stop Gawain, so he goes trotting on and comes to a winding hill. This is the hill of the magician Clinschor (Wagner's Klingsor), and he sees sitting by a spring this glorious woman, Orgeluse. He stops and looks at her and says, "You are the most beautiful woman I've ever seen in my life!"

And she says, "That's no news to me. I know that as well as you do, but it's little joy I take in praise from any old fool that comes along. It's the wise I like to hear talk. Go on, get out of here! The farther away you are, the better it will be for me."

"Well," he said, "reject me or receive me, I am yours."

"If that's the way it is, why don't you just go down the field there and get off your horse, and you'll see some people dancing and playing flutes and a horse tethered to a tree. That's my horse. Bring it here."

This is Gawain's first service to her. He goes across the footpath, and as he approaches the horse, people come up to him and say, "Don't touch that horse." An old man on crutches says, "If you value yourself, don't touch that horse!"

Nevertheless, Gawain untethers the horse, and it follows him back.

Orgeluse then gets on the horse.

He says, "May I help you?"

Orgeluse says, "Don't you touch me." Then she gets on the horse, and the pair of them rides off, Gawain following her. He doesn't know where he's going or where the adventure is leading.

This is Woman. Gawain has gone from woman to woman, but this one has transfixed him, and he's going to remain firmly attached to her, no matter what. This is the *anima* image; it's the image of the woman by the well that is constantly encountered. One thinks of Jacob with Rachael by the well, and Moses with Zantipy by the well—and these women by the well are something to watch out for. And here is Orgeluse, the one he is ready for. This encounter catapults him into another sphere of the feminine altogether. The other women are simply forgotten. She is his soul, and she's a toughie!

As they're riding along he sees a plant, an herb, and he says, "Just a minute." He gets down and picks the herb.

She says, "Oh, I thought I had a knight in my service. I see I have a medical man. You'd probably make a good living if you could sell jars, you know, and put this medicine in there." She goes on kidding him like that.

And he replies, "Well, there's a person down the way I want to bring this to so that it can heal him."

"Oh," she says, "I'm going to witness something interesting, am I?" She follows him back, and he applies this herb to the knight who had been lying in the woman's lap, and what do you know? The knight jumps up and rides off with his girl—on Gawain's horse.

Now Gawain doesn't have a horse and Orgeluse laughs. "Well, now we're going to walk."

So here he is walking along behind her, when this curious creature named Malcreatiure (French, *mal créature*: "bad creature") comes along riding on a terribly decrepit nag with a saddle of straw. This Malcreatiure is Cundrie's brother and looks just like her, with a pig's face and great big tusks—a foul-looking creature. And he is Orgeluse's squire. So here's Gawain walking along, here's this crazy-looking creature riding on his decrepit horse, and here's this beautiful Orgeluse riding with them. (This image is actually right out of an Irish folktale about Cuchullain.)

As Gawain and Malcreatiure start wrangling, Orgeluse laughs and says, "I love to see you fools arguing this way." Then she tells Malcreatiure to go on and to let Gawain have his horse. So now Gawain has this ridiculous horse, which he doesn't even dare mount, because if he put his foot in the stirrup, the whole thing would go to pieces just like that. Even so, he finally manages to get up on this beast just as they come to a great castle.

This is the Castle of Marvels, the one he is supposed to disenchant, where four hundred beautiful princesses and four great queens are all held captive. And it's beyond a great moat, wide as a river, and on this side of the moat is a great plain. Gawain has finally managed to arrive on this crazy mount. He's riding along behind Orgeluse when, *zing*, there comes down the plain a knight in full career.

Orgeluse laughs and says, "This is going to be good! When you fall and split your pants, won't that be a vision for the ladies in the castle?"

So he thinks, *Now what am I going to do? Here comes this knight on a horse.* He works up a stratagem, and thinks, *I'll just ride my horse right up in front of him, and his horse will trip over mine. I'm too low to get caught by his lance. We'll just see how it works.*

And that's exactly what happens. This brilliantly armed knight comes flying down the field on his magnificent steed, and Gawain's idiotic animal trips up the knight's horse so that the warhorse flops over, and the two knights are now afoot, and of course Gawain conquers the other knight.

But the knight will not capitulate. He won't plead for mercy. He says, "Better dead than defeated."

Gawain looks at him and thinks, *Well, why should I kill this man?* He says, "Go on, get up, and sit over there." Gawain notices that the man's horse is Gawain's own, the one that the wounded knight stole, and now it is in the possession of yet another knight entirely. At that moment, the knight from the castle picks up his sword and comes at Gawain, so Gawain defeats him again.

Finally, the ferryman arrives. Now, when you hear about a ferryman in a story, you know you're on your way to the yonder shore, the realm of the great adventure. This ferryman is a lovely character. He says, "There's a custom here that the defeated knight's horse is given to me, and this knight has been defeated, and that's his horse."

"No," says Gawain, "that's my horse. If you want his horse, look at that other one. But if you'll accept a knight instead of a horse, I'll give him to you."

"That's fine with me," says the boatman. "Come across."

The boatman ferries Gawain across to the boatman's house. This is a charming scene! It turns out that this is not only the ferryman but also the guardian of the threshold to the Castle of Marvels. We're at the porter's place to the land of magic. He has a little daughter named Bene, and a son, and this darling family takes Gawain in. They've put new straw on the floor and scattered it with little flowers to make it pretty. They've prepared a bed for him, and Bene has fixed the room up. She is his servant for that night. Gawain goes to sleep.

He wakes up early in the morning and looks out the window. He notices that all the women in the castle are still moving around. We're in the fairyland of no sleep, the land of no time. He has passed out of the realm of time into the magical realm of dream. He goes back to sleep, and when he wakes up, there's little Bene in the room with his breakfast.

Gawain asks her about the castle, but as soon as he does, she begins to cry, and says, "Don't ask that question."

And there he is, still in bed, with the little girl weeping, and her father comes in. The father thinks something else entirely has happened. The ferryman says to Bene, "Oh, darling, don't mind when things like that happen. At first one's angry, but it'll be all right in a little while."

But Gawain says, "No, nothing has happened here," and everything's straightened out.

Gawain then asks the father about the castle, and the father of course says, "Don't ask."

Gawain says, "I am asking."

So the father tells him that this is the Castle of Marvels and that Gawain may either depart or attempt the adventure, but that no one can survive it.

This is the adventure of the Perilous Bed, one of the great adventures in Arthurian romance. The ferryman gives Gawain his shield, since Gawain insists on the adventure. And he tells Gawain, "Just when you think the adventure is over, it has just begun, so stay under that shield."

Gawain approaches the castle, and all is quiet. He enters and goes into the room of the Perilous Bed. The floor is absolutely slick, the bed stands in the middle on wheels, and every time Gawain approaches it—with armor and shield, big heavy gear—the bed jumps away.

The Indologist Heinrich Zimmer, in talking about this adventure, said, "This bed is like a reluctant bride putting up a terrific fight." Zimmer went on to say that this adventure concerns the masculine experience of the female temperament, which seems absolutely irrational from the masculine point of view. The adventure demands, without the man understanding it, that he simply acquiesce. And when he has shown his ability to acquiesce and remain in decent relationship with the feminine, then the boons will appear—and we're going to see them in a minute. But not before the real test.

FIGURE 23. The Perilous Bed (carved ivory, Italy, c. fifteenth century)

Gawain finally makes up his mind and takes a great big leap and lands in the bed, which then begins dashing back and forth against the walls like a bucking bronco, banging so that the whole castle rings with the noise.

After a season of this, the bed stands perfectly still. But Gawain remembers what he was told—that things haven't begun yet—so he stays under his shield. Five hundred crossbow bolts come at him from all directions and bounce off the shield, and then five hundred arrows shoot from all directions, and they, too, bounce off.

Finally, a lion enters the room and begins mauling. Gawain gets up out of the bed and goes to work on the lion and cuts off the lion's paw when the lion strikes at his shield, so that the lion's paw is now gripping his shield and hanging there. The blood from the lion begins to gush all over the place. The two of them are slipping around and don't know what they're doing. Gawain, completely knocked out, flops over, and his sword goes right through the lion's chest. The lion dies and falls on top of him.

All is still and quiet.

And all the ladies are quiet, too.

Two little girls look in and see their knight lying, apparently dead, on the lion. And they go in and they take a bit of fur from his gambeson and hold it up to his nose, and there's a little flutter, so they know he's alive. They bring him a little water and very carefully pour it in his mouth and bring him slowly back to life.

The first thing Gawain says is, "I beg your pardon that you found me in this disgraceful condition. I hope you won't mention it to anybody." So with something like five hundred wounds, he's brought upstairs for healing.

All these glorious women are standing around with the old queen, who happens to be Gawain's own grandmother, but who doesn't know who he is because she's under enchantment. In curing him, she is herself being cured as well. And as he's back in one piece, he looks from one woman to the other and his heart is simply aching. For whom? For Orgeluse—but she isn't there. None of these women means a thing to him. That's the first part of his great ordeal.

Early the next morning, in spite of all his wounds, he gets up and walks through the great hall and climbs into a magical tower that has been brought by Clinschor. For this is Clinschor's palace from the Orient, and in this hall stands a magical mirror in the shape of a pillar. And in this magical mirror one can see reflected everything that's going on in the neighborhood, and no sooner does Gawain look in that mirror than he sees the lady Orgeluse, coming along on the other shore with yet another knight. That means that now Gawain, as the knight of the Castle of Marvels, has to go out and defend it, even with all his wounds, which he does. He goes back across the river and overthrows the knight but can hardly move for pain.

When Orgeluse sees him, she says, "Well, you feel pretty fancy with that lion's paw stuck on your shield, don't you? I have a real adventure for you now that I don't think you'll survive."

Gawain is beginning to get a little tired of this kind of thing, but this adventure—from an anthropologist's point of view—is one of the most interesting in the whole medieval corpus of writings.

James Frazer's 1890 book, *The Golden Bough: A Study in Magic and Religion,* features a similar adventure: There is near Rome, at Lake Nemi, a sacred grove dedicated to the goddess Diana, and there's a tree in that grove that is guarded by a priest. That priest is a criminal who has achieved his role by killing the priest of the tree before him, and he will lose the position when he is killed. But before killing the priest he had to pluck a bough from that tree. This is the Golden Bough of the title.

So it is fascinating when Orgeluse tells Gawain, "There's a grove down the way with a great tree in it, and this tree is guarded by a knight, and that knight killed my husband, for whom I am still lamenting. Before you attack him you must pluck a bough of that tree." In other words, this is the Golden Bough adventure, right here in this romance.

To get to the tree, Gawain and his charger have to hurdle across a great torrent, called the Perilous Ford. The horse misses, and they fall into the torrent, but Gawain gets the horse out and rides up to pluck a bough from the tree.

At once a majestic knight named Gramoflanz comes out. He is beautifully described, riding along in a green costume with his clothing dragging on the ground on either side of the horse. Gramoflanz says, "I have not given up control of this tree; however, I have never presumed to fight fewer than two men at a time, and since you're only one, I will give you a commission, a little job instead of battle. I am in love with the lady in the castle over there, and here is a ring for her. Her name is Itonje."

This is Gawain's own sister.

Gramoflanz continues, "There's only one knight in the world whom I would fight solo, and that is Gawain."

Gawain says, "I am he."

"Well, then," Gramoflanz replies, "we'll arrange for a tournament. You're to bring all the ladies of that castle to the tournament. We'll invite King Arthur's ladies to the tournament, and I have six hundred ladies in my castle. We'll invite all of them, and then we'll see what we will see."

Feirefiz

After Gawain encounters Gramoflanz, the guardian of the tree, a great tournament is arranged by the queens of the Castle of Marvels. Arthur's invited, and a grand scene is built up for this terrific tournament. Yet it's a very bizarre one, because this fight will be to the death, and Gramoflanz wants to marry the sister of the man he wants to kill. The sister doesn't know what's going on.

After all have come together and had yet another banquet, Gawain leaves to exercise in the early morning, but before he does, he sees a

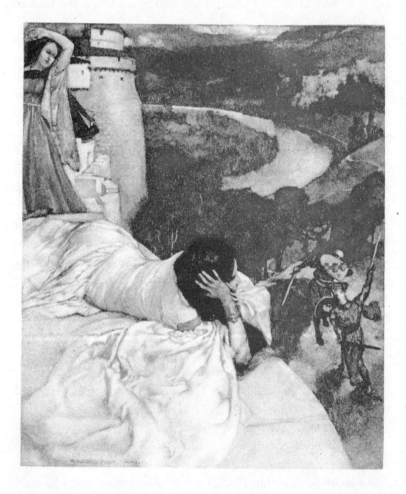

FIGURE 24. Damsel watching Gawain and Parzival (print, England, 1911)

knight in red armor coming. The Red Knight is wearing the wreath plucked from the tree, so Gawain thinks it's Gramoflanz.

We know who it is. It's Parzival, who has plucked the branch to dare Gramoflanz. And so Parzival also sees a knight wearing the wreath: it's Gawain, but he also thinks it's Gramoflanz.

So these two brother knights ride at each other in combat, and they go at it fiercely, with Gawain gradually losing. When Gawain's squires chance by, they shout his name. Parzival tosses his sword away, and says, "I am betrayed! I am fighting my own blood, my own brother." And they stop fighting.

Now no end of weddings take place. Gramoflanz has been assuaged, and he's going to marry Gawain's sister. Gawain is going to marry Orgeluse. And the defeated knights are going to marry other ladies of the castle. And there's a great festival of love, "love in the moonlight among the pavilions," says Wolfram.

Parzival is there, but his wife, Condwiramurs, is not, and he thinks, *Should I participate in this event?* After considering this question, he says, *How can I participate when my heart is somewhere else, and my eyes behold all this joy? I will leave.*

This is a great moment for Parzival: out of loyalty to his love, in the midst of all this temptation, he is not seduced. And in combat, he is never afraid. He is without fear and without desire—in the name of love. The reader may remember the temptation of the Buddha under the Bodhi tree. The Enlightened One, having just achieved *nirvāṇa*, is assailed by the temptation of desire, the temptation of fear, but he has transcended these. This is the same temptation here, and Parzival—not in the way of escaping from the world, but in the way of inhabiting it—has reached that same position.

He rides forth, and has not ridden very far when he sees coming at him a knight in the most gorgeous armor, woven of all kinds of metallic mysteries by gnomes in the Oriental mountains. And again, *we* know who it is: Parzival's half-brother, Feirefiz, son of Gahmuret by Belkane of Zazamanc.

"These two men," says Wolfram, "were born of battle noise. When a lion is born, the lion is born dead, and it is awakened to life by the sound of its father's roar. These men were awakened to life by battle roar." And so they go at each other ferociously. The antagonist is from the Orient, and he has an army of fifteen different nations

FIGURE 25. Feirefiz (print, United States, 1907)

(none speaking the language of any other) hiding in the woods, but he's ridden forth on solo adventure. And each is very angry because he's never fought with another knight who was so powerful.

The two clash and neither is unseated. They wheel, and the battle continues. Presently, both are afoot. Chips fly from their shields as the blows fall.

"I mourn for this," wrote Wolfram. "One could say that 'they' were fighting, if one wished to speak of two. They were, however, one. 'My brother and I' is one body."[4] When Parzival's sword breaks in two, the other tosses his own sword away. "I see, brave man," he says in French, "you would now have to fight with no blade, and no fame would I gain from that." Feirefiz continues, "I've never met a man of such courage. If you'll tell me your name, my voyage will not have been in vain."

And Parzival replies: "Am I to tell you my name out of fear?"

So Feirefiz says, "I'll tell you mine: my name is Feirefiz of

FIGURE 26. Parzival and Feirefiz battle (ink on vellum, Germany, thirteenth century)

Angevin." Then he takes his helmet off, and there's the mottled face. The heathen is piebald, black and white. They realize, to their mutual astonishment, that they're brothers. And it is actually through the heathen's act of compassion, when the sword of the Christian failed, that the two discover their identity.

"Now, these two," says Wolfram—and this is a very important theme and line in his work—"were fighting there, but they are one. They are one, the sons of Gahmuret, each doing the other and himself much harm through courage and through loyalty." These are the

FIGURE 27. Parzival and Feirefiz talk (ink on vellum, Germany, thirteenth century)

two worlds of Islam and Christendom, the two daughter worlds of the Hebrew world. Gahmuret and these two are all one. Wolfram discusses at great length the one that is three, and the one that is two, and how the two fight. But the action comes from the fighting; they must not quit. Each in his honor is in combat with the other.

Feirefiz says, "Come visit my armies."

Parzival replies, "Well, first let's go visit Arthur's court. It's just right by here: lots of tents and pavilions and lots of beautiful ladies and gallant knights."

"Beautiful ladies!" says Feirefiz. "I'm for the castle, then." Of course, all this has already been observed in the castle through that magic mirror, so there is quite a reception for Feirefiz. The ladies gather around him and think he's just marvelous; Wolfram says this attention is probably owing to his interesting complexion. They all say what a wonderful knight he is, and how loyal he must be to his beloved, though of course they would all like very much to destroy that loyalty.

Arthur and the rest of the court prepare for another Round Table party, welcoming Feirefiz and Parzival again.

A lawn party is planned for the next day, and when all have placed themselves around the circular cloth of Oriental silk, Cundrie the Loathly Damsel, riding on her tall horse, appears exactly as before. She gets off the horse, bows weeping before Parzival, begs for forgiveness for what she told him before, and proclaims him the Grail King.

The point here is that he has assumed this role not in direct quest but through the integrity of his character, through his loyalties, courage, and single-minded resolution. Furthermore, this news has been announced to Condwiramurs, who, with their two little sons, Lohengrin and Kardeiz, are on their way. Cundrie tells Parzival—and now we come to the wonderful, crazy resolution—"You must come to the castle with a male companion."

Parzival says, "I will ask Feirefiz." Many a Christian cannot get to the Grail Castle, but this Muslim can. So these two noble men—here's the matter of character that goes way beyond anything like sectarian divisions—ride with Cundrie to the castle, where they are welcomed.

And when Parzival sees the Fisher King, Anfortas, he asks the question, "*Ocheim, was wirret dier?*" ("Uncle, what ails thee?") and instantly the king is healed, and Parzival becomes the new Grail King.

Consider what is happening here: he has become the Grail King *without inheriting the wound.* That is to say, it is possible to be in that position intact and entire. This is a very optimistic work about the powers of man.

Parzival goes to pick up Condwiramurs, whom he is to meet at the same place where he saw the three red drops in the snow. On the way he stops off at Trevrizent's hermitage, and what does Trevrizent say when he hears the news that Parzival has achieved the Grail Castle? He says, "This is a miracle that you have worked. Through your own will you have caused the Trinity to change its mind, to change its rules. Just as through hate you evoke God's hate, through love you evoke God's love." He is saying, that is, through your own integrity, you evoke your destiny, which is a destiny that never existed before.

On the way back with Condwiramurs to the Grail Castle, they stop off at Sigune's hermitage. She is kneeling over a coffin, and she is dead. (This is a very poignant theme running throughout the poem.) They lift the coffin, and there is her beloved, as fresh as the morning. She is laid beside him, and then they go back to the castle, and the great procession of the Grail takes place.

And a curious thing happens: Feirefiz can't see the Grail. All he sees are the eyes and the beauty of the girl carrying it, with whom he is absolutely infatuated. And the court gradually begins to realize that Feirefiz can't see the Grail. There it is right in front of him, the Grail Stone, an abundant, magical thing; people take from it any food they want, any wine they want. It is related, in Wolfram's thinking, to the Ka'aba, the black stone of Islam. The legend of the Ka'aba is that when it was carried down from heaven by angels, it was white. It's a piece of a heavenly mansion, and the kissing of it by sinful lips has turned it. The Grail Stone was brought down by what Wolfram calls the neutral angels, those who in the battle between good and evil, at the time of Satan's fall, took neither side—the Middle Way, again.

Word gets out about this strange Muslim who doesn't see the Grail, and the message comes in that he can't see it because he hasn't been baptized.

When I first read this, I thought, *Good God! After all this, is Wolfram going to let us down here?*

What happens next, of course, is that they tell him he's got to be baptized.

"I don't care about seeing the Grail," he says, "but I want to marry that girl."

"Well," they respond, "you can't marry her unless you're baptized."

So they bring in a baptismal font, which is empty of water. An old priest comes in and begins to instruct Fierefiz about the doctrine of the Trinity—a very complicated doctrine to communicate to anybody. This is an old priest who has converted many heathens.

And so Feirefiz says, "Is that her God?"

When they answer yes, he says, "Well, all right, that's my God. I renounce my God and accept hers."

Wolfram is telling us that this is the way people are converted. Now we come to the actual baptism. What they do—and this is a very interesting moment—is to tip the baptismal font in the direction of the Grail, and it fills up with water streaming from the Grail. Now, the name of the Grail is also a name that is given to the philosopher's stone, *lapis exilis*; anyone who knows Jung's writings on alchemy will recognize this immediately. The water from that stone is the elixir of the philosopher's transmuting power, so this is no ordinary baptism. And this is a very interesting point: the forms of the orthodox tradition are carried out with water of a totally esoteric tradition.

There then appears on the Grail an inscription: *ANY TEMPLAR APPOINTED BY GOD'S HAND TO BE MASTER OVER A FOREIGN FOLK MUST FORBID THE ASKING OF HIS NAME OR RACE AND HELP THEM TO THEIR RIGHTS.*[5]

The date of this writing, c. 1210 A.D., was about five years earlier than that of England's Magna Carta. That document was to be forced from the Norman King John by his barons claiming their own rights, whereas this statement in Wolfram's Castle of the Grail is a free declaration of the rights of others. It is a document entailing a covenant of service, a document of compassion, sprung from the same spiritual ground as the requisite question of the Grail ceremonial. There's nothing like this in the history of political thinking up to this date. This is the first statement, I think anywhere, in the traditions of international law, of the notion of bringing people together, and of maintaining their political rights, through colonial rule, you might say. It is an expression of the Western concept of a united world, which underlies this bringing of these two visions together.

Feirefiz does indeed marry the beautiful girl who carries the Grail. Her name, as we know, is Repanse de Schoye, and they go to India, where his first wife has meanwhile died, and their little son is born, Prester John, whose legends are legion. That is the end of Parzival's story.

FIGURE 28. Parzival and Condwiramurs (print, United States, 1912)

ORIENTAL REFLECTIONS ON WOLFRAM'S *PARZIVAL*

The fact that the Christianized Celts of the early period tended to place no less emphasis on the inward, mystical aspects of a story than on the outward, historical aspect, combined with the implications of the Gospel legend, prepared the way for a later recognition of analogies in the mystical tradition of India; and the number of such analogies immediately apparent to anyone familiar with both worlds is amazing. For in India, whether in its Hindu or its Buddhist teachings, the accent is again on the mystical side. It is not on the importance of historical events that may or may not have taken place, but on the requirement that something should happen, here and now, in one's mind and will. And this brings me to what is a crucial, if not *the* crucial problem of this whole subject, namely, that of the radical distinction between the esoteric (mystical) and exoteric (historical) ways of reading mythological symbols: as references, on the one hand, to powers operative in the human heart as agents of transformation, and, on the other, to actual or imagined historical events.

Take the symbol of the Virgin Birth, for example. This motif occurs in all the mythologies of the world. Consequently, it cannot have referred originally to one extraordinary event that occurred at a certain time and place in Israel. What it refers to in its inward, mystical sense is the birth in the awakened mind and heart of a realization of the Kingdom of the Father. The first birth of man, as a physical creature motivated by the animal energies of the body, is biological. Man's second, properly human birth, is spiritual, of the heart and mind—or, as represented in the Indian symbolic science of the *kuṇḍalinī*, of the heart—a lotus opening to the radiant sound *AUM* that is the divine creative energy resounding through all things.

Teachers of the ways to such a spiritual realization are commonly, in the myths of the world, represented as themselves born of the awakening, since the meaning of their lives and messages to humankind—or to their various tribes—is of this knowledge, not of the "once-born" biological ends of survival, reproduction, and conquest. Demythologizing a symbol such as the Virgin Birth and reading it as referring to a unique, induplicable historical event of the past, impossible to attain ourselves, deprives it of its psychological force, externalizing its message as institutional of some social establishment, upon which, then, our spiritual life depends. The mythologies of India abound in incarnations, with the implication always that we are to become such beings ourselves. And in the Celtic legends also, whether pagan or Christian—of Bran and Brendan, or of Galahad and Parzival, the heroes of the Grail—the accent of the symbolization is typically on the hero life as exceptional indeed, yet paradigmatic of ways to realization that are open to us all.

Galahad entered the fellowship of Arthur's Knights of the Round Table on the feast of the Pentecost, wearing red armor symbolic of the presence in him of the grace of the Spirit, to which his life and character were to be witness (*Galaad* means "mountain of witness"). Parzival, too, began his knightly career in an armor of blazing red. So may we all, when we have caught the meaning of Paul's saying: "It is no longer I who live, but Christ who lives in me" (Galatians 2:20). The reference here is not and cannot be, positivistically, to the corporal person of the historical "incarnation," Jesus of Nazareth, whom Paul never saw or knew, but, mystically, to the ever-living Christ, the knowledge and Knower of the Father, potential within all. This revelation awakened within Paul at that moment on the road to Damascus—and knocked him from his horse. And once one learns this way of reading the symbols, through the imagery of vision and the pictorial script of the religions of humankind, suddenly all the mythologies of the world, each in its own way, become eloquent of the spirit.

In this spirit, then, I will cite the Buddhist legend of the World Savior, Gautama, as a clue to the meaning of the Grail Quest.

This princely youth, Gautama Śakyamuni, had achieved Enlightenment beneath the Bodhi tree, or the Tree of Awakening (*bodhi* means "awakening"), which, as the axial tree at the center of the turning world, is equivalent to that in Saint Brendan's voyage of the Paradise of Birds: there came to him, from the four quarters of the earth, the four guardian kings of those quarters, each with the gift of a begging bowl; and those four bowls became fused into a single bowl of stone, which, like the Celtic Grail, or the cauldron of Manannan, was an inexhaustible vessel. The Buddha came to his realization only after years of trial and seeking, finally coming to the so-called Immovable Spot of the paradisial tree. We are not to seek this place in the world; we are to seek it in our own will. It is the place where the will is moved neither by the quest for life nor by the fear of death; the Buddha, seated there, had been approached by the antagonist, the Tempter, as Christ had been, in the desert. The Tempter, in his character of the Lord of Desire, Kāma, displayed before the seated one his three voluptuous daughters (whose names, by the way, were Desire, Fulfillment, and Regrets); but the prince, who had already left behind the delusions of the senses, was unmoved. The next temptation was that of the fear of death, the Tempter now in his character of Māra, the lord Death himself. But again the prince, unattached to ego, was unmoved. Then finally, in his character of Dharma, lord of the duties of life imposed on one by society, the master of delusion commanded the meditating prince to give up his seat on the Immovable Spot and

Figure 29. The Buddha tempted by desire and fear (paint on wood,
Thailand, date unknown)

return to his princely throne. The one seated there only moved his
right hand to touch with his fingertips the earth, and the very goddess of the earth, of the tree, and of the all-enclosing sphere of the
sky, with a voice of thunder that resounded from the whole horizon,
declared the unmoved and immovable prince to have already so given
of himself in compassion to the world that there was in fact no historical person there anymore, and he was eligible for that seat. With that,
the deluding ruler of the world—the lord Kāma, of lust; Māra, of the
fear of death; and Dharma, of socially imposed duty—was humbled,
his power broken, and the prince, that night, achieved the Enlightenment, which he then, for fifty years, made known as the Middle Way
of releasing humankind from delusion.

Gahmuret and Feirefiz

Wolfram's poem opens with the life of Parzival's father, Gahmuret, who was a Christian knight in the service of the caliph of Baghdad. In the course of this exotic career he arrives, one day, before the city and castle of the black queen, Belkane of Zazamanc, under siege from two armies simultaneously, a Muslim army and a Christian one. The situation is standard Celtic-Arthurian, concerning the queen of the fairy hill, to be saved by the blade of an errant knight. The adventure in Wolfram's tale, however, takes place in the actual world. The name of the queen, Belkane, when rendered in its proper form, Balakana, means "wife or widow of Bala," actually, of Nur-uddin Balak ben Bahram, who recovered Aleppo from the crusader-king Baldwin II of Jerusalem and married there a Seljuk princess. When he was later killed by an arrow, she and her son came under the protection of another Muslim prince named Timurtash: as in Wolfram's work, the protector of the black queen-widow Belkane is named Isenhart, which is a translation of the Turkish name Timurtash. Baldwin II of Jerusalem, to recover Aleppo, joined forces with an exiled Seljuk prince, Sultan Shah by name, and thus there were indeed two armies before Aleppo, a Muslim and a Christian one, at the famous siege (1122–1123). Timurtash (Isenhart) was slain, and defense of the city was undertaken by a Shi'ite leader whose banner displayed a star and crescent on a green field. The flag of Wolfram's Gahmuret displayed an anchor (emblematic of the Christian Church), likewise on a green field. The flag of the people of Aleppo displayed a silver hand (the Hand of Fatima) and a crowned staff on a black field: such was the flag of Belkane also. Thus we have indubitable evidence in this first great section of *Parzival* of precise information about the Muslim world having come into the poet's ken, as well as evidence of the poet's intention to represent the Muslim and Christian knightly modes as equivalent.

Queen Belkane of Zazamanc, having been rescued, along with her city, by the Christian knight Gahmuret, married and conceived by him. She would not allow him to go off adventuring in the good old way, however, and thoroughly bored with her domestic happiness, he one night secretly departed and returned to Wales. The queen subsequently bore a son, whose complexion was piebald, black and white. He was given the name Feirefiz, "son (*fils*) of varied hue," and when he grew to young manhood, he became the Muslim protector of a young Hindu widow and her son. The widow's name was Secondille, a transformation of the Sanskrit Sanyogīta, which was the name of an actual Indian princess, protected by an actual Muslim warrior-prince, Qutb-ud-din Aibak, who in the years 1206–1210 (the years of Wolfram's writing of his romance) became the sultan of Delhi and builder of its first mosque, with its famous polished-iron pillar, the Qutb-Minar. This appears in Wolfram's story as Secondille's magical pillar, which reflected on its shining surface events and people far away. Moreover, the name of her Muslim protector, Aibak, means "Moon *(ai)* Prince (*beg* or *bei*)," and is a reference to his beauty. But the moon is mottled, as was the complexion of Wolfram's Feirefiz; and so, again we have a playful substitution of the poet's fictional character for a known historical figure.

The story of Sanyogīta, by the way, is worth retelling. She was the daughter, about twenty years old, of King Jayacandra of Kanauj, and had fallen in love with the young Rajput king, Prithvi Raj III, of Ajmer and Delhi. Perceiving that she was ready for marriage, her father arranged for a *svayamvara:* an occasion, once customary in Indian aristocratic circles, in which a young princess would herself choose her husband from among a number of assembled candidates by placing a garland around the young man's neck. Sanyogīta's father had no use for the Rajput Prithvi Raj, who was a youth of about thirty; and so, instead of inviting him to the occasion, he had a statue made of an ugly demon, a *rakshasa,* to be placed in the young king's seat. Sanyogīta, when the moment came, placed her garland around the *rakshasa's* neck, at which instant, with a great clatter of arms, King Prithvi Raj III himself broke into the hall and carried the maiden away.

Popular ballads were sung in celebration of this brilliant romance. In the year 1192, however, Prithvi Raj was overwhelmed by the Afghan sultan Mu'zz-ud-din Muhammad; his city of Ajmer was taken, and he himself and his bride were made captive; and when his second city, Delhi, had also been destroyed, he was slain. The victorious sultan went on to conquer the city of Sanyogīta's father, Kanauj; next, Benares, in 1195; Gwalior, in 1197; and Gaur, in Bengal, in 1206. Before returning to Iran, he confided the young widow queen, with her small son, to the care of Aibak, his viceroy, who, in turn, became the first sultan of the slain King Prithvi Raj's former capital, Delhi.

These were tremendous events, and the noise of them resounded through all Islam.

Not only the rumors of such great events but also accounts of the *wonders* of the great Orient were coming back into Europe, and of these, four can be named as of immediate relevance to our topic. The first is the polished iron column, already mentioned, of the Qutb-Minar, which Wolfram celebrates and pictures as the magician Clinschor's magical reflecting column, stolen without her knowledge from Secondille, and set standing in a marvelous cupola on the roof of the magician's enchanted Castle of Marvels, where five hundred knights and five hundred ladies are magically imprisoned. The second is the Qasr-at-Taj, the truly fabulous palace of the Abbassid caliphs on the River Tigris, built by the Caliph al-Mu'tadid (892–902) and leveled to the ground when the Mongols wiped out Baghdad in 1258. In Wolfram's time it was still standing, and many of its known details appear in his description of Clinschor's halls. The third marvel was the great Buddhist stupa built by Emperor Kaniṣka (r. first century A.D.) of Kuṣāna, near Peshawar, which with its tower of steel, nearly nine hundred feet high and bearing twenty-five umbrellas, was at that time the tallest temple in all of India. Wolfram refers to it specifically as "the coffin of Lady Camille (*froun Camillon sarc*),[6] confusing the title of the Buddha as the Perfected One (*al-kamil*) with the name of Virgil's heroic Amazon, Camilla, of the *Aeneid* (books 1 and 7). He mentions it in his description, again, of Clinschor's Castle of Marvels. And finally, there was the famous stone begging bowl of the Buddha, preserved in a temple in Gandhara, described by the Chinese pilgrims Fa Hsien and Hsuan Tsang.[7]

This begging bowl, magically amalgamated of the four bowls brought to the Buddha at the moment of his illumination by the four guardian kings of the quarters, had become joined in Wolfram's imagination with the green "stone" relic in the treasury of San Lorenzo, which once had held the blood of the Christian Savior. Add the cauldron of Manannan, in his palace of immortal life, under the waves; the inheritance of that cauldron by the voyager Bran on the Isle of Women, who appears in the *Queste del Saint Graal* as the Grail King; the philosopher's stone, *lapis exilis,* from which spring the Waters of Life, and through which crude matter is turned into spiritual gold; and, perhaps, the Ka'aba, the stone brought down by Gabriel from heaven, now revered as the world center of Islam in the Great Mosque of pilgrimage in Mecca! Mythologically, symbolically, these are all variants of the one great revelation of the world's abundance—in Christian terms, the radiance of the Kingdom of the Father, spread upon the earth and made known to those who have died to themselves and become reborn in the vision of the All in all.

In Wolfram's *Parzival,* as in the legend of the three temptations of the Buddha, the Middle Way between heaven and hell is entered through the exercise of three virtues, plus a fourth: 1) disengagement from the fury of the passions, 2) fearlessness in the face of death, 3) indifference to the opinion of the world, and 4) compassion. Throughout Arthurian romance, these are the four tests of the heroes, as in the Orient they have been, and remain to this day, the supreme openers to saints of the mystical passage through what in Buddhism is known as the Gateless Gate.

Cundrie

Hermann Goetz points out in his article "Der Orient der Kreuzzüge in Wolframs *Parzival*" (The Orient of the Crusades in Wolfram's *Parzival*) that the attributes of this Grail messenger, Cundrie—her boar's snout and tusks and her boar's-bristle hair, astride her tall mule—are exactly those of certain Indian representations of the goddess Kālī in her terrible aspect. There is also a Tibetan version of this figure—Lhamo by name—who appears, like Cundrie, riding a tall pink mule for the chastisement of those who reject the gospel of compassion. But as we know from many Irish legends of the goddess of the Celtic Land of Youth Below Waves, this goddess, too, may appear with the unappetizing head and face of a pig. When she appears in this guise, for example, to Finn McCool's son Ossian, hinting that he should marry her, he boldly kisses her muzzle·and she is transformed. And he spends many a happy year as king with her in the Land of Youth.[8]

Frazer, in *The Golden Bough,* has shown that both Demeter and Persephone were at one time pig goddesses,[9] and there is evidence enough to suggest that the Irish, Greek, and Indian forms of these goddesses are related variants of a single Neolithic and Bronze Age heritage, where both the wild boar and the domestic pig were associated with a mythology of death and rebirth.[10]

The Grail Knights

Professor Goetz has suggested (rightly, I think) that the vow of absolute anonymity required of Wolfram's knights of the Castle of the Grail —which was something very different from anything required of a Round Table knight—can have had as a model only the vow of the Fidai of the Mohammedan Assassins: a mystico-revolutionary, fanatical Shi'ite sect of Islam, devoted to the service of the Hidden Imam, who, as the "true" leader of Islam, in secret opposition to the orthodox caliphate, might be thought comparable in import to the hidden Castle of the Grail, in contrast to the visible Church of Rome. The hidden fairy hills of the old Celtic gods; the Hidden Imam of Islam; the Kingdom of the Father, spread upon the earth, unseen; and the Land under Waves, of Eternal Life! In the Indian Katha Upaniṣad we read:

> *Though It is hidden in all things*
> *That Universal Self (*ātman*) does not shine forth,*
> *Yet is seen by subtle seers*
> *Of subtle mind and subtle sight.*[11]

In his beautiful essay "On the Basis of Morality," Schopenhauer asks the following question: How is it that a human being can so experience the pain and peril of another, that, forgetting his own well-being, he comes spontaneously to that other person's rescue? How is it that what we generally take to be the first law of nature, self-preservation, can be thus suddenly suspended, so that even at the risk of death one moves on impulse to another's rescue? And the answer he gives is this: such a move is inspired by a metaphysical truth and realization, namely, that we and that other *are* one, our sense and experience of separateness being of a secondary order, a mere effect of the way in which the light-world consciousness experiences objects within a conditioning frame of space and time. More deeply, more truly, we are of one consciousness and one life. Compassion (German: *Mitleid,* "cosuffering"), unself-conscious love, transcends the divisive experience of opposites: *I* and *thou, good* and *evil, Christian* and *heathen, birth* and *death.* And the experience of the Grail, in Wolfram's reading, is of this unity, or identity beyond contrariety. Indeed, the very sense of his hero's name, Parzival, he reads as *perce le val,* "right through the middle" (*rehte enmitten durch*).[12] And not righteousness or self-righteousness but compassion alone is the key to the opening of this all-uniting Middle Way.

The Question and the Turning Wheel

I have had the relationship between Anfortas's wound and Parzival's question in mind for a long, long time. I started work on the Grail romances when I was a young man. In the course of my interest in the Oriental material, I've been watching for parallels, and I ran into a most astounding one some time ago. In the *Pancatantra*, a textbook of animal stories devoted to the art of politics, there's a charming story of four brahmins who had been wealthy and suddenly find themselves poor. And they decided to get rich again somehow.

FIGURE 30. The wheel of *dharma* (carved stone, India, thirteenth century)

So the four of them get together and start off on an expedition. They go north, and as they approach the Himalayas, they encounter a great yogi, whose name is Bhairavananda, which is one of the names of Śiva in his most horrific aspect—Bhairavananda really means "terror lives."

They approach Bhairavananda and tell him their story. He says, "I'll tell you how to get rich. I'll give you four fellows four quills, one quill each. And you just walk north, up over the Himalayas in the Tibetan direction. And when the quills drop, you will find wealth proffered to you."

So the four start north, and the first quill drops. They burrow in the soil, and sure enough, it's all copper. And the first chap says, "You fellows can share this with me," but they say, "Oh, no, we're going on. We have our own quills to find." The first chap stays with the copper, and the other three go on.

Next the second quill drops, they dig in the soil, and there's silver. "You fellows can share this with me," he says.

"Oh, no, we're going on." The third quill drops, and it's gold.

What's going to be beyond this? The fourth fellow says, "Don't you see? Copper? Silver? Gold?" So he goes on.

He comes into the land of a vast desert. There's no one there. It's the land of terrible fairies. And he's parched with thirst. One of these typical desert scenes is of a man marooned in the desert, and off in the distance he sees a strange, solitary sight: a man standing on a table that is slowly turning. This is the world axis, really. And this man, standing on the table, has on his head a wheel that is slowly revolving with great cutting edges so that the blood is pouring down his body from these wounds.

Our friend approaches, and on seeing the man there, asks, "What is that wheel doing on your head?" And when he does, the wheel pops off the other man's head and onto *his* head.

The other man is released. And he says, "Thank you very much!"

The one who now has the wheel, now called in the story the wheel bearer, then asks, "How long have you been here?"

And the released man says, "Who is king in the world now?"

And the new wheel bearer gives the answer, "Rāma."

"Never heard of him. When that wheel came onto my head, so-and-so was king." And this ruler lived millennia earlier.

"But when is this wheel going to leave my head?"

"When someone comes along with a quill, as you came, and asks, 'What's that wheel doing on your head?'"

This figure, in this little fable, is a warning against being too greedy. But the original tale is a Buddhist one. And that figure with the wheel is the Bodhisattva, the one who is the boon-bearer to the world. And it is a precise parallel to the crucified Christ with the crown of thorns; he's in exactly the same role. And so our wounded king, Anfortas, is also the wounded Christ.

FIGURE 31. Crucifixion (etching, Germany, 1498)

Wagner brings up this point in his adaptation of the Grail's romance also. In the very last line of the opera, the king has been healed by Parsifal during his second visit, and from the loft come the boys' angelic voices, singing of redemption for the redeemer. The one who redeems the world must himself be redeemed—because, through the will of ignorance, his blood has become, as it were, petrified. The blood must be liquefied, and made to flow again, in its redeeming form. That is to say, the sense of the Crucifixion must be experienced.

Figure 32. Gottfried von Strassburg, author of *Tristan and Iseult* (ink on vellum, c. 1304)

CHAPTER 5

Tristan and Iseult

ALONG WITH WOLFRAM'S *Parzival,* the other great tale of this era is that of the adulterous love affair between Tristan and Iseult.

We have the manuscripts of six or eight different tellings of the romance from the Middle Ages. The most important is that of Gottfried von Strassburg, who died before he finished, so that you have to continue with the story on which he was modeling his own, the version told by Thomas of Britain. One characteristic of medieval storytelling is that the poet didn't invent the story; he developed it. The bards, troubadours, and minnesingers would take a traditional story and interpret it, giving it new depth and meaning in keeping with the conditions of their particular day and place.

The story of Tristan is that of a typical epic hero whose parents have died. He is the orphan son. His mother's brother is the king of Cornwall (here we have the uncle-nephew relationship), but Tristan himself was born in Brittany. So we have the whole Celtic world. Tristan goes to his uncle's castle in Cornwall and arrives at the same time that an emissary has come from the court of Ireland. The Irish king conquered the Cornish king and requires a tribute: every four or five years young boys and girls must be brought to the service of the Irish throne. The queen of the Irish court is Iseult's mother, whose name is also Iseult, and her brother Morholt is the emissary who has come to collect the tribute: the Dragon Knight, whose shield bears the emblem of a dragon.

This tale is based, of course, on the story of Athens and Crete, of Theseus and the Minotaur. In other words, we can see a perfectly standard mythological syndrome in this sequence, and that will continue. The arrival of the Irish champion, the queen's brother Morholt, marks Tristan's call to the hero adventure.[1] His journey will continue with a dragon battle, an underworld journey, a bride theft, and a return. Tristan's story and Iseult's look closely at the themes of death and resurrection on the one hand and sickness and healing on the other, ringing changes on the myth of Orpheus and Eurydice, with the elder Iseult as Persephone, Queen of the Netherworld, in whom—as in Medusa and many other female monsters of this kind—the powers both of healing and of death reside. And the poet Gottfried von Strassburg, obviously, was perfectly aware of these analogies.

FIGURE 33. Morholt and Tristan (glazed tile, England, c. 1260)

So Tristan arrives in Cornwall just as Morholt arrives from Ireland to collect the youths and maidens to bring to the Irish court. And Iseult the Elder has prepared a poison and placed it on Morholt's sword. Tristan says to his uncle, King Mark, "Let me handle that guy."

His uncle says, "Are you sure? This is very dangerous."

Tristan, says, "This is the only way." So he issues a challenge to the Irish knight, and a jousting champion's battle is prepared between Morholt and Tristan. When Tristan rides against Morholt, Morholt's sword comes down on Tristan's knee, cutting him and injecting the poison into Tristan's blood. The young man is as good as dead, but he manages to bring his sword down on Morholt's head, and it splits the Irishman's helmet, and a chink from Tristan's sword remains in Morholt's skull.

Morholt is brought back dead to Ireland. And his niece, Iseult, who loved her uncle, takes the piece of the sword out of his head and puts it in her little treasure chest to remember her uncle by.

Back in Cornwall, Tristan has become terribly ill. The wound is festering; gangrene sets in, and he says to his uncle, "Just put me in a little boat with my harp, and the boat will carry me to the source of this poison." And indeed, by magic, the boat carries him to Dublin Bay.

FIGURE 34. Tristan sailing to Dublin Bay (glazed tile, England, c. 1260)

When Tristan arrives, the people hear the beautiful music of his harp. Clearly, he is a miraculous young man, so they bring him to Queen Iseult to be cured. She seems not to recognize that it is her own poison that is killing Tristan, nor does she work out who this chap really is. To disguise his identity, he calls himself *Tantris* (French: *tant trist,* "very sad").

In any case, Queen Iseult nurses him. And when the wound has healed sufficiently that the stench of his presence can be tolerated, she invites her daughter, Iseult the Younger, to hear him play the harp, he plays so wonderfully.

Immediately, of course, the two fall in love—only they don't know it. They are crazy in love with each other, but they have no idea. He plays the harp better than he has ever played it in his life, and so Tristan becomes her music teacher.

FIGURE 35. Tristan teaching Iseult to play the harp (glazed tile, England, c. 1260)

The model here is the real-life twelfth-century love story of Abelard and Heloise. Abelard was Heloise's teacher and seduced her. Tristan is the teacher of Iseult, but he doesn't even know to try. Furthermore, when he's cured, this silly boy goes back to Cornwall and says to his uncle Mark, "I met the most wonderful girl. She'd be just the wife for you!"

He speaks so gloriously of this girl that Mark tells Tristan, "Well, why don't you go fetch her for me?"

So, Tristan, calling himself Tantris again, goes back to fetch Iseult for his uncle.

Do you see the courtly love problem here? Tristan has fallen in love. His uncle has never seen Iseult. Mark and Iseult's marriage is to be standard medieval violence: there's no love in it, just political expediency.

Still, Tristan returns to Ireland to present Mark's suit. Unfortunately, there is a rival suitor for the princess's hand: the queen's seneschal, who's a bit of a creep. And, of course, more than a few other courtiers would love to snag the princess.

"Well," says the queen, "Iseult is the sole heir to our throne. With her hand comes Ireland. So we'll have a quest to earn her hand. Whoever slays the terrible dragon that has been marauding through our countryside shall win our daughter in marriage."

Well, the seneschal who has his eye on Iseult is not much at killing dragons. Instead he's always snooping around, in case anyone kills the dragon, so that he can make the claim.

Meanwhile, Tristan goes questing, and he arrives at this huge, fire-belching dragon. The dragon opens his mouth and bites off the whole front half of Tristan's horse.

FIGURE 36. Tristan and the dragon (tapestry, Austria, fourteenth century)

Somehow Tristan manages to kill the dragon. He cuts its tongue out and puts it in his shirt to prove that it's he who's killed the beast. That's the wrong thing to do with the tongue of a dragon, because that tongue is poisonous. So he's walking along and the poison overcomes him, and he falls into a puddle of water, and all that's sticking out is his nose.

Meanwhile, here's this other fellow, the seneschal, who hears the dragon sounds, and when he first sees the dead dragon, he's so frightened he runs away, and it takes him a little while to get back.

Finally he works up the courage to carve off the head of the dragon, and he brings it to court.

Meanwhile, Iseult and her mother are out walking, and they notice a nose sticking up out of a puddle, and they pull this chap out—Tantris!—and they find the dragon tongue. So they take him back to the court, and once again the queen starts nursing him back to life.

Tristan is in the bathtub, recovering from being poisoned once more.

Outside, Iseult the Younger is fooling around with his sword and sheath. She pulls the sword out of the sheath, and *wow!* There's a familiar-looking nick in the sword. She runs to her little treasure chest, and there is the piece that came out of Uncle Morholt's skull. It fits. She mutters to herself, "Tan-tris, Tris-tan, Tan-tris, Tristan..." Tristan and Tantris are one and the same, and his sword killed Morholt!

FIGURE 37. Iseult attacks Tristan in the tub (ink and gold on vellum, France, c. 1320)

With sword in hand, Iseult finds Tristan in the bathtub. She raises the sword up, but he says, "Hold on! You kill me, and that other guy gets you."

Well, the sword is getting kind of heavy anyway, so she puts it down and drops the issue. When Tristan is cured, then comes this wonderful affair of the giving of Iseult to the killer of the dragon—and (coincidently) of her uncle. And this lout, the queen's steward, comes in with the dragon's head.

Tristan says, "Well, let's open the mouth and see what is inside." What do you know! There is no tongue. Tristan has it, since he is the one who actually killed the dragon. So Tristan gets the girl.

So now instead of taking her for himself, he is going to take her back to his uncle, King Mark in Cornwall. He's only fifteen years old, and he doesn't know what's happened to him.

Iseult's mother prepares this love potion to take to Mark for the wedding night and gives it to Iseult's nurse, Brangaene. There's a secret here: *the poison and the love potion are essentially the same.* The pain of love is the sickness unto death that no doctors can cure. So the same woman who brought Tristan to Ireland by poisoning him is now preparing the love potion. But it's supposed to be for Iseult and Mark.

Off they go across the Irish Sea, Tristan, Iseult, and Brangaene, little Iseult's nurse, who is to keep the love potion safe and present it to the couple at the time of the wedding.

Next comes the most famous scene in the story. Sailing on the boat across the Irish Sea, Tristan and Iseult decide to have a drink together; but instead of wine, they accidentally drink the love draught.

FIGURE 38. The love potion (print, United States, 1905)

When the two of them, a couple of kids, drink this potion, they have no idea what has happened to them.

They begin to feel sick. They don't know what ails them. And Iseult says—girls are faster than boys in catching on—"I think it's *l'amour.*" But she slurs her words. Did she say *la mère* ("the mother")? Or did she mean *le mer* ("the sea")? If it's the sea, are they seasick, or is this what is called love? Or did she say *la mort* ("death")?

They've just about caught on to what's happened to them, when Brangaene—the nurse who was supposed to make sure that the love potion was drunk by Iseult and King Mark—realizes that she left the draught unguarded. She discovers that the couple has drunk it and is appalled.

She goes to Tristan and says, "Tristan, you have drunk your death!"

This is a wonderful scene in Gottfried's version. Tristan answers, "I don't know what you mean. If by death you mean the pain of my love for Iseult, that's my life. If by death you mean the punishment that I am to suffer in society, I accept that. If by death you mean eternal damnation in hell, then I accept that, too!"

Meister Eckhart said, "Love knows no pain." In Dante's *Divine Comedy* there's a grand scene in the second circle of hell, the Circle of the Carnal Sinners: Tristan and Iseult, Lancelot and Guinevere, Helen and Paris, Paolo and Francesca: everybody worth anything in the whole history of humanity is in there. They come in on a flaming wind, and it looks as though they are in pain. But as William Blake puts it in that wonderful text of his called *The Marriage of Heaven and Hell:* "As I was walking among the fires of Hell…which to angels look like torment and insanity, I collected some of their Proverbs." And among the number of these was the following: "Dip him in the river who loves water." So here we are. These lovers don't want water; aflame themselves, they want the flaming wind.

What we have here is the difference between the Levantine Christian social order, which is imported, and the accent on the individual life that was native to Europe. By what kind of magic can anyone put God in your heart? They can't. That is the sense of the thing. We saw how Wolfram von Eschenbach coordinated the two traditions through his vision of the Grail. That's the problem here—but this is a love story, so no happy endings.

We have arrived at a theological problem: if the love potion compels you to love, then the love of Tristan and Iseult, although it is adulterous, *is not a mortal sin.* To commit a mortal sin, one must have a serious matter, sufficient reflection, and full consent of the will. But if it's magic that has done it, there's no consent of the will and it's a perfectly innocent love. A number of the authors of the Tristan story fixed it up so that the love potion would work for three or four years. And then when it stops, sin begins. Not here, though: this is love to the death.

Now a terrible thing happens: they come to port, and Iseult has to become King Mark's wife. And she plays a dirty game. She puts Brangaene in her place to go to bed with Mark. This proves that Mark wasn't worthy of her. As I always say: inattention to details. He thinks he's sleeping with Iseult, poor slob! He's doubly disqualified for marriage now.

Tristan and Iseult begin an affair, and eventually King Mark becomes aware of it. The proper thing to do, of course, is to have them killed as traitors, but Mark can't bear to do it. He loves them both.

In the coarser versions of this tale, King Mark is an anxious, spying cuckold, little better than a clown, the main interest of long sections of the narrative deriving simply from the cleverness by which he is deceived. Even in his sympathetic treatment of Mark's agony, Gottfried makes the point that Mark himself was at fault, in as much as he was thinking to retain by right and might what he had lost to love. "This is the case against Surveillance," he wrote:

> That it breeds and fosters for the one who cultivates it nothing but briers and thorns....No matter how far it is pressed, such a guard is lost on a woman. For no man can keep watch on a wicked one, whereas the virtuous needs no watch. She keeps guard, as they say, on herself. And if one nevertheless sets a watch on her, he will gain nothing from that but her hate. Indeed, he will ruin his wife, root and branch: and probably to such an extent that she will never reform her ways enough to be quit of whatever clings to her of the briers of his growing.[2]

Gottfried's Mark is a noble man. He simply says, "You're both banished; get out of my sight. Go away."

And off they go into the forest: these are the forest years of Tristan and Iseult.

They come to a cave fashioned by the giants of pre-Christian times. We are back to the old Celtic-Germanic world. And over the entrance there is an inscription that reads "The Chapel for Lovers."

Every detail of this chapel has symbolic meaning: chastity, loyalty, purity, and so forth. All the terms have new meanings, of course, in this context. And where the altar would have been is a bed of crystal. The sacrament of the altar is the sacrament of sex. Gottfried meant this. Medieval people meant this. The sacrament of love is sexual intercourse. And it *is* a sacrament.

Just above the bed are two openings in the cave roof through which light comes. One fine day they hear off in the woods the blowing of hunting horns. These are the horns of King Mark, who is out on a hunt.

And Tristan thinks, *If Mark comes and looks down and sees us asleep together, that would be bad.* So what does he do? He places his sword between himself and Iseult. This is honor against love—and Tristan has sided with honor. This is the sin of Tristan, to have put the sword between them.

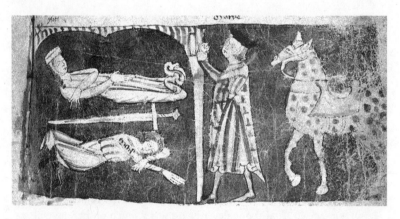

FIGURE 39. Tristan and Isolde sleeping with a sword between them (ink on vellum, Germany, thirteenth century)

And when Mark looks down, he indeed sees the two with the sword between them, and he says, "Oh, I have misunderstood them!" So he invites them back to court.

And that is the beginning of the end of their affair. They are caught again, and this time there is no fooling around. Mark's steward,

Marjodoc, having dreamed of Tristan as a raging wild boar, apprises King Mark of the affair, and the lovers, surrounded by suspicion, became extremely circumspect—during the day. At night Tristan steals out to an olive orchard, where he cuts from a twig some shavings, which he then tosses into a brook that flows past Iseult's apartment; and when Iseult sees these, she sneaks away to their tryst.

One night, King Mark, apprised of their custom by his dwarf Melot, hides himself, along with the dwarf, in the boughs of an olive tree above the brook. But the lovers see his shadow, cast by the moonlight into the water, and their deft conversation throws him off the scent—temporarily.

FIGURE 40. King Mark and Melot spy on Tristan and Iseult (ink on paper, England, fourteenth century)

At last, of course, the affair is exposed, and Tristan is exiled back to Brittany. But before he goes, Iseult has to undergo a trial by ordeal: she has to take an oath that she has not lain with any man but her husband, and having taken this oath she is to grasp in her hand a red-hot iron bar. And if the hand is not burned, she will be vindicated and released from the accusation.

She is on the way to this trial, and they've arranged that she has to cross a river in a boat. Tristan in disguise takes the job of ferryman. He ferries Iseult across and then has to lift her out of the boat. He manages to trip and fall on top of her, so when she goes to the trial she can say, "I have lain with no man but my husband—and the boatman who fell on top of me." So she isn't telling a lie, and the iron doesn't burn her.

"You see," Gottfried says, "Christ is like a weather vane, he blows where the wind goes."[3] That may be why Gottfried didn't finish the book! No one knows how he died, but they were burning people to death in those days for statements of that kind.

Now comes a strange sort of envoi to the whole story. Tristan goes home to Brittany, where he hears of a young lady whose name is also Iseult. She is known as Iseult of the White Hands. This is the kind of thing that happens in medieval romance: he falls in love with her name and marries the lady.

Poor little Iseult of the White Hands. Because she isn't the true Iseult, Tristan can't bring himself to have intercourse with her. She's out riding with her brother, Caerdin, one day and the horse steps into a puddle and the water splashes up on her thigh, and she says to her brother, "The water is bolder than Tristan."

When Caerdin says, "What's this?" she tells him about the situation. Caerdin, being a good brother, is outraged, and goes to Tristan, ready to challenge him. But when Tristan tells him of his love for the other Iseult, Caerdin understands the whole thing.

Gottfried handles with delicacy the infatuation of the lover with the name and then the person of the sensitive, sympathetic, but finally deeply mortified bride. His poem breaks off before the end; for the greatest love poet of the Middle Ages died before completing his masterwork. We know, nevertheless, how the narrative was to have ended, from the version of Thomas of Britain, Gottfried's source.

A youthful knight named, remarkably, Dwarf Tristan, whose mistress has been abducted by a certain Estult l'Orgillus of Castel Fer, comes riding to beg Tristan for assistance. The abductor has six brothers, and Tristan slays all seven; but in the battle, Dwarf Tristan, too, is slain, and Tristan himself—once again—is wounded unto death, pierced by a poisoned weapon through his loins.

Caerdin, our Tristan's brother-in-law, having learned of Tristan's secret love, sails to Cornwall to bring Iseult to him to care for him. The signal of her coming is to be a white sail on the returning ship, but if Iseult was not aboard, the sail is to be black.

After a long delay, the vessel comes into view and the sail is indeed white. The second Iseult, Iseult of the White Hands, says to her mortally wounded spouse, "My love, my brother's ship is coming: I have seen the ship on the sea. God grant it brings the news that is to give comfort to your heart."

Our lover, starting up from his bed of pain cries, "Do you know the ship for sure? My darling, tell me! What color is the sail?"

But instead of telling him the truth, she says, "I see it well. The sail is black."

The whole denouement is again a duplication of the dragon-wound-and-cure motif, with the two Iseults personifying the contrary aspects of the goddess in both her life-giving and life-devouring aspects, and with the seven brothers as a kind of dragon of seven heads.[4] The name Dwarf Tristan itself is enough to suggest the symbolic analogies of the episode.

The most telling item, however, is the fatal sail motif, which comes directly from the classical tale of Theseus's return to Athens from his conquest of the Minotaur in Crete. He departed to the adventure in a vessel with black sails; his father, King Aegeus, has provided a white set, to be used if the vessel returned victorious. Theseus in Crete, we recall, has been enabled to emerge alive from the labyrinth with the aid of King Minos's daughter, sister of the Minotaur, the lovely Ariadne, whom he took with him when he left. But he abandoned her on the island of Dia, and some say she hanged herself. Others tell, however, that Dionysos, the great god of wine and bread, love, death and rebirth, abducted her from Theseus and carried her to Naxos, where first he and then she disappeared.

In any case, such confusion prevails aboard the returning hero's ship as it makes its way back to Athens that the crew forgets to raise the white sails, and as a consequence, when it heaves into view, King Aegeus, Theseus's father, watching for the returning craft from the height of the Acropolis, sees the black sails, and supposing his son to have failed, flings himself from the rock and dies in the sea that now bears his name.

Moreover, it is worth noticing that in the classical legend, when the redeeming hero, Theseus, first arrives as a youth in Athens, his father, King Aegeus, who had begotten him out of wedlock with the daughter of the governor of a small city in Argolis, does not recognize him. The errant king has left a sword and pair of shoes beneath a great stone that had a hollow exactly fitting them; and he has told the girl who had conceived of him—Aethra by name—that if she bore him a son, he should be able, when he came to manhood, to lift the stone and take its trophies, after which he was to come to Athens. The boy is fostered by his grandfather Pittheus.

In due time Theseus lifts the stone, takes the trophies, and comes to Athens incognito—just as Tristan, incognito, comes to Mark. The young hero finds King Aegeus living with the sorceress Medea, who tries to poison the returned son with a cup of wine. In the nick of time the father, recognizing the sword as his own, strikes the cup and spills the poisoned wine, and on the place where it falls an image of Hermes, god of travelers and guide of souls, is erected. There follows the adventure of the labyrinth, within which Theseus slays the Cretan monster the Minotaur and so terminates the custom of the tribute.

Relating this legend to that of Tristan, we may note that the sorceress Medea, furthermore, can be compared to Queen Iseult. Medea's chariot, according to Euripides, is drawn by dragons, and according to Thomas of Britain, the brother of Queen Iseult, Morholt the Mighty, carries on his shield the emblem of a dragon. The goddess patroness of Theseus's voyage to Crete is Aphrodite—as she also guides Tristan's journey to Ireland.

Gertrude Schoepperle, in her exhaustive analysis of the Tristan motifs and their sources, was the first, I believe, to notice that, besides the matter of the sails, there is also a classical Paris-Helen motif suggested in the legend. Paris's nurse (and then wife, before he absconds with Helen) is the ageless nymph Oinone; and his legend tells that, when he is wounded by a poisoned arrow shot by Philoctetes from the bow of Herakles, in those terrible last days of the Trojan War, Paris sends for Oinone, and, on hearing that she refuses to come to him, dies. She is actually at that moment hastening after the messenger with her magical herbs and simples. Arriving too late, she slays herself and is buried with Paris in the same grave.

One thinks here of the relationship of the Valkyrie Brünnhilde to Wagner's hero Siegfried and his defection, then, to Gutrune, with Brünnhilde's subsequent suttee death—Siegfried's funeral pyre. These are ancient, mighty themes, going back at least as far as the Royal Tombs of Ur.[5]

Finally, there is an interesting echo of the Old Irish romance of Diarmuid and Gráinne. As we read above, when Tristan's young wife, Iseult of the White Hands, is riding on her palfrey in the company of her brother Caerdin, the mount splashes into a puddle and some of the water streaks to her thigh, whereupon the brother overhears an exclamation. He asks what she has said, just as Diarmuid asks Gráinne on a like occasion, and she tells him that the water was bolder than her spouse—whereupon Caerdin confronts Tristan with a challenge and learns from him the whole secret of his life.

In the Tristan story, there are echoes of Theseus and the Minotaur all along the line. This is the conflict: love against marriage, *amour* against *honeur*. How do we bring these things together? The marriage situation was that of normal medieval and Oriental custom, with the family arranging the marriage. But the aristocracy of Europe regarded this as intolerable, as is particularly evident in two of the greatest poems of the Middle Ages, Gottfried's *Tristan* and Wolfram von Eschenbach's *Parzival.*

Origins and Transmission of the Tristan Story

We do not know the earliest form of the romance of Tristan and Iseult. The name Tristan itself, however, has been traced far beyond Brittany to a certain King Drustan, son of Talorc, who in the years. 780–785 A.D. ruled the Picts in the marches of Scotland and Northumberland. The Picts (Latin: *Picti*, "the painted, or tattooed, people") were of a Bronze Age, pre-Celtic stock, which, during the period of Roman rule in Britain had remained unsubdued northward of the Antonine Wall. In King Drustan's day they were being harried, both by invading Celts from Christian Ireland, known as Scots (a word meaning approximately "marauders"), who toward the close of the Roman period had begun establishing settlements in Argyll, and, on the other side, by Norwegian Viking raiders from the still-pagan Baltic region. King Drustan would have had little leisure for the dear sorrows and the bitter sweets of love.

However, about the year 843, hardly sixty years after his reign, his battered people were overcome by the Irish Celts of Argyll, and the two royal lines, Scottish and Pictish, were united by a royal marriage—whereupon some sort of legend, or cycle of legends, concerning Drustan son of Talorc passed from Pictland to Ireland, from Ireland to Wales and Cornwall, and finally to Brittany, where the hero now was said to have been born.

We do not know what the Pictish legend was; in Wales, however, where the hero's name became Trystan son of Tallwch, he was celebrated as a master of tricks and as a lover, particularly of Esyllt, the wife of a certain King Marc—known also as Eochaid—whose legend seems to have entered Wales independently from Cornwall, in the south, where he is named as a Celtic king of about Drustan's time. Those were centuries of a tremendous influence and expansion of Celtic Christian civilization from Ireland, not only to Wales, Pictland (now Scotland), and Anglo-Saxon England, but also to the continent, overrun as it had been by pagan German tribes. We may think of Saint Columcille, known also as Columba (521–597), who with twelve disciples founded the church and monastery of Iona in the Hebrides, just off the coast of Argyll, and applied himself from there to the conversion of the Picts. Another of the kind was Saint Columban (543–615), who with twelve disciples went to France, to the Vosges (Haute Saône), where he built the Luxeuil Abbey. Saint Gall (d. 645), in Switzerland, founded the celebrated monastery and seat of learning, St. Gallen; while in Wales, a native son, Saint David (c. 500–600?), established the cathedral town of St. Davids on the westernmost point of Pembrokeshire, which became not only a center of pilgrimage (two to St. Davids equaling one to Rome), but also a point of departure for the very popular pilgrimage to the shrine of Santiago de Compostela in northern Spain. Both Greek and Latin studies were cultivated in the Celtic world at that time. The abbot Ailerán of Clonard (c. 660), writing a work on the mystical meaning of the names in Christ's genealogy, quoted familiarly from Origin, Jerome, Philo, and Augustine. The learned Sedulius, abbot of Kildare (c. 820) corrected his Latin New Testament from a Greek original.

However, the important point to our present reading of the legends of Diarmuid, Drustan, Marc, and the rest is the remarkable fact
that, although in Christian Wales and Ireland the arts of the Druids
had been suppressed, those of the professional literary men, the *filid*
and the bards, with their treasury of ancient pagan stories, were not
only tolerated but even cherished. Saint Columcille himself, at the
Convention of Druim Ceat, in the year 575, secured for the *filid* and
bards a guarantee of honored recognition. Not only was it required of
these masters of narration that they should know all the old stories (of
the *ollaves*, the *filid* of highest rank, 350 were to be known by heart),
but it was also expected that they should know how to amplify and
combine, to fashion new constructions. Moreover, in Wales, during
this period of the Celtic Christian Golden Age (from the sixth to the
twelfth centuries), there was a great infusion not only of Irish lore but
also of Irish stock. Hence, it is by no means surprising that it should
have been in Wales, some time before the year 1000, that the very popular Irish adventure of Diarmuid, Gráinne, and Finn Mac Cumhaill
should have become attached to the names, already joined, of Trystan,
Essylt, and Mark, after which the composite triangle passed to Celtic
Brittany. And there the melancholy final episodes were added of the
second Iseult, Tristan's virgin wife, Iseult of the White Hands.

The fully developed Tristan romance of the French and German
poets of the late twelfth and early thirteenth centuries (c. 1160–1210)
divides broadly into five parts:

1. The parents, birth, and boyhood of the hero
2. The king's champion: first visit to Ireland
3. The bride quest: second visit to Ireland
4. Iseult of Ireland: the love potion
5. Iseult of Brittany: the love death

The earliest versions of the fully developed Tristan romance are
lost. The best scholars now believe, however, that there was a period
of largely oral development (c. 1066–1150) when Welsh and Breton
fabulators were made welcome in the French and Norman courts.
Three of the French poets, for instance, mention a certain Welsh
author Bledri, whose name they variously write as Bréri, Bleherés, and
Bléhés. He is declared by one to have known "all the feats and all the
tales of all the kings and all the courts who had lived in Britain," by
another to have possessed the knowledge of the secret of the Grail, and

by the third to have been "born and begotten in Wales" *(né et engenuï en Galles)*, and to have been the man who introduced the legend of Gawain to the court of the Count of Poitiers.

Thomas of Britain, author of the earliest version of the romance still extant, derived his story from one by this master Bréri. Thomas of Britain was Gottfried's source, and as in Gottfried, so in Thomas (therefore, possibly, also in Bréri), the influence of the love potion lasts throughout the romance. (As I have pointed out, another version states that the love potion lost its effect after a spell of three or four years, thus rendering the lovers fully culpable of committing their sins.)

A number of scholars believe that there must have been a single, basic, literary version of the Tristan romance, now lost, from which the known versions of the legend all derived; and a question arises consequently as to the nature of the potion in that original. The question also arises as to the possible relationship of the master Bréri to that work. The facts and possibilities with which we have to reckon are as follows:

c. 1130–1140: Bréri, Welsh conteur in Poitou

1136: Geoffrey of Monmouth's *Historia Regum Britanniae*, a prose chronicle, purporting to be a history of the kings of Celtic Britain; refers to Arthur as "the Boar of Cornwall": no mention here of Tristan.

c. 1150: an assumed "archetype" of the Tristan romance, a work supposed to have been composed in Norman French, author unknown, from which the earliest extant versions are assumed to have been derived.

1150–1175: the Arthurian *Lais of Marie de France* testifies to an extensive Arthurian tradition already well known; the authoress tells of hearing the tales from minstrels, singing to the music of the rote: "The Lay of the Honeysuckle" is of Tristan and Isolde—"Was it not with them as with the honeysuckle and hazel tree? So sweetly laced in one embrace that thus they might remain while life endured! But should rough hands part them, the hazel would wither at the root and the honeysuckle fail."[6] They were parted indeed, and Tristan is said to have wrought this lay to the music of his harp. He had been banished, it tells, to South Wales, "where he was born," but returned secretly to Cornwall, where he learned of a Pentecost festival at Tintagel, to which the queen would be riding through the wood. He left a hazel wand in her path, peeled of its bark and carved with his name. She spied it, and they enjoyed an hour of love.

1155: Wace's *Roman de Brut,* a Norman French version of Geoffrey of Monmouth's *History.* Here the detail of the Round Table appears for the first time: there is no mention, however, of Tristan.

c. 1160: the Norman French *Tristan* of Thomas of Britain was composed for the Angevin court. Thomas states that he knows many versions of the legend and that it has been his effort to harmonize them. Tristan is represented as having lived one generation later than Arthur. The effect of the love potion remains in force throughout the lives of the couple, and Mark, too, partakes of the cup. Love is here revered as the mark of a generous, well-bred nature.

c. 1170–1175: the Middle High German *Tristan* of the North German poet Eilhart von Oberge. Here the force of the philter abates after three or four years in order to rationalize Tristan's marriage to Iseult of the White Hands. Scholars favoring the archetype theory believe that Eilhart followed a form of the romance from which Thomas is supposed to have departed.

c. 1190–1200: the Norman-French *Tristan* of Béroul, which follows the version of the supposed archetype and of Eilhart.

c. 1210: the Middle High German *Tristan* of Gottfried von Strassburg, which follows Thomas, and is the unquestioned masterwork of the entire tradition, the creation of one of the supreme poets of the Middle Ages. Gottfried's version is the source of Wagner's opera.

c. 1226–1235: the French prose *Tristan*—in the words of historian Myrrha Lot-Borodine, "enormous and insipid...a sort of mosaic composed of bits and pieces, out of which the soul of the elder poetry has departed. In this stillborn work [there is] a brutal suppression of the love that haunts the predestined couple and a pretentious attribution to those immortal heroes, transformed into marionettes, of sentimental adventures quite different from the incomparable unique adventure of their destiny."[7]

1485: the first printing by William Caxton of Sir Thomas Malory's *Le Morte Darthur*. This handy summary of Arthurian romance was translated largely from the Old French Prose Cycles, with approximately one third of its content from the prose *Tristan,* namely, the matter of books 8, 9, and 10, and the last four chapters of book 12. In this massive, extremely popular late compendium of Arthurian matter, Tristan is represented as one of the Knights of the Round Table; Mark is transformed into a cowardly dastard and tyrant; and Tristan is slain by Mark himself, who thrusts a poisoned spear into his back while he is singing to Iseult in her bower. (In this last feature we have something closer to Wagner's wounding of his hero than anything in the earlier poetic works.)

Until recently it was believed that Béroul wrote around the year 1155, and so predated Thomas, and this may have something to do with the fact that a number of authorities even today are still inclined to believe that the Eilhart-Béroul version adheres the more closely of the two to the Welsh or Breton ur-*Tristan* archetype. Gottfried, on the other hand, asserts that Thomas of Britain's version is the one to be regarded as authentic. Those others, he states, "wrote well and with the noblest of intentions, for my good and for the world's good; and they did so in right good faith.... However, they did not follow the correct version, as given by Thomas of Britain, who was the master of adventure tales; for he had read in British books the lives of all lords of the land, which then, for us, he retold."[8]

In the Eilhart-Béroul version of the romance, not only does the power of the potion fade, but Mark is portrayed as the typical *jaloux*—the jealous, befooled spouse of the continental French triangle tradition. In Thomas's and Gottfried's, however, there is a tragic nobility in the king's love for the love-entangled pair by whom he is being deceived. If Thomas, then, was the innovator responsible for this deeper reading, he enriched the legend greatly and well prepared the way for its culminating treatment at the hand of Gottfried von

Strassburg, who is to be ranked as one of the earliest great creative individuals of the modern world.

HORSES, PIGS, AND DRAGONS: KING MARK AND TRISTAN

The name Marc is understood usually as an abridgment of the Latin Marcus, from the name of the war-god Mars. It may also bear some relation, however, to the Middle High German *marc*, meaning "war-horse." This alternative is enforced by King Marc's other name, Eochaid, which is related to the Old Irish *ech* and the Latin *equus*, meaning "horse." In fact, in one Old French version of the romance (that of Béroul) we find the astonishing statement, "*Marc a orelles de cheval*" ("Mark has horse's ears").[9]

This statement plunges us suddenly into a vortex of highly suggestive mythological associations. We think first of the classical legend of King Midas, who has ass's ears and whose touch turned everything, including his daughter, to gold; and we recall, as well, that the leaders of the Anglo-Saxon invasion of Britain (c. 450 A.D.) were named Hengest and Horsa, both of whose names derive from Germanic nouns meaning "horse" (cf. modern German: *Hengst*, "stallion"; English: *horse*).

Figure 41 shows a bronze solar disk ornamented with a gold design of spirals, set on wheels of bronze and with a bronze steed before it, that was found at Trundholm, Nordseeland, Denmark (whence Hengest and Horsa came), and is usually dated c. 1000 B.C.

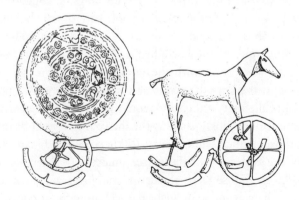

FIGURE 41. Bronze and gold, Denmark, c. 1000 B.C.

Figure 42 shows a pair of late Gaulish coins decorated with horses, each with an eagle, the sunbird, on its back; in one case the horse even bears the head of a man.

FIGURE 42. Bronze, Gallo-Roman, second–third century A.D.

We know that in ancient Rome a ceremony took place every October in which a horse was sacrificed to Mars; and we know also that both the Celts and the Germans celebrated horse sacrifices on Midsummer Day. The Celts had a mule-god, named Mullo, associated with Mars, and this may, indeed, bear some relation not only to the name Marc, as discussed above, but also to the mortifying role that fell to King Mark in his romance.

In Aryan India, where there were many symbolic forms remarkably close to those of the Aryan Celts, the great ceremony of the horse sacrifice (*aśvamedha*) was a rite reserved for kings, in which the noble animal was identified symbolically not only with the sun but also with the king in whose name the rite was to be celebrated. The queen, then, coming from the royal bed, had to enact a frankly obscene ritual of simulated intercourse with the immolated horse, in a pit, all of which gave to the king the status of a solar king, a world monarch, whose light, like that of the sun, should illuminate the earth. In the imperial history of Japan, there is the interesting legend of the birth of the beloved Prince Shōtoku (573–621 A.D.) while his mother was on a tour of inspection of the palace precincts. "When she came," we read, "to the Horse Department and had just come to the door of the stables, she was suddenly delivered of him without effort."[10] It is almost certain that the association of the Celtic-Aryan King Mark of

Cornwall with a horse, and even with horse ears, testifies to an original involvement of some kind in a symbolic context of royal solar rites.

The image of the solar monarch's ritual role, however, became attached to his personal biography (which, in fact, is the way in which a good many of the biographies that pass to this day as history came into being). Possibly some act of his queen gave rise, in popular talk, to suggestions of analogy with the ritual of the dead horse in the pit; and since classical literature was not unfamiliar to the bards and poets of the time, satirical analogies with the King Midas legend could easily have been coined. The Celtic bards and poets (like certain journalists today) took delight and pride in murdering with satire those who had denied them the boons they craved.

In any case, from Cornwall some disreputable story of Mark and his queen must have passed to Wales, where it fused with the Welsh version of the legend of the trickster and lover Trystan, to which ready compound, then, the analogous Irish theme was added of the flight of Diarmuid and Gráinne and pursuit of Finn Mac Cumhaill.

There is an early Welsh triad that lends us another interesting glimpse, even broader and deeper than the last, into the subterranean ocean of story from which the episodes, themes, and even characters of this hero legend were derived. It reads as follows: "Trystan son of Tallwch, disguised as a swineherd,/Tended the pigs of Marc son of Meirchyon,/While the [true] swineherd went with a message to Esyllt."[11] Here we find the celebrated triangle already formed—plus an episode otherwise unknown to the romance, in which Trystan, masquerading as Marc's swineherd, sends his message, by the real swineherd, to Marc's wife.

The stratagem is bold. But it suggests strongly a mythic source, and one of very great interest, furthermore, not merely because the pig and swineherd have, throughout Celtic mythology and far beyond, divine associations, but also because the myths and rites to which these particular associations apply have to do specifically with themes of yonder-world initiation and an immortality to be realized beyond the reach of death. In other words, they concern a dimension of being that transcends the normal fears and desires of the pair of opposites, death and love—or, in the language of Gottfried von Strassburg's introduction to his Tristan romance, "which bears together in one heart its bitter sweet, its dear sorrow, its heart's delight and its pain of longing, dear life and sorrowful death, its dear death and its sorrowful life."[12]

The popular Assyrian divinity Adonis, beloved of Aphrodite, was slain by a wild boar. So, too, was Attis, lover and son of the Phrygian Mother Goddess of the Universe, Cybele. These two gods were but local forms of the repeatedly slain and reborn lunar lord of death and life whose Sumerian name was Dumuzi-apsu, "Child of the Abyss," later known in the Bible as Tammuz. In Egypt the counterpart was the great archetype of the pharaonic principle, Osiris, torn to pieces by his dark brother, Seth, who chanced upon him while out hunting a wild boar. Osiris had been guilty of adultery with Seth's sister-wife, furthermore, which puts him somewhat in the category of Tristan— does it not?—and of Diarmuid slain by the boar let loose at him by Finn.

Let me not repeat the demonstrations, given in *The Masks of God*, of the cultural strata and continuities of the primitive, Oriental, and Occidental myths of the world. Suffice it to recall that in the primitive volume the elaborate ceremonies are discussed, those of the men's secret societies of Melanesia, where the raising and sacrifice of hundreds of boars confers on the owners of the beasts both power on earth and immortality in the yonder world. Associated with such rites are megalithic shrines, together with a mythology of the labyrinth of the yonder world that bears close comparison with the labyrinth symbolism of the early Aegean period, certain aspects of the Eleusinian rites, Orphic mythology, and the Egyptian Book of the Dead.

Apparently the flashing tusks of the boar, at either side of the dark head, were associated by analogy with the waxing and waning crescents of the moon, just as in cattle-raising cultures the horns of the bull and cow were associated with the lunar horns; and even in the later, higher developments of the Bronze Age civilizations, when the ritual lore of cattle-herding acquired precedence over that of the swine, the symbolism of the older, darker rites hung on—particularly with reference to the ultimate, darker mysteries of the generation of life.

In the course of celebrating the Eleusinian Mysteries, commemorating the annual netherworld descent and return of the Maiden Goddess Persephone, there was an offering of young pigs. And the myth associated with this ancient rite tells us that at the time of her

FIGURE 43. Pig sacrifice (red-figure vase, classical, Greece, c. fifth century B.C.)

abduction to the netherworld by Hades, a herd of swine fell into the chasm, along with the maiden, when the earth opened to receive her. Significantly, the name of the swineherd of that adventure was Eubouleus, "the giver of good counsel," which was an ancient appellation also of the god of the netherworld, Hades himself. Is not the Welsh Trystan-as-swineherd sending his message to Esyllt in a role marvelously close to that of the swineherd Hades-Eubouleus of this myth? James Frazer, in *The Golden Bough*, pointed out that Persephone herself, in her animal aspect, was a pig-goddess.

In the *Odyssey* we find the celebrated episode of the magic isle of Circe of the Braided Locks, who turns Odysseus's men into swine, and when she returns them to their former shapes they are younger and fairer than before. She also takes Odysseus to her bed, after which she guides him to the netherworld, where he meets and talks with the living dead. Moreover, on Odysseus's return to his home in Ithaca, it was in his own swineherd's hut that he meets his son, Telemachus, whom he has not seen for twenty years.

In Celtic lore, as well, these themes of the pig as goddess-guide to the mysteries beyond life are readily matched, as, for instance, in the Irish folktale of the Daughter of the King of the Land of Youth, whose head was the head of a pig. She appears on earth and attaches herself to Finn MacCool's magnificent son Oisin (Ossian), who is at first annoyed by her persistent presence, but when occasion gives him the chance to remark that her appearance otherwise is of such beauty as he has never seen on woman before, he kisses the pig snout away, and himself becomes thereby the King of the Land of Youth.[13]

Figure 44 shows a Gallo-Roman altar; the central figure squats on a low dais, holding on his left forearm a cornucopia-like bag from which grain pours, while before the dais stand a bull and stag feeding on the grain. The Roman gods Apollo and Mercury are at either hand of this Gaulish figure, whom the Romans equated with their own lord of the underworld, Dis Pater, Pluto, the Greek Hades, by whom Persephone was abducted to the netherworld.

FIGURE 44. Marble, France, c. 50 A.D.

And so, in a remarkably consistent way, the imagery of the boar and swineherd, with which both Diarmuid and Trystan are linked, appear traditionally in association with early Bronze Age and even Neolithic gods and rites of the underworld. The horse, on the other hand, the noble animal of the patriarchal warrior herdsmen, who entered the British Isles as the iron-wielding, chariot-fighting Celts, was a beast associated not with abyssal, chthonic powers so much as with celestial and, specifically, solar ones: the order of light, reason, law, and waking consciousness, with its own order of decency and virtue, in contrast to the mystery of darkness, feeling, mystical presentiment, and missionary dream, wherein all bounds of definition—ego included—are dissolved, and what Sigmund Freud called the "oceanic feeling" supervenes.

There can be no doubt whatsoever, therefore, of the ultimate derivation of the Tristan romance from the Bronze Age mythological cycle of the dead and resurrected deity, whose death and rebirth, ever recurring, was solemnly—and dreadfully—enacted in rites of lavish human sacrifice throughout the archaic world. A second strain, however, was derived from the Iron Age, which in the British Isles commenced roughly with the entry of the Celtic tribes. And the emphasis here was not on the generative powers of the earth, the heavens, and the waters beneath the earth, the female principle of nature's spontaneity as symbolized in the Magna Mater, but on the war craft and shaping power of the male, as represented chiefly by a type of brilliant hero, very much like the Homeric hero, supported by the deities of an emphatically patriarchal, thunder-hurling pantheon. The characteristic myth concerns the conquest of a monster of some kind, usually of a serpentine, dragonlike form, who, in fact, in the earlier mythology had been the son-husband of Mother Earth (as, for instance, Typhon had been of Gaia). The dragon now is interpreted as the negative, binding, sterile aspect of the masculine principle, and the victory of the hero as the release of life (the gold, the maiden) from its hold. Typical in the Greek context were the deeds of Apollo against the great Python of the Delphic Oracle, of Perseus rescuing Andromeda from the sea beast, and of Theseus overcoming the Minotaur.

It is most remarkable that in the Tristan romance the claims of civilization, reason, law, and honor—in patriarchal terms—are represented by the betrayed and befooled King Mark/Eochaid, who has horse's ears, whereas the Bronze Age mystique of initiation to a sphere of immortal life that can be apprehended only in moments of experience transcending personal loss and gain is represented by a pair of lovers, through whose romance specific references abound to the symbolism of the swineherd and the boar. It is always difficult to tell, when later poets employ images in accord with tradition, whether it has been by coincidence or by design. Many artists today like to pretend to bring forth their own marvels innocently out of their natural genial accord with the ground of being, when they have actually been doing rather a bit of midnight reading in Jung, Freud, Nietzsche, and Joyce.

However, it is also possible—as Jung seems to have proven conclusively—to bring forth symbolic forms spontaneously in dream, vision, and art that perfectly match those of the great traditional mythologies. Such forms have an immediate effect as energy-releasing agents, which comes antecedent to and independent of (indeed, can even contradict) their rational interpretation. I have discussed this problem already at the opening of *Primitive Mythology* and shall not return to it here, beyond suggesting that the motivation of art and the impact of its forms (in contrast to the rhetorical discussion of them) is a function of this energetic potential. And in such works of art as those with which I deal in *Creative Mythology*, the way in which this potential is tapped is my chief concern.

Japanese and South African Reflections
in the Tristan Story

Among the legends of the Japanese *Kojiki* (*Records of Ancient Matters*), a work dating from the same period, approximately, as the beginnings of the Tristan legend, 712 A.D., there is the wonderful tale of the heavenly hero Susano–O–no–Mikoto ("His Brave Swift Impetuous Male Augustness"), who, when sitting alone at a place near the source of the river Hi in Izumo, saw some chopsticks floating down the stream, and thinking there must be people upstream, proceeded upward, where he found a family of earth spirits whose sole remaining daughter was about to be given to an eight-headed dragon, which the hero then contrived to kill.[14]

Furthermore, there is a legend from Southwest Africa, from the neighborhood of the great Zimbabwe ruins of about the sixth to ninth centuries A.D., telling of two sisters, of whom the elder had been betrothed from childhood to an older man. A youth who, having fallen in love with the elder sister, was rejected, threw himself into a pond, into which he sank. But he did not drown; he remained alive. One day the two sisters came to that pond to bathe, and the youth at the bottom, knowing they were there, released a pearl bead, which came floating up to the middle of the surface. The younger sister, seeing it, begged her sister to fetch it. When the elder sister swam out, however, the youth from beneath seized her by the legs and drew her down. He made her his wife down there, and when their child was born, they returned from that watery dwelling place to the village.

Apparently, both the episode of the bathtub and the idea of the love potion also belonged to the earliest mythological and magical stages of the Tristan legend. For in connection with the African tale from of the boy in the pond, a tale is told, as well, of a brother and sister, Runde and Munjari by name, who grew up together. When the girl one day sees her brother naked in his bath, she thinks, "Runde is more of a man than others: I want to sleep with Runde." She goes to a sorcerer and says, "Make me a magic potion. There is a man whom I desire." The sorcerer prepares a charm, a little seed, which he gives to Munjari. That evening, after eating, Runde says to her, "I am thirsty; give me a drink." She puts the little seed under her thumbnail, and when she brings him the calabash full of water, she holds it so that her thumbnail is in the water. Runde takes a drink and swallows the seed.

The next day Runde comes to his parents and says, "No one shall marry my sister, Munjari; I myself will marry her." The parents answer, "You are outdoing yourself; only kings marry their sisters." He replies, "I have to marry my sister." They answer, "You are neither a king nor a beast. We won't allow you to marry your sister." Runde replies, "If you don't let me take my sister, Munjari, as my wife, I shall kill myself." They repeat, "You will not be allowed to marry your sister, Munjari."

The youth goes away. He takes white clothes, spears, and dogs, and walks to a pond. He enters the water with all those things. His clothes become a red sparkle on the surface of the water; his spears turn into reeds; his dogs become crocodiles; and he himself resides as a lion at the bottom of the pond.

One day an old woman comes to the edge of the pond to wash clothes. The clothes become red, frightening her. Runde sings: "Grandmother, dear, you there who are washing something, go and declare that Runde is in the pond. His clothes are the red color of the standing water; his dogs are crocodiles; his spears are reeds; he has died for his Munjari."

The old woman, having heard his song, hurries to the village, to his parents. She says to them, "Your son Runde has gone into the pond; his clothes have become the red sparkle on the surface of the water; his spears have become reeds; his dogs crocodiles; and he has died for his Munjari."

The parents, afraid, declare they would do all they could. They go to the pond with a beautiful girl and call, "Here is your sister, Munjari." Runde answers from the water, "If you are my sister, Munjari, jump into the pond." The girl is terrified and runs back to the village. Runde calls, "That was not my sister, Munjari," and the parents return home. They bring another girl to the pond, and the event goes as before. Then they go with their daughter, Munjari, to the pond. They call, "Here is your sister, Munjari," and Runde calls from the water, "If you are my sister, Munjari, jump into the water." Munjari removes her clothes, anklets, and her bracelets. She takes the pearl ornaments from her hair. And she goes into the pond.

When Munjari enters the water, the reeds become spears, the crocodiles turn into dogs, the red sparkle on the surface of the water turns into white clothes, and Runde comes out of the pond in his white clothes. Munjari comes behind him. Munjari puts the pearl ornaments back in her hair, slips her bracelets on, attaches her anklets, and dons her clothes. Runde and Munjari then go into the village and marry. And Runde becomes the first king of that land.[15]

In southeast Africa these folk legends are gathered in a rich body of lore reflecting the old Bronze Age rites of the Sacred Regicide.[16] At the time of a certain heavenly juncture of the moon and the planets (usually marked by Venus or Jupiter), the god-kings of this area—until as late, apparently, as about 1810—were ritually slain as incarnations of the dying god, and their favorite queens, ceremonially stripped naked, were then strangled and interred with the remains. In the great Bronze Age communities of Egypt, Southwest Asia, India, and China, the entire population of the court was buried alive with the body of the king, in elaborate palaces underground. And the later dragon-killer myths point back to a time when this inhuman custom—associated especially with a mythology of the death and resurrection of the moon god—was discontinued under the influence of a warrior aristocracy for which the old fertility pageant of the death and rebirth of the lord of the rhythms of time no longer held any meaning. In Japan, as well as in Africa and Europe, this succession of traditions, from the Age of Bronze to that of Iron, has left vestiges in the mythic lore that can be readily recognized. The pearl bead floating up from the bottom of the African pond of death and rebirth is matched in Japan by the pair of chopsticks floating down a stream from the site where a dragon was to consume an offered maiden.

FIGURE 45. Inscription (carved marble, France, first century A.D.)

CHAPTER 6

The Knights of the Round Table

Arthur

Just to the west of Lourdes, in the French Pyrenees, is a little place called Saint-Pé-d'Ardet, where we have a monument engraved, as shown in figure 45. The date is the Gallo-Roman Period, and it reads, "Lexeia Odanni filia. Artehe vslm" ("Lexeia the daughter of Odan, thus acquires merit through her dedicated vows to Artehe.") This shows that already in the period of Roman Europe, Arthur was revered by the Celts as a god. And the name Artehe (Artus, Arthur) is related to Artemis and Arcturus; all these are related to the bear, the oldest worshipped deity in the world. We have bear shrines going back to Neanderthal times in just this part of the world from perhaps 10,000 B.C. So this is a bear god; the valley, and the river here, running by Lourdes, is called the River of the Bear (the Ourse). This is the God Arthur. I think I can make the point here that Lake Geneva is therefore the source of the whole idea of King Arthur's departure on a boat after his death to the Isle of the Golden Apples, the Isle of Avalon. The philosopher Charles Musès, who discovered the inscription above, also makes a very good point: these traditions, which in our literature we associate with Britain, are in the preliterate period associated with the Celtic sense of the La Tène culture in the middle of France.

Another early continental site associated with Arthur is in Modena, Italy, where, as early as about 1090 A.D., baby boys were being named Artusius; and between the years 1099 and 1106, when the cathedral of Modena was being constructed in Lombardy, a group of sculptors carved on the archivolt of the north portal a scene of Arthurian romance.

The bas-relief in figure 46 illustrates an episode in the legend of the abduction and rescue of Guinevere. Most of the figures in the bas-relief are labeled, the forms of their names being of Breton origin.

FIGURE 46. Carved granite, Italy, c. 1100 A.D.

From left to right, we see an unnamed knight, along with Isdernus (Sir Ydier) and Artus de Bretanica (King Arthur), encountering a churl with a *baston cornu* (Old French: "battle-ax") named Burmalt, who is defending one portal of the keep; within the castle, surrounded by water, stand Winlogee (Guinevere) and Mardoc (Mordred, King Death); while at the second gate, Carrado (Sir Caradoc, the giant guardian of the Dolorous Tower) confronts Galvagian (Sir Gawain), Galvariun (Sir Galeschin), and Che (Sir Keie).

Noteworthy is the absence of the name Lancelot, to whom, in all later romance, the rescue of Queen Guinevere from the Dolorous Tower is ascribed. In this earlier version of the romance, Gawain, Arthur's nephew, not Lancelot, rescues the queen. Compare this situation to the Tristan triangle, in which Tristan is Mark's nephew; and to the Irish legend, in which Diarmuid is the nephew of Finn. Here Sir Gawain, the king's nephew, the ladies' knight, rides to free Guinevere.

The point of importance here is the evidence at Modena of the widespread popularity of Arthurian romance in early-twelfth-century

Europe even before the earliest known written versions of the tales appeared, and the indication, by way of the forms of the names, of a Celtic Breton source.

Arthur appears in the old chronicles of Gildas and Nennius in the sixth and eighth centuries as a *dux bellorum* ("leader in war"; this is the origin of the English word *duke*). And what the scholars now picture with regards to Arthur is a sort of Roman trained military man who helped the kings of southern Britain in their battle against the invading Germans—that is to say, against the Anglo-Saxons and Jutes from what is now Denmark. The southern part of Britain was the field of the collisions. The chronicles tell of twelve great battles in which Arthur, *dux bellorum*, this Roman-trained military man (like, say, some Senegalese officer trained by the French), assisted the kings of the south; at the last battle Arthur is killed, and the German triumph is confirmed.

During this invasion there were, of course, refugees, particularly from southwest England, who went to what is now called Brittany in France. The whole Breton peninsula is populated by people who were refugees from Britain, and there grows up what is called the Hope of the Britons—the hope that Arthur, the once and future king, will return and restore to them their homeland in the south of England.

So we have the period of these invasions in the late fifth and early sixth centuries as the historical moment underlying the legend of Arthur—that is to say, about 450–550 A.D. Then we have a period of oral legendry, of reciting the deeds of this great man, building up the legend of the Hope of the Britons, namely, of Arthur as the one who will return to restore their lost world to them. It's a bit like the hope that inspired the ghost dance religion at the end of the last century in America: the hope that the ghost dancers would dance and dance and that another land would come over the land that the white people had taken, and that only the Indians would be able to jump up onto that land, and the buffalo would be there, and the old world would be there again. This is a common motif in the traditions of defeated peoples.

Where is Arthur supposed to be in the meanwhile? There are three principle interpretations of where Arthur is residing. One is that he is under a burial mound sleeping in the hill. This is a motif that we get throughout the world, too, the sleeping giant, the sleeping savior in the tomb, waiting out the eons in the great burial mound until the time is right. Another view is that he's residing in the lower half of the world, in the Antipodes, among the pygmies and dwarfs of the South Pole. But the most charming and most popular was the story of him sleeping in the Island of the West, Avalon. Now, Avalon is a Celtic formation of the word *apple*. This is the Isle of the Golden Apples, the counterpart to the classical Greek Hesperides: an eternal land, a timeless land, just like the timeless world of the sleeping giant in the hill. This is the world of the unconscious; it is the world beyond time and space, the world of the *Sambhogakāya* ("body of enjoyment"), of the mythological forms that endure beyond time and yet are not the void. It's between the realm of the void and the realm of phenomenality, the realm of dream and vision, where the savior sleeps, and that realm was in the past, and is in the present, and is to come. It's around us like the silence around *AUM*.

This body of oral mythology does not break into writing until 1136. On that date there is published a work by a monk named Geoffrey of Monmouth called *Historia Regum Britanniae* (*The History of the Kings of Britain*). This book purports to be an account of the kings ruling in the British Isles—specifically in Britain—from the time of the fall of Troy until the coming of the Germans. The model for the book is Virgil's *Aeneid*, which tells the story of the fall of Troy, the escape of the Trojan prince Aeneas, his voyages until he arrives in Italy, and his establishment of Rome. Geoffrey uses the same model to tell how a figure named Brut, after whom Britain is named, flees from Troy, traveling the length of the Mediterranean, sails up and around to Britain, and establishes there the line of the British kings.

Geoffrey of Monmouth's book is a compendium of Celtic lore, which up to that time had not been known to the literary world, and it broke like a bomb upon the world. It was translated almost immediately into Norman French by an author named Wace, in a work called *Roman de Brut*. Wace's version gives us the first Round Table. Soon thereafter a clergyman in the south of England named Layamon published a work in Middle English again called *Brut*, and it was also enormously popular.

What took place in England before the writing of *The History of the Kings of Britain* was an event of no less importance than the invasion by the Germans, and this was William the Conqueror's conquest of the last of the English kings, in 1066, at the battle of Hastings, when King Harold was overcome and the Norman-French dynasties of England were established. So now we have Geoffrey writing these legends in Latin, Wace translating them into the Norman French of the court, and Layamon translating it into the mélange of French and the Anglo-Saxon spoken by the commoners, Middle English.

When you read *The History of the Kings of Britain*, you find Shakespeare's King Lear with his three daughters, as well as Cymbeline, and you find at the end Vortigern, the last of the British kings, who invited Hengest and Horsa, with their hordes of Angles, Saxons, Frisians, and Jutes, into Britain to defend him against the Picts and the Celts. You also find the legend of Arthur, as it then had developed.

From there a whole literature sprang, cycles of stories that we call the Arthurian romances. In England, King Arthur himself was the most important figure in these cycles. When the material was brought by bards to the courts in France, Arthur was not as important. France already had its hero king—Charlemagne. What the French and then the Germans found more interesting were the Knights of the Round Table and their various careers.

Look at what we've got here. We've got the early Bronze Age mother right people, we've got the patriarchal Celts, we've got the Roman Empire, we've got the invasion of the Germans, and we've got the invasion of the Norman French. If we take the last three groups, what we see is this: the Celts are at the bottom of English society, the Anglo-Saxons are on top of them, and the Normans are on top of the Anglo-Saxons. That was the situation in England.

The Normans had conquered the Anglo-Saxons, not the Celts, and they put the Anglo-Saxons out in the yard, taking care of the pigs, whereas at the table where the pig's flesh was being eaten, people were speaking French, not that vulgar English. So when food is outside it's pig or swine, and when it's on the table it's *porc*. When it's outside it's a cow or a calf, and when it's on the table it's *boeuf* or *veau*, French indoors, and English out there in the pantry and in the servants' quarters. But we have to have entertainment at our meals, and the favorite entertainers are the Celtic bards. So you've got all three strata coming together in the dining hall.

We have two new things running: one, Geoffrey of Monmouth's *The History of the Kings of Britain*, written for a Norman king, Henry

II. Henry II's domain included a large portion of France, and this new empire was to have a mythological background just as Rome had, and this *History*, now it seems very clear, was composed with the patronage of the House of Plantagenet.

Let us explore the whole history of Arthur as Geoffrey of Monmouth gives it to us.

Behind Arthur is this wonderful figure, Merlin. Geoffrey of Monmouth wrote another work, a shorter one called the *Vita Merlini*, *The Life of Merlin*. And in that work appears the figure of the Druid, the Celtic magical priest—the counterpart to the Indian brahmin. Just as the brahmin in the Hindu caste system is priest-magician to the *ksatriya*, or warrior, so, too, is Merlin the magician and mystic master of the warrior princes. *The Life of Merlin* is modeled on the image of the Druid priest, but with certain specific characters of Arthur's time involved, particularly a man named Ambrosius, who seems largely responsible for overthrowing Vortigern, who was the traitor to England, and so forth and so on. The story of Merlin is, briefly, that of a boy whose mother had conceived him of a devil. Of course, in good Christian tradition, whenever you have a miracle that's not a miracle of God, it's a miracle of a devil, and of course, the devils are simply the earlier deities.

So here we have the old story of a virgin birth. Merlin could appear either as a boy or as an old wise man. As a little boy, he uttered a prophecy to King Vortigern, telling him that his empire was going to collapse, and he described it in the way of an allegory: "You are trying to build a tower," Merlin tells Vortigern, "but the tower won't stand firm because in the ground underneath are two contending dragons, a white and a red dragon." These are the two races that are contending, and Merlin goes about it later to make sure that Vortigern is defeated.

Merlin's next work was to produce the king who would now govern the happy new world, and this is going to be Arthur. Now we get the famous tale of the begetting of Arthur: He was to be from the house of a certain queen Igerne, and his father was to be Uther Pendragon, who was not Igerne's husband. Merlin arranged that Uther Pendragon should assume the form of Igerne's husband, and while the husband was away, have intercourse with her, with Igerne thinking it was her husband. Thus Arthur was begotten in extramarital magic.

Next Merlin arranges the whole theme of the sword in the stone;

the sword is the sword of destiny. One of the great powers recognized in early times was that of the smith to draw steel from a stone—iron and charcoal combined to create something stronger than either—and this steel of the sword represents the virtue and triumph of whatever people we're talking about. So there's this legend of the stone with the sword in it that could be drawn only by the one for whom it was destined. Merlin produces Arthur, who draws the sword. There's the beginning of a whole context of the imperial story and its development.

Guinevere becomes Arthur's wife. The emperor of Rome sends a challenge to Arthur to submit to him. Arthur arranges an expedition to campaign against Rome, but while Arthur is away, his nephew Mordred seduces Guinevere and attempts to take over the throne. Before he's had a chance to conquer Rome, therefore, Arthur is called back. He gives battle to Mordred, whom Arthur slays, but who wounds Arthur mortally. Arthur is carried off to Avalon.

That's the whole history of Arthur. You see there the germ of what comes up later in the Lancelot story with Mordred, only Lancelot is an honorable man and simply caught in this invincible passion, which Arthur recognizes as something more important and sacred than marriage itself. In this earlier view, Guinevere is cursed and downgraded, and the female is not celebrated and valued as she is in the later stories—Geoffrey's *History* is a monastic work for dynastic purposes, not an entertainment for court ladies and their beaux.

Now the stories go to the continent. There are certain bards to whom the stories have been attributed: there's one named Bledri, whom I have mentioned, and another named Kyot.

The tradition of medieval storytelling did not value free invention; there is what is called the "matter," and there is what is called the "sense." The poet takes the matter and interprets it in his own sense. So these Celtic bards brought the matter of the Arthurian romances—what was known as the Matter of England—to the French courts, transmuting them from Celtic story, and then this matter was picked up by writers and turned into literary form in the courts of the glorious Eleanor of Aquitaine (1122–1209). She is *it*: Eleanor, Duchess of Aquitaine, on the southwest coast of France, queen to both Louis VII of France and Henry II of England, mother of two English kings (Richard I and John). She is the source of the whole romantic period we're talking about. She'd been married to Louis when she was a little girl, but she despised him. Apparently she went with him on a crusade to the Holy Lands, and there was a scandal of her having an affair with Saladin, the great Muslim warrior monarch. She couldn't have had an affair with Saladin because he at that time was a little boy of about three years old, but that's how the story goes. At any rate, when she returned she managed to get the pope to annul her marriage to Louis, and then she sailed to England and married King Henry II. So she was the wife of two kings and the mother of two, and two of her daughters became queens: Marie (her daughter by Louis) was queen and queen-regnant of France, and Eleanor (her daughter by Henry) was queen of Castille. Three generations later, she was the ancestress of every royal head in Europe.

Her grandfather, William IX of Poitiers, was, in fact, the first of the troubadours, who fought against the Moors on the Iberian Penin-sula as part of the Reconquista. He brought the lyric traditions of the Moorish love poets with him back across the Pyrenees.

You see what a complicated thing this is: we have the Moorish-Sufi stories and poems of love inspiring the songs of the troubadours, which in a slightly later period, the end of the twelfth century, move over into Germany with the minnesingers. There are also Celtic bards in the Norman courts—of which Aquitaine was one—and these Celtic bards are telling the old Celtic stories in twelfth-century cos-tume, with the gods and heroes of the old Celtic tales parading about in the armor of medieval knighthood: these are the Knights of the Round Table.

GALAHAD, BORS, AND PERCEVAL

The monastic Grail story, which I mentioned earlier, was composed about fifteen years after Wolfram's *Parzival.* The Fourth Lateran Council in the year 1215 proclaimed as authorized dogma the real pres-ence of Jesus in the Eucharist. Christ's participation in the Eucharist is not a symbolic presence, but literal: the wine *is* Christ's blood, and the wafer his body. This created great excitement in the ecclesiastical world, and the whole story of the Grail became associated with that doctrine.

FIGURE 47. Galahad, Bors, and Percival receiving the Grail (ink on parchment, France, fifteenth century)

The Cistercian series of Grail romances are *La Queste del Saint Graal* and after that *L'Estoire del Saint Graal.* The two Cistercian monks (whose names we don't know) both followed a man called Robert de Boron, who also had dealt with this story as concerning the vessel of Christ's suffering. The story here is that the Grail was brought to England (along with the Spear of Longinus) by Joseph of

Arimathea. So now we have an ecclesiastical version of the Grail, in which the central hero is not Parzival, the married man, but Galahad, whose name is supposed to have come from a Hebrew word meaning "mountain of witness," and there's definitely an ecclesiastical accent. In that story we see the disqualification of most of the knights because of their secular character. The only three that come through are Sir Bors, Sir Perceval, and Sir Galahad.

You all know the story of the begetting of Galahad by Lancelot on the Grail keeper's daughter, and so Galahad is brought up really under the shadow of the Grail in this wonderful romance. The Grail shows itself to Arthur's court, and the whole court decides, on the initiative of Gawain, to go questing for it. The Grail had appeared with a covering over it, and they are to go on a quest to behold the Grail without its covering. Arthur is greatly disturbed by this, because his entire court is going to depart.

The reason I bring this up is that one of the greatest lines in medieval romance comes right at the opening of this adventure. The knights are all going to start out on the same morning. They're going to leave Arthur, and so they say good-bye to him. The text then says: "They thought it would be a disgrace to start out in a group, in the same direction. Each entered the forest at that point which he himself had selected, and where there was no trail or path, at its darkest point." The message is that if you follow a trail or path, you're following someone else's adventure, not your own. Every human being is unique, and must find his or her adventure by entering the forest where there is no way or path.

In this adventure of the Cistercian quest, however, no matter what way you go, the path leads to the renunciation of the world, the confession of sins, and the sacraments. However—and this is again associated with the work of Joachim of Floris, who wrote about the three ages of manifestation of God—the Christ who is responsible for the Grail in the hands of Joseph of Arimathea is the *resurrected* Christ, the Christ Who Is to Come. That is to say, in this work the Grail represents the Hermetic rather than the ecclesiastical tradition. So always associated with the Grail we have the background, not the foreground, of the Christian tradition. In Wolfram's *Parzival*, it is a secular life that leads to this realization of transcending the sacraments. In the Cistercian quest, it is the religious life that leads to this experience, again, of transcending the sacraments.

So in both the secular and the monastic Grail tradition we have the same kind of secret esoteric notion that we find in the Oriental texts, and particularly in *Parzival,* where there is a line you won't find in Hinduism or Buddhism anywhere. In the Orient, the ways of initiation are mapped out—you know what stage you're in, you find your guru, you submit to the guru, you do not criticize, you do what he tells you, and he leads you to your own experience. Not so in this European quest. In *Parzival,* you are to follow your own nature, your own inspiration; following someone else will lead you only to ruin. That is the sense of Parzival's journey, and that is the sense you get, briefly, here, as the knights set out on the quest for the Holy Grail.

I offer this as our counterpart and one to be remembered, and not to be mixed up with Wagner or Thomas Malory. Malory comes along in the fifteenth century. His translation is right from the *Quest.* The Grail story that you get in Malory is that of the Cistercian monks. This is also the one Tennyson took over, and it's the one that influenced Wagner. And I think it's too bad that the image of the Grail that has come down to us has been in the monastic tradition, while the secular one—the layman's movement, you might say—has been left in the woods. The story, as we have seen, was developed to the full by Wolfram von Eschenbach. He understood knighthood and what it was about in a way that Gottfried never did and that the monks couldn't.

The author of the next two tales, the great Chrétien de Troyes, was also no knight. He was, however, a courtier: he was court poet to Marie de Champagne, Eleanor of Aquitaine's granddaughter. It has been said that Chrétien could "shake perfectly turned couplets out of his sleeves." He wrote one of the first adaptations of the Tristan and Iseult romance, as well as *Perceval ou le Conte du Graal,* the other great secular telling of Parzival's quest for the Grail. Here, however, we are going to examine his stories about two other knights: Lancelot and Yvain.

LANCELOT

Poor Lancelot also comes very close to an experience of the Grail in the Cistercian work. He arrives at the same castle that Perceval, Bors, and Galahad come to, with a very different outcome. Lancelot enters a room where a very old priest is celebrating a Mass; when the priest elevates the host, he almost falls down, because the host becomes, in fact, the body of the young Christ. And Lancelot is moved by compassion to rescue him, and when he tries to do so he is struck down because he is unworthy of being present. Why? Because of his love for Guinevere. Now, to be healed of a sin you have to have true contrition. But he cannot experience contrition for his love for Guinevere—like Tristan, he cannot repent. That is beautiful. That a monk could work that in speaks very well for him.

That love was the subject of Chrétien de Troyes's finest—and best-known—romance, "Lancelot, the Knight of the Cart," in which Lancelot falls in love with Guinevere and goes through quite an ordeal. He becomes *Le Fou* ("The Madman"), the one who is absolutely mad for love, and the two become completely swept up in a torrent of passion.

FIGURE 48. The trials of Lancelot (ivory, France, 1330–1350)

The great story, the basis of which served as the inspiration for that carving over the portal in Modena, is that Guinevere is abducted. These women in the Middle Ages, like those in the earlier Greek tradition, have a habit of being kidnapped and then saved. Helen of Troy was abducted several times; the whole Trojan War took place to get her back for Menelaus. This time, Guinevere is abducted by the lord of a castle that Chrétien equates with the underworld.

Arthur himself doesn't go to get her back; Lancelot does. And he goes with such speed that he rides two horses to death. He is walking along in a suit of armor, not getting very far very fast. And a cart, driven by a churl, a peasant, catches up with him. As it passes, Lancelot thinks, *If I were in that cart I'd get to Guinevere faster.* But then he worries about his loss of honor and his reputation as a knight. So he hesitates for three steps about getting into the cart. Why? Because people who ride in the cart are being taken to be hanged or punished in some way. It's a dishonor to get into the cart. But finally he does.

Next he comes to a castle where he finds a trial we recognize: the Perilous Bed. Once he's overcome that obstacle—as Zimmer would say, integrating himself with the masculine experience of the feminine—the next trial for our friend Lancelot is what is known as the Sword Bridge. This is a bridge spanning a roaring torrent that is made of a sword, and he has to go across with bare hands and feet on the sharp edge of the blade.

FIGURE 49. The Knight of the Cart (print, United States, 1903)

You may know Somerset Maugham's novel *The Razor's Edge.* The title is a motif from the Katha Upaniṣad: any trip along your own path is a razor's edge.[1] It really is; nobody's done it before. And it's so easy, particularly if what you're following is your bliss, your own path, to tip over and fall into a torrent of passion that sweeps you away. This is a real lesson.

Having survived the Perilous Bed, Lancelot also survives the Sword Bridge. And then he disenchants the Dolorous Tower, the castle in which Guinevere has been held. When he comes in to receive her greeting and gratitude, however, she's as cold as ice. Why? Because he hesitated for three steps before getting on that cart. How did she know? Because she's the goddess. Women know these things.

YVAIN

Chrétien's next story appears also in a Welsh version known as "The Lady of the Fountain." The knight here is called Yvain, the Knight of the Lion. I won't go through the whole story, just give an outline.

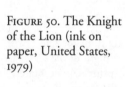

FIGURE 50. The Knight of the Lion (ink on paper, United States, 1979)

One day, a knight named Calogrenant comes to Arthur's court and tells of an adventure in which he has failed. The knight came to a glade with a castle and a tree, and under the tree was a spring. And beside the spring was a stone, and hanging from the tree was a ladle. The adventure consisted of dipping water from the spring onto the stone, at which moment a terrific storm arose. Suddenly, all the leaves and birds were blown from the tree; out of the castle came storming the Black Knight, the Thunder Knight. And he engaged in combat the one who had dared to sip the water. Calogrenant was overthrown.

On hearing this story, Sir Yvain says, "I'm going to attempt the adventure!" And he does. When the knight comes out, Yvain kills him. His lance goes through the knight's body, but the knight turns and rides his horse, even though he is dying, escaping into the castle.

Yvain follows close behind, but he gets caught by the portcullis. These castles had trap gates that would drop in front of the main gate, and he's gotten caught between the two, with his horse cut in half.

A beautiful young girl in the castle, the queen's handmaid, sees him trapped, and she thinks, *This is a beautiful knight. He should become the husband of my lady, who has just lost her husband.*

This is right out of Frazer's *The Golden Bough*, where the one who kills the priest becomes the new priest and consort of the queen. It's a holdover of an old, old mythological theme.

Yvain does become the lady's spouse. He forgets all about Arthur's court. He has found his bliss, but it has disengaged him from the world of duties. He's there with Laudine, the Lady of the Fountain, when Arthur's knights come and pour water on the stone. Yvain has to come out then as the Thunder Knight, and he defeats a whole series of knights before he finally engages with Gawain. Neither can defeat the other. Neither knows who the other is.

FIGURE 51. Leaving the Castle (ink on paper, United States, 1979)

Finally they take their helmets off, and Gawain says, "Oh, hi, Yvain! Come on back to the court!"

Yvain then goes with Arthur's knights back to the court—and forgets Laudine. This is a basic spiritual problem: the split between the worlds of social and personal responsibility.

And she sends a messenger and tells him that he has lost her and must quest forth on the adventure of getting back to her, which, of course, he finally does. The whole story is about the ordeal of recovering the relationship to your true being, and then bringing this to the court; it is the problem of integrating an authentic life with duty.

Sir Gawain and the Green Knight

And now we come to another wonderful story. The tale of *Sir Gawain and the Green Knight* appears in the late period, the fourteenth century.

In Arthur's court the company is at table for a Christmas feast, when in comes a great knight dressed all in green, riding a green horse, and carrying a great battle-ax, and he bellows, "I propose an adventure! Any knight here may cut off my head. Then he shall come to the Green Chapel on New Year's Day a year from now, and I'll return the favor, and cut off his head."

Strange!

Only one knight dares to attempt the adventure, and that is Gawain, Arthur's nephew. He cuts off the Green Knight's head—but the knight just stoops down, picks up the head, and rides out, saying, "See you in a year!"

People are very good to Gawain that year.

Finally, Gawain sets off on All Soul's Day (Halloween) to find the Green Chapel and meet the knight. He rides for some time and comes on Christmas Eve to the magnificent house of a hunter. He stops at the door and says, "I'm looking for the Green Chapel. Do you have any idea where it is?"

His host says, "Yes. It is only a couple hundred yards from here, actually. You have three days until New Year's, so why don't you just stay with us until the time comes?"

This sounds very good to Gawain. At bedtime, the hunter says, "I'm going off to hunt tomorrow. You stay in bed and rest up. When

FIGURE 52. The Green Knight lifting his own head (ink on vellum, England, c. 1375–1400)

I come back I'll give you everything that I've caught during the day, and you give me whatever you might catch."

Well and good. The hunter goes off in the morning and Gawain is in bed—when in comes the hunter's wife. She tickles his chin and invites him to love. Now here's a young man, with only two more days to live, perhaps, when the most beautiful woman in the world comes to him; but he's a courteous knight of Arthur's court, so he does not act disloyally to his host, and so he refuses her.

"Well," she says, "maybe just one kiss?" And she gives him a good strong kiss.

That evening the hunter returns and presents the head of a magnificent stag, and then asks Gawain, "What did you catch during the day?"

Gawain gives him a kiss, and they laugh and retire for the evening.

The next day, when the hunter goes out, Gawain is in bed, and the wife comes in again, and she tickles his chin, saying, "Please, please, please?" And then, when he once more demurs, she gives him two kisses.

FIGURE 53. The
hunter's wife and
Gawain (ink on
vellum, England,
fourteenth century)

When the hunter returns that night, with a big wild boar, Gawain
reciprocates with the two kisses.

On the third day, the hunter goes out and the lady comes in,
tickles his chin, gives Gawain three kisses, tempts him with a ring
(which he rejects), and then gives him her garter, telling him that it
will protect him against all harm.

That evening when the hunter comes back with one smelly fox,
he gets three kisses—but no garter.

Now comes the adventure of the chapel. Gawain sets off on the
morning of New Year's Day toward the chapel, at the bottom of a
deep ravine beside a rushing river, when he hears something.

The great battle-ax is being honed.

The huge Green Knight comes crashing down the steep hill and
says, "Well, then, stretch out your neck!"

Gawain, being an honorable knight, kneels and stretches out his
neck.

The giant lifts up the ax, swings—and misses.

He tries a second time, once again missing the extended neck.

On the third swing, down comes the ax, and nicks Gawain's neck —just enough for the red blood to spurt out onto the white snow.

And the Green Knight says, "*That* is for the garter." The knight, of course, is the hunter.

That's the origin of the legend of the Knights of the Garter.

It concerns the two great temptations of lust for life and fear of death. Those are the same temptations faced by the Buddha. What you have here in these knightly adventures are spiritual adventures, and the tests are those of lust and fear. Gawain has not succumbed to the temptation of Kāma, the god of Desire, and he had felt just a bit of fear at the brink of death (the god Māra). He was fearless, but not without fault. He was human, after all, and this is what keeps him in the world, you might say.

PART THREE

THEMES AND MOTIFS

FIGURE 54. Parzival in the Waste Land (print, United States, 1911)

CHAPTER 7

————————●————————

The Waste Land

IN THE MIDDLE AGES we find two principles of social life: living as one ought on the one hand; and on the other hand love, which ripped one out of this social norm. The dislocation between these two is represented in the Grail legend as the Waste Land.

In the Waste Land, life is a fake. People are living in a manner that is not that of their nature; they are living according to a system of rules. And this is represented in turn by a wounded king whose wound has turned the whole country to waste. The aim of the Grail Knight, then, is to heal that king. How can that king be healed, that wounded king? And where does this Waste Land come from? And where do the heroes come from?

Overwhelmed with grief at her husband's death, Herzeloyde withdraws from the world of courts and battle to a solitary cottage in the woods, where she gives birth to a son, Parzival, whom she plans to keep there all to herself and in ignorance of knighthood. But there was at that time a great need in the world for such an authentic hero as her little son was to grow to be, and there is no way a mother can defend her child from the summons of his own nature.

This need of the medieval world was symbolized in the Grail romances in the image of the Waste Land: an enchantment of sterility cast over the whole society, which it is to be the task of the hero to undo. T. S. Eliot, in his poem *The Waste Land*, published in 1922, applied the motif to a characterization of our own day and general problem. Many will recognize the memorable lines: "What are the roots that clutch, what branches grow/Out of this stony rubbish?"[1]

As told in Chrétien de Troyes's legend and again in the Cistercian *Queste*, the Grail King has been wounded by a lance thrust through his thighs, and his land, as a result, is laid waste. Modern commentators have recognized in this motif a reflection of the well-known primitive superstition discussed by Frazer, in *The Golden Bough*, of the king's health and well-being as the cause and support of his realm's well-being. It is a primitive, magical idea: What could it have meant to a modern poet like Eliot, or to a medieval poet like Wolfram?

As I've said before, the period of the flowering of Arthurian romance lasted roughly from the mid-twelfth to the mid-thirteenth century. The earliest work in which Arthur's name appears, Geoffrey of Monmouth's *The History of the Kings of Britain,* dates from 1136, and all the great Grail romances, from Chrétien's *Perceval* to the *Queste* and Wolfram's *Parzival,* appeared between 1180 and 1230. It was a glorious, primal time for Europe, comparable in importance to the Homeric period for the classical world. But there was a grim, negative side to the picture, as well. "Hard by the Cathedral," as the historian Oswald Spengler reminds us, "were the gallows and the wheel."[2] And there was the Albigensian Crusade of Innocent III.

In brief: people were being forced to profess beliefs they did not hold; others, through inheritance and political intrigue, were holding high positions in a politically oriented Church for which they were not spiritually qualified; marriages were being contracted for social and political ends that a clergy was then blessing and binding in the way of what was called a sacrament; and love could enter lives only in the way of a disaster, of a so-called mortal sin, the sin, namely, of adultery, which was punishable by death. And in this light, we can read with interest the passage in Gottfried von Strassburg's *Tristan* where the poet tells of the young couple's drinking of the love potion. It is, of course, an accident, and when the maid Brangaene, who was responsible for the potion and for Iseult, realizes what has happened, she comes to Tristan, appalled, and says to him: "That flask and what it contained will be your death."

To which he answers: "So, then, God's will be done.…If Iseult is to be my death this way, I shall gladly court an eternal death."[3] That is to say, he accepts not only the physical death of the Church and society's punishment for the crime of love, but even eternal death in the fires of an actual hell. Such spiritual courage in the prospect even of torture everlasting typifies the heroism of anyone of that period thinking to live a life of his own. It says something to us also of the power and courage of a perfect love in any age. As Meister Eckhart declared: "Love knows no pain." The Middle Way, the way of one who would, in Wolfram's gloss of Parzival's name, *pierce the valley*, is not an easy way, and may require of its traveler indifference to the opinion not only of the world but also of its God; and to this, another line of the mystic Eckhart: "Man's last leave-taking is the leaving of God for God."[4] And as Lao-tzu put it, "The Way that can be named is not the Way."[5] The God named and supposed to be known, together with his opposite, the Devil, is to be left behind in the passage by the Middle Way to the tree by the well, where the white birds merrily sing.

The Waste Land, then, is the land of people living inauthentic lives, doing what they think they must do to live, not spontaneously in the affirmation of life, but dutifully, obediently, and even grudgingly, because that is the way people are living. That is what T. S. Eliot saw in the Waste Land of the twentieth century; and that is what Wolfram von Eschenbach—Eliot's model—saw in the Waste Land of the thirteenth.

Such a condition is epitomized and personified in Wolfram's figure of the wounded Grail King, Anfortas, whose name, as we saw, is drawn from the Old French word meaning "infirmity." He is a beautiful and gentle youth but inherited rather than earned his position and role as guardian of the highest symbol of the spiritual life. And in the way of youth, moved by nature, he rides forth one day from the Castle of the Grail with the battle cry, "*Amor!*"—which for a young knight of the world was fitting, but for the Grail Guardian inappropriate. Anfortas's spiritual role, that is to say, was formal and external, not consistent with his will. And as he rode, he saw charging toward him from a neighboring forest a pagan knight. Anfortas couched his lance. The two collided and the pagan challenger was slain; Anfortas, however, was wounded sore, the other's lance having unmanned him. Its poisoned head remained in the wound, and on it was inscribed the words *The Grail.*

Thus the sense of the wound in Wolfram's version of the legend was that in the Europe of his day the spontaneity of nature had been annulled. Nature, represented by the pagan knight emerging from the forest, aspiring to its own spiritual fulfillment as symbolized in the

words *The Grail* inscribed on the head of the pagan lance, had been
struck down by the Christian, whose own nature had been thereby
undone. For spirit, in the medieval Christian view, was not *of* nature
but against it, since nature had been rendered corrupt by the Fall in
the Garden, and the repository of the spirit was the Church, not the
heart corrupt. Moreover, at the helm of the ship of the Church was
a crew of master politicians: their Albigensian Crusade had already
been launched in 1209, and their Inquisition (established 1233) was in
preparation. Spirit and nature were conceived and taught as contrary
to each other: not the spiritual life as the flowering and completion of
the natural, but as the abnegation of the natural. That was the meaning, in Wolfram's work, of the Waste Land: a people's own inherent
spirituality cut down by an order of values radically out of accord with
the order of nature itself.

In anguish, the destroyed young Grail King returns to his castle,
where the presence of the marvelous stone, *lapis exilis*, keeps him alive
but of itself cannot heal the wound. He remains in such pain that, as
Wolfram states: "He can neither ride nor walk, the king can neither
lie nor stand: he leans but cannot sit."[6] Eliot repeats the words: "Here
one can neither stand nor lie nor sit."[7]

The people of the hidden castle live on in helpless sorrow, waiting
for that one to arrive who will, out of the impulse of his own noble
heart, pronounce the words that will break the spell.

ENCHANTMENT AND DISENCHANTMENT

The Waste Land of T. S. Eliot refers to Jessie Laidlay Weston's famous
book from the early 1920s, *From Ritual to Romance,* in which she
argues that the Grail legend—and indeed all the Arthurian legends—
derived from Celtic mythologies that became associated in the period
of the Roman occupation of Britain with mystery cult themes. And
although her theory has been challenged, these challenges have not
been serious. The theory has to be modified a little bit here and there,
but essentially it is correct. The knights and ladies of the Arthurian
romances are indeed Celtic gods and goddesses masquerading in
human costume. And this is one way of saying that in all of us, in our
human activities, deities are operating.

Now, the particular theme of the Grail story is one of enchantment and disenchantment. This is a very well-known mythological motif.

One of the strongest influences on the troubadour tradition, of course, was that of the Sufis—the mystic Persian and Muslim poets in Spain. And the magnum opus of this tradition—at least in terms of popular culture—was *The Arabian Nights.*

There are some beautiful examples in these wonderful tales of just the kind of storytelling that we've been examining. One that is very close in sentiment to the Grail story is "Judar and His Brothers." This is a dandy story, and it shows that this theme of enchantment and disenchantment is not peculiar just to the Arthurian system. In fact, the tales of *The Arabian Nights* and the tales of the Arthurian romances are in many cases exact contemporaries. These two worlds of the Muslims and the medieval Christian knights were in intimate interplay, not only in the Holy Land at the time and in the place of the Crusades but also in Spain, where the Christians were trying to recover what they had lost in 711 to the Muslims, and which they did not completely recover until 1492. The whole history of the Middle Ages in Spain is one of interplay between the Muslim and Christian worlds. And in southern Italy and Sicily, in the court particularly of Frederick II, we have very strong communication between these two worlds. So not only were the theological discourses, the knightly activities, and the social contacts closely connected, but so were the philosophical and popular story worlds.

The idea of enchantment and disenchantment is that people at a certain time and place are forced to perceive the world in a way that is inadequate or improper to its character. This makes me think of the Gnostic aphorism in the Gospel according to Thomas in which Christ is asked when the Kingdom will come. And Christ says, "It will not come by expectation. It is here now. The Kingdom of the Father is spread over the earth and men do not see it."[8] Men do not see it because of an enchantment. In these legends the savior who is to disenchant the world is the equivalent of Christ, the Savior who opens men's eyes.

In the Oriental tradition of Buddhism, it is the Buddha who releases you from the enchantment of *māyā.* And the enchantment of *māyā,* in modern psychological terms, is exactly the image of the world that you have as a consequence of your fears and desires. If you could break away from your ego limitations, you would behold the world of paradise right here and now. There is a Buddhist saying: "This world with all its ills, with all its horrors, with all its stupidities, with all its darkness, is the golden lotus world." *This* is the golden lotus world, right now as it is. And if you cannot see it as such, it is not the world's fault. What must be corrected is not the world, but your own perspective.[9] And so we find in the Grail legend that everything needed is all there, only it is not being seen. And what the hero is to do is to clarify the situation.

FIGURE 55. Clinschor the enchanter (print, United States, 1911)

Another enchantment in Wolfram's story runs parallel to the enchantment of the Grail Castle. This is the enchantment of the Castle of Marvels, which concerns not the realm of the spirit but the realm of love—physical, erotic love. It concerns the world of the troubadours.

This part of the story tells of Clinschor, a very powerful, well-known, and distinguished duke, who falls in love with the wife of a noble king of Sicily, probably Frederick II. And in the way of the twelfth-century troubadours, he becomes the lover of the king's wife. But when the king discovers the two together, the king castrates this man, who is so mortified, as well as physically stricken, that he decides on revenge. He goes to Persia and learns tremendously powerful magic. And then he comes back and enchants the whole aristocracy of Europe in a castle known as the Castle of Marvels. All the queens, countesses, and beautiful women, and all the glorious knights, are separated from one another, even forgetting who they all are.

On the one hand we have the Castle of Marvels enchanted in the wasteland of love of which I spoke earlier in connection with the *Tristan* story. And on the other, we have the Castle of the Grail, lost in the Waste Land of the spiritual life. Both the spiritual and the secular worlds of spiritual experience, love and beauty, are under this pall of enchantment through these two *castrati*, Clinschor and poor young Anfortas. (Here we can see the influence on Wagner already.) That's the situation. That's what has to be healed. And two heroes are available, one for each task. One hero is Parzival, who starts out as a young, callow fool. And the other is graceful, courteous, lovely Gawain, a highly sophisticated philanderer. Wolfram presents Gawain as he goes in and out of bed and in and out of the battlefield, and all of it in grand style. But all that represents part of the enchantment situation. Each hero must disenchant himself before he is able to disenchant the Waste Land.

THE ANOINTED KING

It was Wolfram von Eschenbach who picked up the theme, and declared in his preface and his conclusion that Chrétien had misrepresented it. Wolfram developed it in full. And this is the great *Parzival* that Wagner took over—and I would say, in a certain way, destroyed. (I'll explain why a little later.) Now, according to Wolfram, who really knew what he was talking about, the reason for the enchantment was that the Grail King had been very severely wounded by a pagan lance. The character of the Grail King is the crux of this whole situation. This young man inherited his role; he had not earned it.

He was simply anointed as king. The whole problem in the Middle Ages was that the religious life was under the control of the anointed. The salvation of man transpired through the sacraments, which were handed down through anointed clergy. And whether you were a person of great majestic spirituality or a very trivial character who had made a good confession, you would be saved through the ritual magic of the sacraments. You might ask, Why should anyone go in quest of the Grail in the Middle Ages when the holy sacrifice of the Mass was being celebrated every day, and all one had to do was go around the corner, and there was Christ himself in the sacrament of the altar?

The point is that the sacrament of the altar was simply ritualistic, available to anyone who went through the paces, while the Grail Castle is to be entered only by one who is *worthy* of it. An unworthy person, no matter how many Hail Marys or Our Fathers he might have said sacramentally, is not guaranteed to be eligible for it. Wolfram shows the Grail Castle entered not only by the Grail hero but also by his Muslim half brother. So in Wolfram's context you don't even have to be a baptized Christian to get to the Grail Castle. It is the majesty of spirit that counts.

One of the characteristics of an enchantment is that there are people all around who know the rules of the enchantment. These are the people of the Grail Castle community. They know what the curse is and how it works, but they can't dispel it. The only way the enchantment can be broken is by some naive person doing the thing that has to be done unintentionally, out of his true nature. To do something intentionally will not break the spell. In other words, the rescue of the world occurs through an intrinsic nobility of nature expressed by the hero. In this tradition the hero is called the Great Fool, one who is uninstructed in the secret of the enchantment. Nevertheless, because of his purity—and I don't mean purity in the Galahad sense but rather in the sense of the integrity, honesty, courage, and forthrightness of his character—he is able to restore the proper natural order, as against the enforced social order of the anointments. Here is a king, the Grail King, who was not naturally competent for his job but has been anointed. And he right away becomes interested in the adventure of love.

The Wound

The Grail King, who represents the champion, the guardian of the highest spiritual symbol, goes forth in quest of love. And he encounters on the way a man, a pagan who represents the natural principle in quest of the Grail. And these two, one a Christian and the other a Muslim, immediately go into combat. And what happens is that the Moor, the Muslim, sends his lance through the genitals of the king so that he is rendered impotent. That is the symbol of the Waste Land. The king who represents the land's health, its spiritual fertilization, is symbolically rendered impotent. And that king, at the same time, slays the Muslim. So as a result of the fact that the lord of the spirit is inadequate to his function, both the world of the spirit and the world of nature are rendered impotent. A pall falls over the Grail Castle. The king, in terrific anguish, is carried home. And when the head of the lance is extracted from the wound, the words *The Grail* are seen

FIGURE 56. Anfortas receives the wound (print, United States, 1911)

written on it. This Muslim was in quest of the Grail. What you have here is spirit in quest of nature, and nature in quest of spirit. And neither is helping the other but is in collision with the other. What we've got to do now is unite the two.

There's another aspect to the Grail. When the question is finally asked, the king will be healed, but he will lose his position. The position of the Grail King will go to Parzival, the one who asked the question. You might say the secret problem of the quest is to heal the Grail King and to achieve his role, but without the wound—that is to say, to become the supporter of the spiritual principles, without the emasculating, literally sterilizing wound.

I'd like to make two points before going into the rest of our story. Wagner, when working on his opera *Tristan und Isolde*, had the sudden realization that the Tristan wound, the wound from which Tristan died, was the same wound as that of Anfortas. And that is why, while working on the *Tristan* opera, he commenced work on his *Parsifal*. And what is that wound? It is the wound of lust, life thrown off balance by compulsive lust, rather than by controlled *amor*—only Wagner interpreted the healing of lust in terms of *agapē*, impersonal spiritual love, and not in terms of *amor*.

A further point of interest is that Wagner himself, while working on his *Tristan*, was violently in love with the poet Mathilde Wesendonck, another man's wife, in whose arms he hoped he would die. He identified himself with Tristan, and Mathilde with Isolde, and her very generous, and—I must say—noble husband, Otto, with King Mark. In Gottfried's version, Mark is a noble, wonderful man—lacking, however, the gentle heart of love. He sends for Iseult to be his wife on the urging of his nephew and his council without ever having seen her. He has neither the eye to scout out love nor the heart to feel it, as Borneilh would say. And one woman, for him, was as another—he had no idea on his wedding night that he had bedded the maid Brangaene rather than his bride, Iseult. Thus he was ineligible to be her real consort. So here we have this Wagnerian concept, and it is borne out in both his *Tristan* and his *Parsifal,* which share this theme of the wound.

Wagner's recognition is an important one. One notes immediately a number of themes already shared by Wolfram's *Parzival* with the

Tristan romance of Gottfried. Like the sword cut on Tristan's thigh, delivered by the blade of Morholt, Anfortas's wound, too, was poisoned and incurable, save by magic of a certain kind; it's incurable, yet the victim does not die. The one who delivered the wound is slain. Furthermore, as Morholt the Mighty had been the emissary of the Irish king and queen, so this alien warrior was also from a land of heathenness, which, like Ireland, was a land of magic, an Earthly Paradise. However, the main point of Wolfram's account is to be seen in the association of the young Grail King's wound with his sensual erotic urge, which is obviously an appetite contrary to the order of spiritual realization signified by his sacred office as guardian of the Grail.

No such sense of the symbolic relevance of the wound appears in Chrétien's fragment; the dolorous stroke there was a mere battle accident, of no spiritual significance; in other versions of the tale, it is the magical result of an impiety of some kind, usually the impudent or accidental approach to, and touching of, some sacred object. Thus it is only in Wolfram that a significant psychological, as opposed to merely magical, wondrous, fairyland reading is given to the mythic theme of the wound that we have traced now of the ever-dying, ever-living, castrated-yet-all-generating consort of the Cosmic Goddess.

And indeed, it therefore would now appear that Wagner's brilliant equation of Tristan's wound with that of the Grail King was precisely what had been in Wolfram's mind: and not Wolfram's only, since Wolfram and the *Tristan* poet Gottfried were exact contemporaries, the leading European narrative poets of their generation; and they were in open rivalry, furthermore, as representing diametrically opposed attitudes to the leading spiritual as well as literary problem of the Middle Ages—which is to say, the relevance of conscience (integrity of character) to salvation.

It was the aim and achievement of Wolfram to represent the crises of a youth's attainment to an order of honorable, freely rendered love that should lead not to the timeless state of an otherworldly rapture— whether of Dante's sort or Saint Bernard's, in the Empyrean, or of Gottfried's, on a crystalline bed, immune to the universe and to the terrors even of hell—but of a living significance here on this moving earth and in the social context of the day, this day, which so quickly comes—and goes.

THE FISHER KING

As we know, Anfortas has another role to play in *Parzival*: that of the Fisher King. In the Orphic tradition, Orpheus is "the Fisher." Christ said to his apostles, "I shall make you fishers of men."[10] The ring worn by the pope is called the Ring of the Fisherman. It represents the spiritual principle going down into the unconscious waters to pull souls, or beings, out of the unconscious state into the realm of the light.

And so Parzival is going to render this boon. These preliminaries really carry a sense of the depth hidden behind the maimed king, the Fisher King, the one who is fishing for men. Christ crucified is the Fisher King.

According to Abelard's view, this was a great problem for the Church. Why did Christ have to die? What was the sense of his death? There were two approved views. One was a very early view that you find already in the doctrine of Original Sin, and in some of the very early interpretations: that the Devil, through his deception of Adam and Eve, had gained legal power over their souls. And the only way he could be relieved of that power was by being deceived himself.

So if God the Father made a kind of contract with the Devil with the intention of deceiving him, though the Devil had already deceived man, he would have to swap Christ's soul for man's soul. "If you will release man," he says, "I will give you my son."

The Devil, like people of the same character, mistakes shadow for substance. He thinks he should make the swap. As a result, God goes fishing for the Devil with Christ. The image is of Christ on the cross as the bait on the hook. And there's an image that comes from the twelfth century in a little work written by a nun named Herrad of Landsberg called *Hortus Deliciarum* (The garden of delights)—it's a kind of handbook for the nuns teaching children—that shows God the Father fishing. And the weights on the fishing lines are the kings of the house of David, with Christ at the end on the fishhook, and Leviathan, the Devil, is rising to be caught by the bait. He was caught, all right, on the hook—namely, the cross. But Christ, since he was deathless, not subject to death, escaped. So the Devil was tricked.

This was one notion of the atonement: Christ redeeming us, in the sense of a bank loan or a debt being redeemed. The next great crisis in the Christian view of the Crucifixion comes in the eleventh

FIGURE 57. God fishing for
Leviathan (artist's representation of ink on vellum, France,
c. 1185)

century with Saint Anselm, who says that nobody owes the Devil anything; it was God the Father who was owed something because of the
offense to him, which man was responsible for because of disobeying
him in the Garden. This was a horrendous offense, because God pos-
sesses infinite virtue, and nobody could possibly pay God the redemption. There was no man who could do it.

So out of love for man, Christ assumed the role of *being* man—he
was both God and man, and therefore eligible to make atonement.
And he died voluntarily, because living a good life wouldn't have been
enough to atone. The death itself was the atonement. But he didn't
have to receive any merit for the death, being infinitely virtuous, so
he passed the merit on to man, and through Christ's merit we are all
redeemed.

Can you have these two views at the same time?

Abelard saw both as perfectly ridiculous, and his notion was that
Christ came to win us through *love* back to God, from whom we had
been alienated through our rejection of him. And it was simply to
prove God's love and to invoke our love that Christ came to us. So we
can compare this to Christ offering himself as bait to man. The Fisher
of Men is what he was, like our Fisher King in the Grail romances, in
this role of the redeemer, of Christ, of the Bodhisattva.

The Grail

The mythological theme of the inexhaustible vessel is associated in Celtic mythology with the hidden presence of the Earthly Paradise. The Grail is a vessel of this kind, and behind it is the earlier inexhaustible cauldron of the Irish sea-god Manannan.

There is an old, old story of the sea voyage of Bran, the son of Fefbal, to the Isle of Joy and the Isle of Women; on the way, he encounters Manannan. Bran hears one day, in the neighborhood of his stronghold, lovely music behind him. He turns around quickly, and it is still behind him: the music of the Sidhe, the people of the fairy hills, who are here among us, unseen. For just as the Kingdom of the Father is spread upon the earth and men do not see it, so is the fairy world of the Sidhe.

And the music was so sweet that Bran falls asleep, and when he wakes he sees beside him a branch of silver with white blossoms, which he carries in his hand to his royal house. And when his company has assembled, a woman in strange raiment appears who sings in fifty quatrains of the land of apples, the land without grief, sorrow, sickness, or any debility. And when Bran and his company of three times nine sail to that land, they see a godlike man coming toward them over the waters in a chariot, and they are amazed. The charioteer is Manannan, the Hospitable Host of the Land under Waves, and he sings to them thirty quatrains. "Bran thinks this a marvelous sea," he sings. "For me it is a flowery plain. Speckled salmon leap from the womb of your sea; they are calves and colored lambs." Again we have a Celtic counterpart to the image of the Kingdom already here: the interface of the two worlds, of Eternity and Time.[11] Manannan is the counterpart to Śiva in India and to Poseidon and Neptune in the Mediterranean system. These lords are the initiators into the abyss. And they are the lords and consorts of the goddess Mother Earth.

Manannan is especially famous for his palace at the bottom of the sea. It is a spinning castle, a whirling castle of glass, where he entertains all who come to him with an inexhaustible meal, serving the flesh of his immortal pigs, which, killed and eaten one day, are alive the next and fit again for use; along with this, he serves an immortal ale that preserves those who consume it from disease, old age, and death. The cauldron of plenty, the inexhaustible flesh of the pigs, and the ale of immortality are in the later, Christian context of the Grail translated into the chalice, the body, and blood of Christ. And in this we have an intentional recognition of equivalent symbols, themes, and meanings in the earlier, mythological and later, theological traditions—the art of recognizing equivalencies of this kind having been a major interest of the old druidic diviners and bards.

In 1837 a gold ceremonial bowl was discovered in Pietroasa, Romania. It seems to have been part of the ritual regalia of one of the mystery cults that spread throughout the Hellenistic world in the centuries before the coming of Christ. This work is of especial pertinence to our present topic. First, the general region in which it was found is that from which the Manichaean religion (which would attempt to synthesize the Christian religion with the mystery cults) finally entered Europe in the Middle Ages, to flourish in southern France in the period of the Tristan and Grail romances. Second, the female figure in the center (see fig. 59) seems to be holding in her hands something resembling at least one form of the Holy Grail. Third, the general organization of the composition resembles that of the alabaster bowl of approximately the same date, having just sixteen figures in the circle, but the Bronze Age goddess, instead of her serpent-spouse, in

FIGURE 58. Pietroasa bowl (cast gold, Hellenistic, Romania, third or fourth century B.C.)

FIGURE 59. Serpent bowl (carved alabaster, provenance unknown, second or third century A.D.)

the center. Finally, the cult references of the surrounding figures relate directly to the Orphic mysteries.

Let us note, for instance, the vine about the seat or mound upon which the goddess sits, and compare this with the serpent wrapped about the mound in the center of the alabaster bowl. In India the same symbolic statement is made with the symbol of the *lingam-yoni*: a more or less stylized representation of the female organ (*yoni*) of the world-enclosing goddess, penetrated from below by the male organ (*lingam*) of her spouse, the world-generating Lord God, Śiva. Returning to the alabaster bowl, we see the same relationship of the serpent (*lingam*) to the bowl (*yoni*). The Christian words of consecration are taken from those pronounced by Christ himself at the love feast of the Last Supper, for when he took the chalice into his holy and venerable hands, and giving thanks to God the Father, with whom he was in substance one, he blessed the cup and gave it to his disciples saying: "Take and drink ye all of this, for this is the chalice of my Blood, of the New and Eternal Testament: the Mystery of Faith: which shall be shed for you and for many unto the remission of sins. As often as ye shall do these things ye shall do them in remembrance of me."[12]

There is, furthermore, an extremely archaic biological theory involved in the offices of this cult that is still largely held among primal peoples; namely, that the miracle of reproduction is effected in the womb through a conjunction of menstrual blood and semen. The interruption of a woman's period during pregnancy led to the assumption that the blood withheld was formed into the body of the child by virtue of its influence upon the sperm. Just as in the symbolism of the Grail procession, where—if Weston's theory is correct—in the two symbols of the cup (representing the female) and the lance (representing the male) the one life-force was represented in the more primitive mysteries of nature from which the symbols of processing were derived, the menstrual blood and the semen were revered as the vehicles of a life that also was revered.

The earliest surviving version of the Grail legend is, as we know, *Perceval, le Conte del Graal* of Chrétien de Troyes, who declared that he adapted the tale—"the best tale ever told in a royal court"—from a book that had been given to him by the Count Philip of Flanders. The date of his writing of the Grail romance was somewhere between 1175 and the departure of Count Philip for the Holy Land in 1190. We do not know why Chrétien left the tale unfinished, but he did; and we do not know how he would have carried it to conclusion. All the great themes are left in the air. As far as it goes, it is a tale of the type known as the Great Fool: a youth, Perceval, of noble heart, brought up in ignorance of the rules of knighthood, nevertheless sets forth to become a knight, and though in the beginning he is boorish and clumsy, he becomes in time the very model of a knightly champion; whereupon, by what appears to him to be mere chance, he enters, without knowing, upon the adventure of the enchanted Castle of the Grail.

There he is introduced to the Maimed King, "wounded by a javelin through his two thighs," and in the great hall observes a mysterious procession of squires and damsels bearing tokens of unknown import: a sword in its sheath, a white lance bleeding from its point, the golden Grail, set with precious stones, carried by a damsel of great beauty, and a silver carving dish, carried by another very young woman. He fails, however, to ask a certain expected question (in this version, "Who is served by the Grail?") that would have healed the king and broken the enchantment. And so his quest has failed. And the poem ends with its hero, Perceval, receiving religious instruction from, and practicing penance with, a hermit.

One cannot but feel that Chrétien either did not know what his legend was all about and here broke off in frustration, or did know and could not sympathize with its increasingly evident heretical implications. In any case, though gracefully and fluently rendered in delicious verse, his legend of the Grail is unresolved; the hermit's instruction of Perceval has little or nothing to do either with the sense of the enchantment or with the meaning of Chrétien's version of the question to be asked; and what the book of Count Philip of Flanders may have made of it all, we neither know nor likely shall ever know.

In the later ecclesiastical and monastic tradition, the Grail is identified explicitly with the cup, bowl, or dish (variously) of the Last Supper, the lance with the Lance of Longinus that pierced the side of the Crucified, and the Grail Hero with Galahad—that saintly, virginal youth, wearing a red armor symbolic of the Holy Spirit, who was introduced to Arthur's dining hall at the feast of Pentecost, the festival of the descent of the Holy Spirit in tongues of flame upon the heads of the assembled apostles. The principal texts are three: first, *Joseph d'Arimathie*, by a Burgundian poet, Robert de Boron; next, *L'Estoire del Saint Graal*, by an unidentified Cistercian monk; and finally, *La Queste del Saint Graal*, by another unknown Cistercian, this being the version of the legend translated by Sir Thomas Malory in *Le Morte d'Arthur* (originally spelled *Le Morte Darthur*).

A prodigious mass of material is associated with this version of the legend, containing many inconsistent passages; and modern scholarship on the subject is as complex and confused as the medieval texts themselves—which have been roughly dated to the years between 1199 and 1230 or so.[13] Robert de Boron mentions, without naming it, a certain "great book" (*le grand livre*) from which his knowledge of the tale was drawn, and there is evidence that a version of the same may have inspired *L'Estoire* as well. The *Queste*, on the other hand, is apparently original, and from the hand of an inspired master. It is a magnificent work, expressing, as one major critic has observed, "the mystical spirit of the Middle Ages with a power that is hardly equaled elsewhere."[14]

Briefly, the main themes of this tradition of special relevance to our topic are those touching the history and mystery of the Grail itself. It had been bestowed by the risen Christ himself upon Joseph of Arimathea, while the latter was in prison for having offered his own sepulcher as a repository for Christ's body; and the risen savior, bearing the instruments of his passion, had appeared to him in the locked cell, charging him to fare with the relics to Glastonbury (which in folk memory had become identified with Avalon), there to establish the blessed sanctuary of the Grail.

The vital point here, which I very much want to stress, is that the Grail Castle was founded by the *risen* Christ, whereas the Church of Rome, of Peter, which everyone can see and enter, was founded by the historical Jesus, teaching and preaching at a time when anyone in Palestine at the time might have seen, heard, and known him. Only those spiritually gifted and especially blessed, on the other hand, would ever see in vision the risen Christ. Likewise, only those spiritually and blessed in a very special way would ever discover and enter in vision the otherwise invisible church or Castle of the Grail.

This legend, then, represents an elite tradition—elite in a mystical sense. And in this sense it represents the challenge of a Celtic type of alternative mystical Christianity to the historical and historically oriented Church of Rome. Indeed, not only was Glastonbury here identified with Avalon, but in de Boron's poem the Grail was passed from Joseph to a younger relative named Bron; and it was this Bron, then, who, as its guardian, sailed with the Grail to Britain—just as, in the old pagan legend, Bran sailed to the everlasting Isle of Women. The name Bron has been identified by the leading modern scholars with Bran, who, when he arrived in the blessed isle, became identified with Manannan, and even served his guests, like that Hospitable Host, from an inexhaustible cauldron—which, in the opinion of most modern scholars of the legend, was the first and foremost model of the vessel of the Grail. Not only in the *Queste*, but in all versions of the legend, questing heroes may ride back and forth over the very ground of the Grail without seeing it: and I am told that in Ireland, one may walk around and right past a fairy hill without seeing it. One seems to be walking a straight line, but actually the line is curving past an invisible fairy hill of glass, which is right there, but hidden—like the Hidden Truth.

As I have said, Wolfram's Grail, in contrast to Chrétien's and Robert de Boron's, is a stone. And that stone is called the philosopher's stone. Now, the philosopher's stone is that alchemical marvel that can transmute gross matter into subtle matter, can transmute primal filth into gold. It can transmute the life of the world into the golden life of the spirit. That's what the Grail can do. Furthermore, it is a vessel, as it were, that will give to everyone what he or she asks for. It is the vessel of plenty, a symbol of the spiritual conduit that carries the inexhaustible of the eternal into the inexhaustible forms of temporal world. There is a *sloka* in one of the Upaniṣads that says, "From that inexhaustible this inexhaustible."[15] And that one is not even tapped. It cannot be exhausted. And the Grail is the source through which this comes.

Now, the source to which Wolfram attributes his version of the legend is not Chrétien's but that of an otherwise unknown poet, Kyot of Catalonia, who, he declares, discovered in Toledo the manuscript of a heathen alchemist and astronomer named Flegetanis.[16] It was from this source that he had derived his knowledge of the Grail, not as a vessel but as a stone carried from heaven by the neutral angels, who had sided neither with Lucifer nor with God. Its name was *lapis exilis*, which is one of the terms applied in alchemy to the philosopher's stone, translating from Latin to "the uncomely stone, the small or paltry stone."

There is in the treasury of the cathedral of San Lorenzo of Genoa (which was consecrated in 1118) a flat, quadrangular bowl of green glass, which, until broken in Napoleon's time, was thought to have been carved of a single gigantic sapphire. It was taken as booty by the Genoese at the time of their conquest of Caesarea, 1001–1002 A.D., where it was supposed to have been the vessel in which, according to a Byzantine legend, Joseph of Arimathea and Nicodemus had caught and preserved the blood of the Savior. Hermann Goetz, from whose splendid article I have drawn my information for this part of my discussion, has suggested that it may have been this bowl, allegedly of precious stone, that suggested to Wolfram the idea of the Grail as a vessel of stone.

AVALON

In 1191 the fabulous isle of Avalon was equated with Glastonbury, when the monks that year claimed to have discovered in their cemetery the skeletons of Arthur and Guinevere, Saint Patrick of Ireland, Saint David of Wales, and Saint Gildas of Brittany. They also brought forward an old tradition, recorded around 1000, that the first missionaries to Britain had founded a church at Glastonbury, built by no skill of man, and consecrated by Christ himself to the honor of the Virgin: it was the same, they now claimed, as the little wattled structure that had burned in 1184, on the site of what is now St. Mary's Chapel. Moreover, there were in Glastonbury many relics: a piece of the table of the Last Supper; a piece of the pillar at which Christ had been scourged; parts of the scourge itself, and of the garment in which Herod caused him to be clothed; the sponges from which Christ had been given wine mixed with myrrh and vinegar mingled with gall to drink; many pieces of his cross, and a stone from where it stood and even part of the hole in which it was fixed; a thorn from the crown of thorns; and six fragments of the Holy Sepulcher. In addition, a series of forgeries were perpetrated from this *officine des faux,* "laboratory of forgeries," as one great scholar has termed the abbey, which, after about 1240, included the name of Joseph of Arimathea himself among those whose presence had been found. And all this was taken so seriously that, as Professor Loomis recounts in his delightful account of the pious fraud: "At four great Church Councils the English delegation vigorously asserted their right to precedence over the representatives of other nations of Western Christendom on the ground of prior conversion": at Pisa in 1409, Constance in 1417, Siena in 1424, and Basel in 1434.[17] It required the legal mind of Spain in the person of Alfonso García de Santa María, doctor of laws, to demonstrate that Joseph of Arimathea could not have arrived, as claimed, in Britain in 63 A.D., since he was not released from his dungeon by Vespasian until 70 A.D.

FIGURE 60. The Dolorous Stroke (print, United States, 1880)

APPENDIX A

A Study of the Dolorous Stroke

"THEN SAID MERLIN TO BALIN...thou shalt strike a stroke most dolorous that ever man struck,' except the stroke of our Lord, for thou shalt hurt the truest knight and the man of most worship that now liveth, and through that stroke three kingdoms shall be in great poverty, misery and wretchedness twelve years, and the knight shall not be whole of that wound for many years."[1] Balin, to his sorrow, wrought fulfillment of this prophecy, and the blow which he dealt has been known as the dolorous stroke.

Modern questers for secrets of the grail swarm along a well worn route, and battle their ways through the multitude around them. As a consequence of their impassioned activities grail questing has retained much of its ancient, perilous character, and the highway to the dim vessel has been rendered almost unpassable. But the dolorous stroke has been favored with little more than cursory notice, and therefore I should like to distract some attention from the main highway. The path which I propose to follow lies aloof from the main road, and no one has ever pressed it to conclusion.

My plan is to seek the pristine significance of Balin's pagan deed, and to scrutinize, then, the history of its transfiguration to Christian purpose.

A STUDY OF THE DOLOROUS STROKE

By Joseph J. Campbell

Submitted in partial fulfillment of the requirement:
for the degree of Master of Arts in the Department of English
and Comparative Literature, Faculty of Philosophy, Columbia
University, March 15, 1927.

FIGURE 61. Title page (typed manuscript, United States, 1927)

PART I

I.

The French Huth Merlin furnishes our earliest tale of Balin. Extant in a single defective manuscript, it is preserved in the library of Mr. Alfred H. Huth, of London. According to the Messrs. Gaston Paris and Jacob Ulrich,[2] and to Dr. Oskar Sommer,[3] this manuscript was written at the end of the thirteenth or the beginning of the fourteenth century. Two of its important leaves (ff 136 & 137) are missing,[4] and consequently, from the killing of Garlon, to Balin's exit from the castle of Pellean, the story has to be supplied by the *Demanda del Sancto Grail,* which is an ancient Spanish translation, and by book two, chapter fifteen, of Malory's *Morte Darthur.*[5] The *Demanda* furnishes many more details than Malory, and therefore I shall prefer it as a point of departure.

One day Balin was escorting a young knight to the tent of Arthur, when, suddenly, a spear directed by an invisible hand struck the young man from his horse. Balin, grieved at the good knight's death, drew the spear from the bleeding wound, and set forth eager for revenge. With him he carried the shaft of the deadly weapon.

Not long after this tragic misadventure, Balin, riding with another young knight, met Merlin, who told him that the invisible murderer of his first companion was Garlon, brother of King Pellean. Then Merlin disappeared, and the two knights continued on their way. But, suddenly Balin's companion was killed with another invisible lance-thrust, and Balin, more than ever, was filled with a lust for revenge.

At a time when King Pellean was feasting, Balin arrived at his palace; and though a prohibition there in force forbade anyone to enter with weapons, he gained admittance full-armed. Spying Garlon eating there, our hero split his head without ado, and killed him by shoving the broken shaft of Garlon's own spear into the wound. Then the king waxed exceeding wroth, and straightway seized a beam with which to attack Balin. In the struggle which naturally enough ensued Balin's sword was broken, and weaponless our gallant rushed, with the king full tilt behind him, from one room of the castle to another.

"And he looked everywhere and saw another chamber open and entered into it, thinking to find there something with which to defend himself, and the King, who was following very closely when he sought to enter heard a voice that said to him: 'To your misfortune will you enter there; for you are not such an one that you ought to enter into so very holy a place.' He (Balin) heard indeed the voice but did not refrain from entering; and he saw the chamber so beautiful and rich that he did not suppose that in the world could exist its equal. And the chamber was very large and square, of a very rich fragrance as if all the fine spices in the world had been there. And in the midst of the chamber was a great table, and of very rich silver, placed upon four legs of silver; and upon this table was a great basin of gold, and within this basin stood a lance, perpendicularly, point downward, and any one looking at it would have marveled because it was not inserted, nor supported, nor fastened anywhere. And the Knight of the Two Swords saw the lance but did not consider it carefully, and he was on the point of taking it, and a voice said to him: 'Do not take it, sinner!' But he did not refrain on this account from taking it with both hands, and he struck with it Pellean who was coming against him so vehemently that he thrust it through both of his thighs, and the King perceiving himself severely wounded fell to the earth. And the knight returned the lance to the place from which he had taken it, and, when he had replaced it, it stood as before."[6]

At this instant the castle walls began to totter and fall, and there was heard a voice which said:

"Now commence the adventures of the Adventurous Realm, which will never cease until shall be dearly paid for the deed of that one who took with his filthy and vile hands the Sacred Lance, and therewith wounded the best man among the princes, and the great Master will take vengeance for it so that those who may deserve to do so shall suffer in consequence."

Then the castle crashed to ruins, and everyone within it lay as dead for two days and nights. Later it was found that more than half of them were killed, and that the surrounding countryside was desolate.

Balin lay with the victims till a sudden shouting of Merlin revived him. The wizard showed him his host and damsel, dead beneath the wreckage. Then he procured a horse for Balin, and vanished.

Balin rode off and saw all about him people dead and wounded. Malory tells us that all who were alive cried out to him, "O Balin, thou has caused great damage in these countries; for the dolorous stroke thou gavest unto King Pellean, three countries are destroyed, and doubt not but the vengeance will fall on thee at the last."[7]

2.

After a careful analysis of the grail quest romances, Miss J. L. Weston writes as follows:

"There is a general consensus of evidence to the effect that the main object of the Quest is the restoration to health and vigour of a King suffering from infirmity, caused by wounds, sickness, or old age; and whose infirmity, for some mysterious and unexplained reason, reacts disastrously upon his kingdom, either depriving it of vegetation, or exposing it to the ravages of war."[8]

To this therapeutic quest Balin's dolorous stroke is a prelude. It tells how the king was wounded, and how his kingdom was sore smitten; and it emphasizes with a good deal of vivid colour, a close connection between the vitality of the king, and the happy prosperity of his kingdom.

Professor A. C. L. Brown observes that this Balin story "is in the whole range of Arthurian romance...the most coherent and detailed explanation of the machinery of the grail quest. It tells why and by whom the king was wounded and his land laid waste."[9]

In an extract printed by Sommer from Ms. Bib. Nat. Fr. 343, Professor Brown has found a grail quest conclusion which links itself closely with the Balin dolorous stroke. Here Galahad arrives at Corbenic and enters "la mestre forteresce trés devant le palleis aventureux."[10] He and his companions leave their arms at the door. An old man leads Galahad from chamber to chamber, and then points him to the room where the king lies wounded, bidding him enter alone. Then we have the chamber of the grail described as though it were the chamber of the Balin story: large and rich, with a table of silver, and above this, pointing downward, the bleeding lance which pierced the side of Christ, poised miraculously in the air.

"Et voit maintenant en mi leu de la chamber qui mult estroit granz et riche la table dargent et le santime vessel si hautement et si bel aorne com nostre estoire a la autre fois devise...et il voit tres de sus la table dargent celle meesmes lance dont la santime car ihesu christ avoit este navree. Et ele estoit mise en lair le pointe de soux et li fust de sus, et pendoit merueilleusement que mortex hom ne peust pas ueoir qui la sostenoit, et sachiez que ele rendoit par la pointe gotes de sanc qui chooient en un moult riche vesse dargent assez espessement. Mes apres ce que eles estoient venues el vexel ne pooit nus savoir qui li sans devenoit. Quant Galahas voit ceste merveille il pense bien que ce est sanz faille la lance aventureuse."[11]

This unique version finally refers the wound of King Pellean to the Knight of the Two Swords—who is Balin.

Thus Balin's dolorous stroke appears to be related to the grail quest, and the grail quest has been revealed as an attempt to restore an infirm king to good health. A close connection has been observed between the vitality of the king and the fertility of his kingdom, and the dolorous stroke has appeared as an elucidation of the circumstances which made this grail quest necessary.

The first phase of our problem, then presents itself as follows:

A king is struck through the thighs by a marvelous spear wielded by a young man and straightway his kingdom is stricken with death and barren waste.

Our effort will be to discover, (a) who the king can have been whose vitality and good health so obviously supported the prosperity of his kingdom; (b) who the young man can have been who so nearly killed him; (c) what the origin and nature can have been, of the marvelous lance with which the dolorous stroke was dealt the king.

To do this we shall have to turn for a glance at gods and magic.

3.

Primitive man seems to have arrived at the fundamental notion of soul, or spirit, through speculations based upon comparisons of sleep with death. To him sleep appeared as a short absence of the vitality which departs forever at death; and in dreams, consequently, he could imagine himself wandering in the death world, seeing for himself what spirits look like. But in dreams he saw not friends alone, but lodges, fish-hooks, pebbles, and trees. Thus everything in this wide world exhibited ghostly essence, and behind every natural phenomenon some spirit seemed to reside. With dreamland for his model the savage seems to have conjured up a furtive pantheon of occult beings. In this lay the smouldering germs of deity.[12]

But as man grew his gods drew away from their intimate, earthly associations; assuming a seemly and aloof dignity they progressed from the graveyard to the sky. Behind them remains a bizarre trail of curious, haphazard vestiges, to reveal the course of a picturesque ascension.

In *The Golden Bough* Frazer has shown that primitive communities scarcely discern the great gulf which later thought finds between gods and men.[13] The savage draws no sharp distinctions between a god and a powerful magician. Often his gods are merely sorcerers invisible, who work, behind the veil of nature, charms and incantations like those which human magicians work among their fellows. And furthermore, the gods are commonly supposed to exhibit themselves to their worshippers, clothed in the likeness of men. Thus it is easy for the magician, with his supposed miraculous powers, to acquire the reputation of being a deity incarnate.

When the welfare of a tribe is supposed to depend on the performance of magical rites, the magician rises into a position of much influence and repute, and he may readily acquire the rank and authority of a chief or king. "Thus beginning as little more than a simple conjuror, the medicine-man or magician tends to blossom out into a full-blown god and king in one."[14]

In an agricultural community, where happiness depends upon propitious rain and sunshine rather than upon anything else, the duties of a public magician have a great deal to do with the weather. Therefore the magician comes into the character of one who can call up rain or sunshine; and since savages, as we have noted, draw no fixed distinctions between gods and men, he becomes identified with the rain gods, sun gods, or water gods. The powers animating the storm and the sunshine seem to have taken up residence in his being, and, therefore he is thought to hold the prosperity of his people in the very palm of his hand. If he will he can summon sunshine or rain—if he will he can drive them away. And upon the success of his magical endeavor depend not only his crown, but also his head which sustains it.

Savages very often personify the powers of nature as male and female; and on the principle of homeopathic or imitative magic they attempt to assist the growth of trees and plants by imitating the marriage of these powers. When this idea of sex in nature becomes developed further, feminine characteristics are attributed to the earth with its teeming produce, whilst to the rain and sunshine which quicken the earth, masculine qualities are assigned.

Because of the tendency to anthropomorphize—a tendency characteristic of ignorant peoples—the feminine earth notion takes definite form, finally, of a goddess, and the masculine fertilizing principle takes shape in a vigorous god. The union of god and goddess, it is thought, results in the abundant fertility of nature.

But through careless anthropomorphizing godhead is enjoyed not only by the great deities themselves, but also by their marvelous manifestations. Thus the forces which work behind sun, storm, and water, while they are essentially forces which tend to the fertility of nature, are nevertheless quite independent of each other, and liable to separate deification. We have, therefore, lesser fertility gods who tend to be most commonly associated with one or another of the obvious means to fertility. Sun gods, storm gods, and water gods are common enough examples.

But because these gods are so obviously related, and because they all serve, finally, the same important purpose, they are often confused with each other. Therefore it is impossible to limit with any degree of exactitude the precise nature of any given fertility god, or to determine conclusively just what his powers and duties are. He is apt to assume the aspects of any one of his relatives—or of them all.

The magician, we have learned from Frazer, tends to become a full-blown god and king in one; and the gods, we have seen, which he incarnates, are rulers of sunshine and storm. But the sunshine and storm are means to the fertility of the earth goddess. Therefore the magician very often combines in his single personality a great variety of vaguely distinguished characteristics which have to do with the god or gods in charge of impregnating the earth. He acquires the dignity of a veritable pantheon incarnate.

To some extent it appears to be assumed that the god-king's power over nature is exerted through definite acts of will. Therefore if drought, pestilence, or storm arises, the people attribute the misfortune to the negligence or guilt of their king, and punish him accordingly. "Sometimes, however, the course of nature, while regarded as dependent on the king, is supposed to be partly independent of his will. His person is considered, if we may express it so, as the dynamical centre of the universe, from which lines of force radiate to all quarters of the heavens; so that any motion of his—the turning of his head, the lifting of his hand—instantaneously affects and may seriously disturb some part of nature. He is the point of support on which hangs the balance of the world, and the slightest irregularity on his part may overthrow the delicate equipoise. The greatest care must, therefore, be taken both by and of him; and his whole life, down to its minutest details, must be so regulated that no act of his, voluntary or involuntary, may disarrange or upset the established order of nature."[15]

"But no amount of care and precaution will prevent the man-god from growing old and feeble and at last dying...(and) if the course of nature is dependent on the man-god's life, what catastrophes may not be expected from the gradual enfeeblement of his powers and their final extinction in death? There is only one way of averting these dangers. The man-god must be killed as soon as he shews symptoms that his powers are beginning to fail, and his soul must be transferred to a vigorous successor before it has been seriously impaired by the threatened decay....If the man-god dies what we call a natural death, it means, according to the savage, that his soul has either voluntarily departed from his body and refuses to return, or more commonly that it has been extricated, or at least detained in its wanderings, by a demon or sorcerer. In any of these cases the soul of the man-god is lost to his worshippers, and with it their prosperity is gone and their very existence endangered....By slaying him, (however) his worshippers could in the first place, make sure of catching his soul as it escaped and transferring it to a suitable successor; and, in the second place, by putting him to death before his natural force was abated, they would secure that the world should not fall into decay with the decay of the man-god. Every purpose, therefore, was answered, and all dangers were averted by thus killing the man-god and transferring his soul, while yet at its prime, to a vigorous successor."[16]

Dr. Lowie has shown[17] that these general principles formulated by Frazer probably do not hold good throughout the world. But they seem, nevertheless, to have materially affected the thought of Europe.[18] From Ireland to the Hellespont they flourished, and the mythology which survives to this day bears distinctly the vestiges of the god-kings and the nature cults upon it. In Ireland, especially, these venerable notions persist in the shape of vague traditions. Read in the light furnished by old relics and manuscripts, which fortunately outlived the rest of their generation, these vague traditions take on some significance. Judiciously retouched by a careful imagination they become eloquent explanations for myriad enigmas.

The Irish king at Tara was certainly a fertility god incarnate.[19] He was expected to be a source of fertility to the land, and of fecundity to the cattle. A canon attributed to Saint Patrick enumerates among the blessings which attend the reign of a just king, fine weather, calm seas, crops abundant, and trees laden with fruit. On the other hand, dearth, dryness of cows, blight of fruit, and scarcity of corn were regarded as infallible proofs that the reigning king was bad.

The marriage of the king was considered essential to the security of the benefits expected of his reign. With his wife playing the role of earth goddess, and himself in the part of fertility god, the exercise of his marital functions was thought to act sympathetically upon the fecundity of lands, cattle, and mankind. A king sexually impotent, or otherwise physically imperfect, would certainly be to his people a source of woe. To guard, therefore, his healthy divinity, the king of Ireland had to submit to the hedging restrictions of "gessa."

The Irish god-king achieved his position usually by killing his predecessor, and he enjoyed his office till a day when a stronger man than he arrived to wrest the divine spark from him. Whenever he was inconsiderate enough to die a natural death his successor had to be determined by methods cleverly designed to discover the will of the gods. These gods, of course, immediately after the coronation ceremony, took up residence in the personality of the newly appointed king. And then, after a tense and usually exciting lapse, things could move on as before.[20]

Thus the god-king flourished in Ireland, and upon his persistent vigour the flourishing crops all depended—upon his health fertility hung, and abundance. The phenomenon, therefore, of which King Pellean is a shadow, our investigation has tended to explain; and the dolorous stroke has begun to assume an aspect of new significance. It seems to be a polished fragment of savage mythology, wherein gods, beneath a thin guise of armor, masqueraded as medieval gentlemen. Pellean, himself, seems to have been, originally, a Zeus of a northern pantheon. He is the old god-king upon whose domestic habits the fruitful produce of the earth depends. When he is injured the land becomes desolate; the consort of the earth mother loses his ability to fulfill the obligations of his office; the source of the earth's fertility is withdrawn; all life must languish and decline. Pellean is, essentially, the last step in a business of anthropomorphism. He is our god-king notion translated to paradise, governing the universe from his Irish-other-world castle, as king of nature. He is our masculine principle cumbered not only with human shape, but also with human costume. He is our god-king become king-god.

4.

In *The Bleeding Lance* Professor Brown has attempted to link the grail lance with a marvelous weapon of Irish myth, but he has not tried to associate either with the subject of fertility. My own intention is to show that Balin and the lance are related fertility symbols. I shall try to summon both to the support of my suspicions concerning the nature of the dolorous stroke.

Professor Roger Loomis has pointed out to me parallels which suggest that the Irish *Fate of the Children of Tuireann* may be homologous with the tale of Balin. These parallels go a long way toward explaining the strange juxtaposition characteristic of the miraculous lance and cauldron, and therefore the story may serve as an auspicious start to this phase of our investigation.

The children of Tuireann killed the father of Lugh. They were forced consequently to pay an astonishing fine. They had to set out and obtain for Lugh a number of supernatural objects which he carefully named. Among these was the flaming spear of Pisear, who was king of Persia. "And do ye know what spear it is I have demanded from ye?" Lugh asked them. "We know not," said the Children of Tuireann. "An excellent poisoned spear," Lugh replied, "of which Pisear, the King of Persia (is possessed); Ar-eadbair it is called; and every choicest deed is performed with it; and its blade is always in a pot of water, in order that it should not (by its fiery heat) melt down the city in which it is kept."[21]

The three children of Tuireann were at a loss to know how they might set about procuring these marvelous objects. Then it was suggested that nothing but the magic Curach of Manannan could take them to their prizes. Now Lugh was subject to many "gessa," and one of these required that he should grant every second boon which anyone might ask of him. Therefore, when the children of Tuireann, with their second question, asked him to lend them the Curach of Manannan, Lugh, in spite of himself, had to grant their request.

"'....give us a loan of Manannan's Curach,' said Brian, son of Tuireann. 'I shall give it,' said Lugh. 'What place is it in?' said they. 'At brugh na Boinne,' said Lugh.

"And they came again to where Tuireann was, and Eithne, the daughter of Tuireann, their sister: and they told them that they had obtained the Curach.

"....They then set forward, and left Tuireann in sorrow and lamentation, and Eithne accompanied them to the port in which the Curach was. . . .

"....(Then) this warrior band pushed their canoe out from the beautiful, clear-bayed borders of Erinn...'we demand of thee, thou canoe of Manannan, which art under us, to sail with us to the garden of the Hesperides.'

"And this command was not neglected by the canoe...for it sailed forward in its career upon the tops of the green-sided waves..."[22]

After procuring some magic apples, which were items of the fine, they arrived at the Persian palace disguised as poets. The king was feasting, and they proceeded to entertain him with a bit of extempore singing. But the king was displeased, for their songs dwelt overlong upon the lance, Ar-eadbair, which he owned. And he bid them fiercely to be silent with their ominous entertainment.

"When Brian heard this conversation from the king, he bethought him of the apple which he held in his hand, and he made a successful cast of it at the king (and struck him) in the flesh of the forehead, so that he drove his brain back out through the pole of his head; and he bared his sword and fell to hewing down the hosts around him."[23]

After a great battle the three brothers gained access to the room where the spear was kept, and they found it, "with a cauldron full of water under its blade in order that its heat should not scorch the people of the court."[24] They found it "deep in a great cauldron of water, which hissed and bubbled round it. And Brian, seizing it boldly in his hand, drew it forth; after which the three brothers left the palace and went to their canoe."[25]

This story immediately suggests that of the dolorous stroke. The two lances involved correspond exactly in position, and, significantly in general setting. In both tales questers employed with avenging a murder arrive when the king is feasting; a fight immediately precedes the discovery of the lance; and the king is severely wounded. Furthermore, in this Irish story there exists a curious parallel to a Galahad quest situation. We shall quote briefly from Malory for comparison:

"And the good knight, Galahad, rode so long till he came that night to the Castle of Carboneck; and it befell him thus that he was benighted in an hermitage. So the good man was fain when he saw he was a knight errant. Then when they were at rest there came a gentlewoman knocking at the door, and called Galahad, and so the good man came to the door to wit what she would. Then she called the hermit: Sir Ulfin, I am a gentlewoman that would speak with the knight which is with you. Then the good man awakened Galahad, and bad him: Arise, and speak with a gentlewoman that seemeth hath great need of you. Then Galahad went to her and asked her what she would. Galahad, said she, I will that ye arm you, and mount upon your horse and follow me, for I shall show you within these three days the highest adventure that ever any knight saw. Anon Galahad armed him, and took his horse, and commended him to God, and bad the gentlewoman go, and he would follow there as she liked.

"....they found the ship where Bors and Perceval were in, the which cried on the ship's board: Sir Galahad, ye be welcome, we have abiden you long....And the two knights received them both with great joy, and every each knew other: and so the wind arose, and drove them through the sea in a marvelous place....Then said the gentlewoman: Perceval, wot ye what I am? Certes, said he, nay to my witing.

Wit ye well, said she that I am thy sister, which am daughter of King Pellinore."[26]

This situation seems to relate Galahad and his companions to the unhappy children of Tuireann. It presents us again with three questing heroes, accompanied by their sister to a magic, self-propelled craft. And it starts them on a journey to unearthly chambers where marvelous weapons are preserved.

After the lance of Pisear was brought to Ireland it enjoyed a spectacular career. It came to be known as the Luin of Celtchar, and it is described in the *Bruden da Derga* as follows:[27]

"I beheld the room that is next to Conaire. Three chief champions in their first greyness are therein....A great lance in the hand of the midmost man, with fifty rivets through it. The shaft therein is a good load for the yoke of a plough-team. The midmost man brandishes that lance so that its edge-studs hardly stay therein, and he strikes the shaft thrice against his palm. There is a great boiler in front of them, as big as a calf's cauldron, wherein is a black and horrible liquid. Moreover he plunges the lance into that black fluid. If its quenching be delayed it flames on its shaft and then thou wouldst suppose that there is a fiery dragon in the top of the house.

"....A cauldron full of poison is needed to quench it when a deed of manslaying is expected. Unless this come to the lance, it flames on its haft, and will go through its bearer or the master of the palace wherein it is."

Another account of the Luin of Celtchar is in the *Mesca Ulad*. That version reads:[28]

"....A large knightly spear to the height of his shoulder. When its spear-ardour seized it, he would deal a blow of the handle of the mighty spear upon his hand, when the full measure of a sack of fiery particles would burst over its side and edge, when its spear-ardour seized it. A blood-black cauldron of horrid, noxious liquid before him, composed through sorcery of the blood of dogs, cats, and Druids. And the head of the spear was plunged in that poisonous liquid when its spear-ardour came.

"The quick, deedful Luin of Celtchar is in his hand, on loan, and a cauldron of crimson blood is before it, for it would burn its handle, or the man that is bearing it unless it was bathed in the cauldron of noxious blood. And fortelling battle it is."

And, finally, in the *Battle of Rosnarig*, appears the following passage:[29]

"Wonderful indeed were the attributes of that spear; for flood-great streams of fire used to burst out through its sides, and there were four hired soldiers before him with a brazen bright cauldron between them filled with blood in which that venomous spear was dipped every hour to quench its venom."

This ancient spear would seem to be, if anything, a domesticated lightning flash, in constant need of watching and cooling down.

The conclusions which Professor Brown draws from his examination of this material are not altogether pertinent to our present task, and I should like, therefore, to emphasize the tendency of my own argument. My suggestion is that the Luin of Celtchar is a lightning weapon: that in Pisear's palace it appears in a situation similar to that of the lance which dealt the dolorous stroke: and that consequently it may stand as a connecting link between Balin's spear and the lightning.

Now lightning is a convenient weapon for fertility gods. Therefore it is interesting to discover that in one case, at least, a fertility god has employed the Luin of Celtchar as Balin employed the lance of the dolorous stroke. Professor Brown has considered the case in question, and recognized its similarity to the tale of Balin. But he has not indicated the fertility god connection in which I am most interested. It seems to me exciting to find a lance which exhibits lightning characteristics in the supernatural hands of an angry fertility god. The tale is supplied by the *Book of Aicill*, an ancient treatise of Irish law.[30]

King Cormac owned many marvelous objects derived from the Tuatha De Danaan. One of these was Crimall, a remarkable, bloody spear. Oengus was impelled to seek Cormac, one day, by a great desire to revenge an injury suffered at the hands of the king. At a time when King Cormac was celebrating a feast, Oengus arrived at his palace, and because a prohibition there in force forbade anyone to enter with his arms, Oengus left his weapons at the door. But on a wall inside the palace, hanging on its rack, was Crimall, the bloody spear of King Cormac. Oengus, in his anger, quickly seized it, and dealt Cellach, the son of Cormac, a fatal blow. And the spear edge "grazed one of Cormac's eyes and destroyed it: and in drawing it back out of Cellach its handle struck the chief of the king's household of Tara in the back and killed him. And it was a prohibited thing that one with a blemish should be king at Tara. And Cormac was therefore sent out to be cured to Aicill close to Tara: and Tara could be seen from Aicill but Aicill could not be seen from Tara. And the sovereignty of Ireland was given to Coirpri Lifechair son of Cormac."

Professor Brown has pointed out many of the parallels between this story and the dolorous stroke. "In both, the hero comes to the palace of a king at the time of a feast as an avenger of personal wrong. In both is the prohibition against carrying arms into a royal palace.... In both tales the mischief is wrought by a spear kept in the palace as a relic or a marvel. In both cases the king's chief steward or seneschal is slain, although not quite in the same manner. In both, the aggressor escapes and the king is left wounded in such a way as to be left incapacitated for kingship."[31] To these parallels it may be added that in both cases the first person to be slain is a very near relative to the king.

Thus in its general plot, as well as in many of its details, the *Blinding of King Cormac* seems to be definitely related to the story of the dolorous stroke. Two modern newspaper versions of a single event might easily vary more.

Oengus seems to have been primarily an historical character of pre-Celtic Ireland;[32] but in the course of time divine characteristics came to be associated with the dim definitions of his personality. If, originally, he was a prominent magician-king, it is natural enough that godhead should have been in some measure attributed to him during his lifetime—and since he must have been considerably eulogized after his death, it is also natural enough that mythology should finally have effected his complete apotheosis, naming him as one of the fertility gods.

But no matter what may have been his origin, the Oengus of tradition is certainly a god. He is the subject for some colorful mythology, and we find him worshipped in Ireland down to the seventh century A.D. Macalister has identified Oengus as a storm god[33]—and to this character the titles "Oengus of the Dread Lance," and "Oengus of the Great Quencher" may give some evidence. But in any case Oengus was generally associated with the duties and legends of fertility gods, and as one of these he must have been, sometimes, at least, coadjutant of the storm. A fertility god in his most frightful and vigorous aspect is manifest in the thunderstorm, when his weapon is the blazing shaft of the quick and ruthless lightning. Oengus, in a stormy mood, bent upon killing King Cormac, appears to have used this marvelous weapon of gods to fearful purpose.

Thus this Irish god, Oengus, once dealt a dolorous stroke; and in spite of an obvious metamorphosis of names, many details persist which connect his adventure with that of Balin. Furthermore, the Luin of Celtchar, which seems to be not far descended from the lightning, twice appears in settings similar to that of the Balin spear. In one of these it is poised exactly as Balin found his weapon poised. In the other, wielded by a fertility god, it damages a king, and thus truly deals a dolorous stroke. It is possible that these parallels may be consequences rather of convergence than of homology, but it seems to me not probable. Balin, wielding his supernatural weapon, comes doubly into the character of a fertility god.

5.

Following one trail of evidence we have been led to believe that Pellean is a fertility god. Following another trail we have found that Balin, too, may be associated with fertility. Approaching from a third point of view we shall try to draw some definite conclusions.

Adonis, fair youth beloved of Aphrodite, was killed by a wild boar that struck him through the thigh, and therefore his goddess was disconsolate. But she pleaded with Zeus till he finally promised to let her lover return to earth every year. And ever since that time poor Adonis has endured an annual ordeal of glorious death and resurrection.

The ancients believed that this death and resurrection explained the succession of the seasons. This fair young god represented to them the anthropomorphic embodiment of the principle upon which nature depends for its vitality. He survives as one of our typical examples of the fertility god.

Attis was the Phrygian counterpart of Adonis. The myths and barbarous rites connected with his worship are suggestive. "Two different accounts of the death of Attis were current. According to the one he was killed by a boar, like Adonis. According to the other he unmanned himself under a pine-tree, and bled to death on the spot.... The story of the self-mutilation of Attis is clearly an attempt to account for the self-mutilation of his priests, who regularly castrated themselves on entering the service of the goddess (Cybele)."[34]

But Frazer believes that the boar is an embodiment of the divinity himself. The analogies of Dionysius, Demeter, Osiris, and Virbius seem to show that the story of the hostility of an animal to a god is only a late misrepresentation of the old view of the god as embodied in the animal. Thus the boar was once the embodiment of Adonis.[35] Furthermore, the wound in the thigh of Adonis is a euphemized emasculation.[36]

The Adonis myth, then, tells us how the consort of the earth goddess was emasculated. The natural result was that the earth failed in its fertility, and that life lapsed into languishment. The situation is euphemized by representing the god as wounded by a boar in the thigh. This boar was originally the god himself in another form.

When we turn now to consider King Pellean, we find that he too was stricken through the thigh, but by a young man wielding a spear. The fact that he was originally described as having been emasculated is made clear by the fact that in some less euphemized versions, such as the *Parzival* of Wolfram von Eschenbach, and the *Sone de Nausay*, the exact nature of his injury is less cryptically explained. Lines 1388–1392 of *Parzival* read as follows:

einen gelüpten spar
wart er ze tjostieren wunt,
so daz er nimmer mer gesunt
wart, der süeze oeheim din,
durch die heidruose sin.[37]

And lines 4775–4776 of the *Sone de Nausay* explain the plight of the maimed king (who is Joseph himself in this version) in language hardly less clear:

Es rains et desous l'afola
de coi grant dolor endura.[38]

Therefore the story of the dolorous stroke appears as a parallel to the Adonis myth. It tells how the consort of the earth goddess was emasculated. The natural result was that the earth failed in its fertility, and that life lapsed into languishment. The situation is euphemized by representing the god as wounded by a young knight in the thigh.

This young knight is simply a vigorous embodiment of the cosmical vitality which is waning with the strength of the old god.

PART II

Our study has identified Balin's dolorous stroke as the upshot of an attempt to refer the progress of seasons to the alternate waxing and waning of a celestial vitality. Beneath its disguise of lively cast and action we have discerned the gods who govern nature.

Thus the lance-stroke dealt the king-god Pellean has been accounted for. But an undeniable challenge still confronts us. Before we may call it secure, our theory will have to take into account the dolorous stroke of a strangely ubiquitous sword.

I.

In the continuation appended by Gautier to the *Perceval* of Chrétien de Troyes, appears an adventure of Sir Gawain, which has for its basis a dolorous sword stroke dealt by the Knight of the Two Swords. Balin, we have noted already, was nicknamed the Knight of the Two Swords; and therefore this reference bears upon our problem.

Professor Nutt has summarized the Gawain section of Gautier's romance as follows:[39]

"An unknown knight comes to Arthur's court; Keie, who demands his name, is unhorsed; Gauvain brings the unknown to the court, but the latter is slain by a javelin cast by invisible hands. Gauvain equips himself in the unknown's armour and starts forth to learn the latter's name . . . he rides through Brittany and Normandy, and comes to a castle where, owing to his armour, he is at first hailed as lord. In one of the rooms stands a bier, whereon lies a knight, cross and broken sword upon his body, his left hand bleeding.

"A crowned knight enters and goes to battle with Gauvain; canons and clerks come and perform the Vigil of the Dead; whilst at table Gauvain sees the rich Grail serving out bread and wine to the knights. Gauvain remains alone after the meal; he sees a lance which bleeds into a silver cup. The crowned knight again enters, bearing in his hand a broken sword which had belonged to the unknown knight, over whom he mourns. He hands the sword to Gauvain and asks him to put the pieces together. Gauvain cannot, whereupon the knight declares him unfit to fulfill the quest (Old French: *li besoin*) on which he came. Later he may try again. Gauvain asks concerning the lance, sword, and bier. The lance, he is told, is the one wherewith the Son of God was pierced in the side, 'Twill bleed till doomsday.' With regard to the sword the crowned knight explains that 'the kingdom of Logres was destroyed, and the country laid waste by the stroke of this sword.'..."[40] but here Gauvain falls fast asleep. On the morrow he wakes, and finds himself on the sea strand. He rides off, and behold the country has burst into green leaf, and the reason thereof is his having asked concerning the lance. The country folk both bless and curse him for having so far delivered them and for not having completed the deliverance by asking concerning the Grail."[41]

This curious tale is clearly related to that of Balin. Both stories open in precisely the same way. Both adventurers travel far before they reach the grail castle. Both stories know the broken swords. Both refer to the waste kingdom, and conclude with an explicit statement that the kingdom of Logres was destroyed by the dolorous stroke.

Miss Weston, comparing them, thinks, "that there can be little doubt that the same original lies at the root of both tales, but both alike have suffered contamination and are far from clear and coherent."[42] Dr. Oskar Sommer believes that Balin and Gawain must be related. And Professor Brown supposes that the two adventures "represent the introduction and the termination of some lost grail story, which must have been of an exceedingly primitive character, and may have been one of the pagan originals to which Chrétien and the other grail writers ultimately go back."[43]

But in spite of the clear connections, Balin dealt a dolorous lance stroke, whereas this Gawain adventure refers to the stroke of a sword. I shall attempt two possible explanations.

2.

In the tale of Balin a sword figures about as prominently as the lance. Balin acquired his first distinction by drawing a sword which King Arthur and his entire court were unable to budge from its sheath; Balin struck his first blow in the palace of Pellean with a sword; and this sword broke when he parried the beam which Pellean swung in his direction. Balin struck his final blow with a sword, unwittingly killing his own brother. It is possible, therefore, that during the course of transmission the role of the sword may have been confused with that of the lance.

This possibility becomes the more likely when we consider the evidence which bespeaks a confused body of sources for the romance of Gautier. Writing about the account of Gawain's visit to the grail castle Miss Weston remarks: "it is found twice over in the section known as that by Gautier, and when Gawain meets his son he again recounts the experience. Thus in a small space we have three versions of the incident, and none of these agree with each other in detail, though the main outline leaves no room for doubt that they are all versions of the same story. It is clear that the tale must have been well known and very popular for so many variants to have been current at the same moment."[44]

The connection of the Gawain sword with that of Balin becomes even clearer when we consider that both were broken close to the time when the dolorous stroke was dealt.

But this evidence of confusion is not all that can be said for the sword. Swords have been found to constitute popular items in the equipment of fertility gods, and it is possible, therefore, that in its early mythological stage the dolorous stroke may have been associated, sometimes with the blow of a lance, and sometimes with the blow of a sword.

I believe that both of these associations survive in the tale of Balin. Pellean suffered a lance stroke; Garlon was killed by a sword. These neatly dovetailed tragedies have independent sources in what seem to me two dolorous stroke constructions.

We have discussed the lance stroke and found it to be a prelude to the grail quest. Its conclusion we have recognized in the Galahad adventure summarized on pages 174 and 175. But so far as I know, no one has ever suggested that Balin dealt a dolorous sword stroke. In the next section, therefore, I shall offer grounds for my suggestion, and I shall try to show that dolorous sword stroke which Balin dealt Garlon, finds its grail-quest sequel in the Gawain adventure which Gautier has recounted.

3.

In the Gautier Gawain quest the lord of the grail castle is alive, the unnamed knight being designated as victim of the dolorous stroke.

This situation corresponds exactly to the one which would result if the sword stroke dealt Garlon were considered as the dolorous stroke, and if the blow dealt Pellean were omitted from the tale of Balin. Pellean, in that case, would have remained alive to assist at the avenging of his brother, just as the crowned knight, in the Gautier romance, remains alive to assist at the avenging of the unnamed knight. It must be remembered, furthermore, that the crowned knight tells Gawain that the Knight of the Two Swords killed the unnamed knight and that when he committed this deed he broke his sword. That dolorous stroke laid waste the kingdom of Logres.

We know that Balin was called the Knight of the Two Swords, that he broke his sword killing Garlon, and that he laid waste with a dolorous stroke the kingdom of Logres. Gautier, therefore, seems clearly to indicate Balin and Garlon as participators in the dolorous sword stroke. If we can show that Garlon is a fertility god, and that there could be such a thing as a dolorous sword stroke, it will be logical to assume that Gautier was correct when he referred to Balin the wounding of the knight unnamed.

Let us turn first to Malory's account of Garlon's wicked custom:

"And as they were even afore King Arthur's pavilion, there came one invisible, and smote this knight that went with Balin throughout the body with a spear. Alas, said the knight, I am slain under your conduct with a knight called Garlon; therefore take my horse that is better than yours, and ride to the damsel, and follow the quest that I was in as she will lead you, and revenge my death when ye may.... So King Arthur let bury this knight richly, and made a mention on his tomb how there was slain Herlews le Borbous, and by whom the treachery was done, the knight Garlon. But ever the damsel bare the truncheon of the spear with her that Sir Herlews was slain withal.[45]

"So Balin and the damsel rode into a forest, and there met with a knight that had been a-hunting, and that knight asked Balin for what cause he made so great sorrow...said Balin, I am not afeard to tell you, and told him all the cause how it was....And as they came by an hermitage even by a churchyard, there came the knight Garlon invisible, and smote this knight, Perin de Mountbeliard, through the body with a spear...Balin buried the knight under a rich stone and tomb royal. And on the morn they found letters of gold written, how

Sir Gawaine shall revenge his father's death, King Lot, on the King Pellinore."[46]

Garlon is a slayer invisible, and thus a slayer supernatural. He can be killed only by the truncheon of the weapon which he himself used for slaying, and this fact adds to the evidence for his supernatural character. Furthermore, Garlon is the brother of Pellean, whom we canonized in Part I, and it seems not improbable that godhead may have run in the family.

But the supernatural scribe of epitaphs who wrote in gold upon the tomb of Garlon's second victim seems to have confused our villain with King Pellinore. A possible reason for this confusion becomes clear when we review Malory's account of King Pellinore's whimsical customs. We find that Pellinore and Garlon have much in common, and that they appear to belong to a small but picturesque group of fertility gods:

"Thus was the dream of Arthur: Him thought there was come into this land griffins and serpents, and him thought they burnt and slew all the people in the land, and then him thought he fought with them, and they did him passing great harm, and wounded him full sore, but at the last he slew hem. When the king awaked, he was passing heavy of his dream, and so to put it out of thoughts, he made him ready with many knights to ride a-hunting. As soon as he was in the forest the king saw a great hart afore him. This hart will I chase, said King Arthur, and so he spurred the horse, and rode after long, and so by fine force oft was he like to have smitten the hart: whereas the king had chased the hart so long, that his horse lost his breath, and fell down dead; then a yeoman fetched the king another horse. So the king saw the hart embushed, and his horse dead; he set him down by a fountain, and there he fell into great thoughts. And as he sat so, him thought he heard a noise of hounds, to the sum of thirty. And with that the king saw coming toward him the strangest beast that ever he saw or heard of; so the beast went to the well and drank, and the noise was in the beast's belly like unto the questyng of thirty couple hounds; but all the while the beast drank there was no noise in the beast's belly: and therewith the beast departed with a great noise, whereof the king had great marvel. And so he was in great thought, and therewith he fell asleep. Right so there came a knight afoot unto Arthur and said, Knight full of thought and sleepy, tell me if thou sawest a strange beast pass this way. Such one saw I, said King Arthur, that is past two mile; what would ye with the beast? said Arthur. Sir, I have followed that beast long time, and killed mine horse, so would God I had another to follow my quest....I have followed this quest this twelvemonth, and either I shall achieve him, or bleed the best blood of my body....

"Sir knight, said the king, leave that quest, and suffer me to have it, and I will follow it another twelvemonth. Ah, fool, said the knight unto Arthur, it is in vain thy desire, for it shall never be achieved but by me, or my next kin. Therewith he started unto the king's horse and mounted into the saddle, and said, Gramercy, this horse is my own. Well said the king, thou mayst take my horse by force, but an I might prove thee whether thou wert better on horseback or I. Well, said the knight, seek me here when thou wilt, and here nigh this well thou shalt find me, and so he passed on his way. Then the king sat in a study, and bade his men fetch his horse as fast as ever they might...."

Then on a day there came in the court a squire on horseback, leading a knight before him wounded to the death, and told him how there was a knight in the forest had reared up a pavilion by a well, and hath slain my master, a good knight, his name was Miles; wherefore I beseech you that my master may be buried, and that some knight may revenge my master's death....Then came Griflet that was but a squire, and he was but young, of the age of the King Arthur, so he besought the king for all his service that he had done him to give him the order of knighthood....Then took Griflet his horse in great haste, and dressed his shield and took a spear in his hand, and so he rode a great wallop till he came to the fountain, and thereby he saw a rich pavilion, and thereby under a cloth stood a fair horse well saddled and bridled, and on a tree a shield of divers colours and a great spear. Then Griflet smote on the shield with the butt of his spear, that the shield fell down to the ground. With that the knight came out of the pavilion, and said, Fair knight, why smote ye down my shield? For I will joust with you, said Griflet....So the two knights ran together that Griflet's spear all to-shivered; and therewithal he smote Griflet through the shield and the left side, and brake the spear that the truncheon stuck in his body, that horse and knight fell down.

"When the knight saw him lie so on the ground, he alit, and was passing heavy, for he weened he had slain him...and so with the truncheon he set him on his horse and gat him wind, and so betook him to God....And so Griflet rode to the court where great dole was made for him. But through good leeches he was healed and saved... the king was passing wroth for the hurt of Sir Griflet. And so he commanded a privy man of his chamber that or it be day his best horse and armour, with all that longeth unto his person, be without the city or to-morrow day. Right so or to-morrow day he met with his man and his horse, and so mounted up and dressed his shield and took his spear, and bade his chamberlain tarry there till he came again. And so Arthur rode a soft pace till it was day."

Arthur rescued Merlin from a slight distress, and the wizard's gratitude expressed itself in prophecy: "thou art more near thy death than I am, for thou goest to the deathward, an God be not thy friend. So as they went thus talking they came to the fountain, and the rich pavilion there by it. Then King Arthur was ware where sat a knight armed in a chair. Sir knight, said Arthur, for what cause abidest thou here, that there may no knight ride this way but if he joust with thee? said the king. I rede thee leave that custom, said Arthur. This custom, said the knight, have I used and will use maugre who saith nay, and who is grieved with my custom let him amend it that will. I will amend it, said Arthur. I shall defend thee, said the knight." And with that they set upon each other thrice all to-shivering their spears. Then they flung at each other with swords, "But the sword of the knight smote King Arthur's sword in two pieces, wherefore he was heavy." Finally, the knight had Arthur safely under him and would have smitten off his head. But Merlin, therewith, "cast an enchantment to the knight, that he fell to the earth in a great sleep. Then Merlin took up King Arthur, and rode forth on the knight's horse. Alas! Said Arthur, what hast thou done, Merlin? hast thou slain this good knight by thy crafts? There liveth not so worshipful a knight as he was....Care ye not, said Merlin...for he is but asleep...I told you, said Merlin, what a knight he was...there liveth not a bigger knight than he is one...and his name is Pellinore."[47]

This knight, defending his hermitage pavilion, is singularly like Garlon, who committed his first murder close to a pavilion, and his second close to a hermitage. It may be significant that King Arthur buried the first victims both of Garlon and of Pellinore, and that the second victims of the two seem to have been somewhat confused with

each other. Moreover, in his battle with Pellinore, whom he con-
fronted in an effort to avenge the two ruthless murders, King Arthur
broke his sword. This fact coincides unexpectedly with the plan of the
tale of Balin.

But the name Pellinore is an important blessing to our cause.
Professor Loomis[48] believes that the names, Pelle(s), Pellinore, Pellean, and Pellehan(s) are all variants of a single original. Manuscript
errors and translations would originate variations, and these would
be retained because of their tendency to explain slight discrepancies
between versions of the story. Thus Pellinore is probably our fertility-
god-king, Pellean, in disguise.

These connections establish a kind of triangular relationship between Garlon, Pellean, and Pellinore. Garlon and Pellean are brothers,
and each, by a separate trend of evidence, may be related to Pellinore. The latter, curiously enough, seems to represent a combination of the complementary personalities embodied in the two strange
brothers. He is at once a worshipful knight, the biggest in the world,
and a cruel knight who maintains a wicked custom. Both Merlin and
Arthur praise him enthusiastically, in spite of his bloodthirsty nature.

It is possible to associate Pellinore quite closely with a character
who illustrates vividly the eccentricities of a storm god. This association tends to illuminate the character of Garlon, and we shall consider
it, therefore, somewhat carefully. This storm god, whom we are about
to meet, appears in the Welsh *Mabinogion*, in the tale attractively entitled, *The Lady of the Fountain*.[49]

".... and I followed the cross-roads which the man had pointed
out to me, till at length I arrived at the glade. And there was I three
times more astonished at the number of wild animals that I beheld,
than the man had said I should be. And the black man was there sitting upon the top of the mound.... Then I asked him what power he
held over those animals. 'I will show thee, little man,' said he. And he
took his club in his hand, and with it struck a stag a great blow so that
he brayed vehemently, and at his braying the animals came together,
as numerous as the stars in the sky.... And he looked at them, and
bade them feed; and they bowed their heads, and did him homage as
vassals to their lord.

"Then the black man said to me, 'Seest thou now, little man,
what power I hold over these animals?' Then I inquired of him the

way.... 'Take,' said he, 'that path...and ascend the wooded steep until thou comest to its summit; and there thou wilt find an open space like to a large valley, and in the midst of it a tall tree, whose branches are greener than the greenest pine-trees. Under this tree is a fountain, and by the side of the fountain a marble slab, and on the marble slab a silver bowl, attached by a chain of silver, so that it may not be carried away. Take the bowl and throw a bowlful of water upon the slab, and thou wilt hear a mighty peal of thunder, so that thou wilt think that heaven and earth are trembling with its fury. With the thunder there will come a shower so severe that it will be scarce possible for thee to endure it and live. And the shower will be of hailstones; and after the shower, the weather will become fair, but every leaf that was upon the tree will have been carried away by the shower. Then a flight of birds will come and alight upon the tree; and in thine own country thou didst never hear a strain so sweet as that which they will sing. And at the moment thou are most delighted with the song of the birds, thou wilt hear a murmuring and complaining coming towards thee along the valley. And thou wilt see a knight upon a coal-black horse, clothed in black velvet, and with a pennon of black linen upon his lance; and he will ride unto thee to encounter thee with the utmost speed. If thou fleest from him he will overtake thee, and if thou abidest there, as sure as thou art a mounted knight, he will leave thee on foot. And if thou dost not find trouble in that adventure, thou needest not seek it during the rest of thy life."

Clearly the fountain keeper of this adventure is a storm god. He responds with a vengeance to what Frazer has shown to be a very common rain charm, i.e. the stipulation of rain by the sprinkling of water.[50] The knight comes with a roaring, preceded by a fearful storm. He is black as a storm cloud, swift and inescapable as the lightning. The rest of the romance bears out this early fertility god suggestion. Owain delivers a dolorous sword stroke, fatal to the black knight. At the funeral "a vast number of women...both on horseback, and on foot"[51] accompany the mourning hosts that fill the streets to overflowing. After a time the wife of the slain knight marries her husband's murderer, and thus conforms to orthodox earth goddess custom. And Owain, thereafter, "defended the Fountain with lance and sword."[52] The black giant, surrounded with his animals, who gave Kynon directions to the fountain, seems to me related somehow to the Questing

Beast whom King Arthur encountered at the fountain of Pellinore. Both monsters are precursors to the god who defends the woodland fountain, and both are weirdly associated with a multitude of beasts. The connection will be emphasized by the next tale which we shall consider; and though the transformation from giant to beast is fantastic it is certainly not impossible. The mistranslation of a word could perform the miracle.

The Tale of Meriadeuc forms the final link in the chain of evidence by which I have been trying to associate Garlon with gods of fertility. It presents us with another woodland king who lives in a tent by a Fountain of Marvels, and whose appearance is heralded by a grotesque keeper of many beasts. Clearly the king in this tale is akin to Pellinore, and to the Mabinogion keeper of a fountain. Moreover he suffers from a dolorous sword stroke from which Meriadeuc revives him. Meriadeuc and Balin have the same nickname, the Knight of the Two Swords, and many details of their stories are identical.

Thus the tale of Meriadeuc is connected by one ligature with Garlon, and by another with Balin. It presents these two characters in clear association with a dolorous sword stroke, and identifies Garlon quite conclusively as a fertility god.

Following is a summary of the tale of Meriadeuc:

At a Waste Chapel, a damsel, one night, disinters a fresh corpse, ungirds the sword attached to it, and ties it onto herself. Then she discovers she cannot untie it again. Going, therefore, to Carduel, she asks Arthur to give her as husband the man who should relieve her of this sword. After many have failed, Meriadeuc succeeds. Meriadeuc, sometime squire to Sir Gawain, has been nicknamed the Knight of the Two Swords.

The damsel once free, this knight rides away, very much to her mortification. Arthur sends Sagremor, Dadinel, Yvain, and Ellit to retrieve him; but Meriadeuc unhorses them all.

During the next few days, sending to Arthur's court nine vanquished knights and a king, the Knight of the Two Swords piques to excited interest the lady whom he had scorned. Gawain, in search for the young man, unknowingly encounters him at a tournament, and there, until the young knight discovers the familiar name of his opponent, the two engage each other in furious combat.

In the course of their subsequent travel together "Gawain and his companion come upon a squire...who tells the young man that his father had been killed by Gawain and that his mother wished him to avenge her dead husband. The Knight of the Two Swords then accuses his friend of the deed, but leaves him without attacking him, and wearing his father's shield, which he had received from the squire, rides on until he comes upon a sword lying on the ground and stained with fresh blood. These stains only become brighter when our hero tries to wipe them off.

"There is a castle nearby, surrounded by a lake. At the request of a girl from this castle, he crosses the lake and is conducted to an orchard where the lady of the castle (really his mother)"[53] sits grieving over her husband, who has recently been slain.

During the course of the mother's talk it is revealed that her husband was the man exhumed at the Waste Chapel, and thus, originally, the ungirded sword belonged to our hero's father. The Knight of the Two Swords promises to avenge the woe of this widow, and then his kinship with her is discovered. The mother explains to her son that a villain named Brian is really the murderer. By a trick this Brian had induced Gawain to the deed.

Riding forth, then, on his avenging quest, our hero performs some gallant deeds, and takes for his new name Ladies' Knight.

Gawain, meanwhile, delivers the mother from a siege laid by the son of Brian.

Finally, after a reconciliation, Gawain and the Knight of the Two Swords ride to the Fountain of Marvels, "to solve the mystery of the stained sword. In the forest about this fountain the two companions have various experiences—encounter a dwarf followed by a multitude of beasts—also, a company of huntsmen chasing a hart. Later they come to the tent of these huntsmen's master, who is wounded."[54] The knight who had wounded this huntsman had left his sword behind, with a warning that the wound would never heal unless a knight bearing the name (Meriadeuc) inscribed upon this sword should strike him with it. "The wounded man's wife, accordingly, had the sword, with an explanatory inscription attached to it, laid where many adventurous knights were in the habit of passing. This was the stained sword, and when our hero struck the wounded man...with it, the latter was at once able to rise and the stains vanished from the weapon."[55]

After one or two more adventures, Meriadeuc was married to his lady love by the Archbishop of Canterbury.

This tale has been carefully reworked and polished, but the dolorous stroke theme clearly survives at is basis. Two swords appear, and we shall consider them in order:

(a) The Waste Chapel sword has obviously supernatural character. A sword which only the hero can loose from a scabbard, stone, or tree, is a stock figure not of Arthurian romance alone, but of North-European saga in general. The famous sword which Sigmund drew from Branstock, the swords which Arthur and Galahad drew from stones, and the sword which Balin drew from a scabbard, all can be closely connected.

(b) We shall consider later the Meriadeuc-Balin connections, so that we need not dwell upon them here. Let it suffice to say that upon its first appearance this sword of Meriadeuc exhibits a nature typical of swords employed by gods of sunshine and fertility.

It is significant that the sword should have been found at a Waste Chapel. This reference to desolation is certainly a relic of the Waste Land associated generally with the dolorous stroke. In the course of literary reworking the tendency would naturally be for unintelligible situations of barbaric character to be glossed over, minimized, or left out altogether. It is not surprising to discover, therefore, that the wasting effects of the dolorous stroke have been mentioned in this tale simply in a curiously unintentional fashion. Waste places in connection with wounded kings are diagnostic symptoms of a dolorous stroke. In connection with this Waste Chapel sword, Meriadeuc is summoned by a maiden to a castle surrounded by water. Here he finds a widow who mourns for her lately murdered husband. Gawain generally is involved in a quest which brings him across water to a castle inhabited by maidens; and in grail stories access to the maiden castle is gained, very often, through the help of a ferryman who furnishes sage advice with his transportation.

The tale of Meriadeuc has all the ingredients for a maiden-castle adventure. The misappropriation of the mixture is due, no doubt, to the thorough reworking of the story. We have, in the first place, the castle surrounded by water. And we have, in the second place, an unmistakable suggestion of its feminine population. A maiden summons our hero to his visit, and a weeping woman greets him on arrival. Weeping women are frequently found at the grail castle. We have, in the third place, an old squire who preludes the visit of Meriadeuc with warnings, gifts, and news. He may be the kindly old ferryman in a slightly unfamiliar role. We have, finally, an avenging quest in the course of which Meriadeuc arrives at the widow's castle. We have noted already the close connection between the avenging quests and the dolorous stroke.

(c) The blood-stained sword sends Meriadeuc questing for solution to its mystery. This he finds in the neighborhood of a woodland Fountain of Marvels. Here languishes a maimed master huntsman, whom Meriadeuc revives with a stroke from the sword which had injured him. With this homeopathic blow the blood stains vanish from the weapon.

The theme of this incident corresponds in main outline with what we have found to be the primitive theme of the grail quest; the revival of a maimed king and his wasted kingdom. Later we shall find that, pending the achievement of the grail quest, the weapon which dealt the dolorous stroke often bleeds.

The maimed master huntsman, I believe, is a metamorphosed god of beasts and nature. In a tent he lives in the woodlands, surrounded by beasts, and close to a fountain. The hunter guise may simply be an attempt to explain his life in the forest, and his close connection with the animals which surround him. His tent, close to the Fountain of Marvels, and the strange creatures which move past the fountain, link him with Pellinore and the knight of the storm fountain. The dwarf and black giant surrounded by their beasts are certainly kindred. The dwarf, furthermore, appears in connection with a hart hunt, somewhat as the Questing Beast appears. When these coincidences are taken into consideration together with the congruent circumstances which relate our trinity of woodland fountain gods, there seems to be good reason for believing that the tales of Pellinore, of the Knight of the storm fountain, and of Meriadeuc, are descendants of a single source.

Thus through several means Garlon has been identified as a fertility god. He has been related to Pellean, Pellinore, and the Master Huntsman. Pellean we have recognised as a fertility god in Part I of this paper. Pellinore we have recognised as a fertility god, first, through his connection with Pellean, and then, through his connection with the knight of the storm fountain. The Master Huntsman we have recognised as a fertility god, first through his rustic associations, and next through his connections with the knight of the storm fountain, with Pellinore, and, consequently, with Pellean. But gods related to the same god must be related to each other. Therefore Garlon and the knight of the storm fountain must share at least a mathematical relationship.

But the strongest connections between the tales of Balin and Meriadeuc are those which bind the heroes to each other. Both young men are nicknamed the Knight of the Two Swords; both draw, after many have failed, a sword brought to the court of King Arthur by a strange damsel; both rise, through that adventure, from obscurity to fame; both treat the damsel rudely, and ride away; both arrive, on avenging quests, at a castle where momentous events affect them; and both become involved in the theme of a dolorous stroke.

With Garlon identified as a fertility god, and, together with Balin, associated with a tale which bears unmistakable vestiges of a dolorous sword stroke at its basis, it becomes evident that the blow dealt Garlon may qualify as a dolorous stroke. Therefore, it is reasonable to accept at its face value Gautier's reference to a dolorous stroke dealt by Balin. It is also reasonable to believe that this sword stroke was the blow suffered by Garlon, and to conclude, consequently, that Garlon is the unnamed knight whom Gawain finds bemourned in the bier.

4.

Gawain was at one time a solar hero, and his strength was endowed with a curious tendency to wax and wane with the rising and setting of the sun. In a text even so late as Malory we read:[56] "But Sir Gawaine from it passed nine of the clock waxed ever stronger and stronger, for then it came to the hour of noon, and thrice his might was increased.... And then when it was past noon, and when it drew towards evensong, Sir Gawaine's strength feebled, and waxed passing faint that unnethes he might dure any longer...." And again we read in the same text: "Then had Sir Gawaine such a grace and gift that an holy man had given to him, that every day in the year, from underne till high noon, his might increased those three hours as much as thrice his strength, and that caused Sir Gawaine to win great honour. And for his sake King Arthur made an ordinance, that all manner of battles for any quarrels that should be done afore King Arthur should begin at underne; and all was done for Sir Gawaine's love, that by likelihood, if Sir Gawaine were on the one part he should have the better in battle while his strength endureth three hours.... And then when it was past noon Sir Gawaine had no more but his own might."[57]

Miss Weston has enthusiastically demonstrated the solar nature of Gawain,[58] and she concludes her argument as follows:

"We shall scarcely go far astray if we believe that Gawain, at the outset of his career, was equipped as befitted a 'solar' hero, with a steed and sword of exceptional virtue; nor shall we, I believe, be wrong if we accept the statement of the early romance-writers and believe that the sword was Excalibur."[59]

Thus the sword, as well as the lance, may be weapon to a fertility god.

Gawain, throughout the tale of Meriadeuc, is closely associated with the Knight of the Two Swords. In relieving the knight's mother from siege, Gawain performs a task not properly his; and the Knight of the Two Swords, in rescuing the Master Huntsman from his illness, performs a task similar to that typically credited to Gawain. Moreover, the Knight of the Two Swords began his career as squire to Sir Gawain.

The suggestion seems to me clear that Balin, Meriadeuc, and Gawain must spring from a single source. The Balin-Gawain and Balin-Meriadeuc parallels remain, as we have seen. And the Gawain-Meriadeuc association is constantly insisted upon. Thus a strong family resemblance persists in these far-flung scraps of romance.

The master huntsman has been injured with a sword stroke, and he has to suffer the sorry effects of that blow till a younger knight, seeking solution to a question, shall perform an ordained feat with the dolorous sword. But Garlon has been slain with a sword stroke, and at the Gawain grail castle, as an unnamed knight attended by his regal brother, he awaits resurrection. Here, like the master huntsman, he must lie till a young knight seeking solution to a question, shall perform an ordained feat with the dolorous sword. To maintain this striking parallel, we have definitely related Garlon with the knight unnamed, and with the master huntsman, and we have quite as definitely related Balin with Gawain and with Meriadeuc. We have shown, furthermore, that all of these characters are associated with fertility, and that the sword is a popular item in the equipment of fertility gods. Garlon, knight invisible, discovered only through the evidence furnished by the fatal materialization of his sudden lance, is a vivid embodiment of thunderstorm. There seems to be small reason left for doubting the accuracy of the identification which Gautier made when he credited Balin with the dolorous sword stroke which killed the knight unnamed, and laid waste the kingdom of Logres. The evidence seems to indicate that in our tale of Balin we have vestiges of a dolorous sword stroke dealt Garlon as well as clear descriptions of the lance stroke dealt his brother, Pellean. This being the case, the Gawain adventure serves as a sequence to the sword stroke, whereas the Galahad adventure which we have considered serves as a sequence to the lance stroke. Thus in the tale of Balin appears a neat junction of two separate dolorous strokes. Both weapons involved betray supernatural origin, and all the characters may be related closely to the fertility gods who govern somewhat whimsically, the progress of weather and seasons. The dolorous stroke appears more vividly than ever as a relic of primitive European mythology.

5.

Attempting to explain conflicting references to a lance and a sword as weapons employed in dealing the dolorous stroke, I have suggested, (a) that the role of the sword, as it appears in the Balin story, may simply have been confused with the role of the lance in that tale; or (b) that there may have been from the very start two separate versions of the dolorous stroke; a sword stroke, and a lance stroke. The evidence supporting the latter suggestion bears heavily in its favour, and suggests that Balin may have been associated with both versions of the blow.

Of course it is possible that the similarities which I have noted may be the results of convergence rather than of homology; but the nice dovetailing of the far-flung tales, and the persistence of the certain bizarre situations, seems to me strong evidence for the relationships which I have suggested.

Part III

When the young god has supplanted the old, he falls heir to the taboos and tasks of a fertility god. In the course of time he waxes old as gods waxed old before him, and then his own death becomes a kind of agricultural necessity. Winter follows harvest time, and the divinity relapses to its old, unhealthy ways. It is possible, therefore, that our young hero may, at some time, have figured in passive rather than active connection with the dolorous stroke.

In this section I include three adventures which may give testimony to a dolorous stroke dealt the character whom we have been wont to consider as hero. These adventures do not bear directly upon the development of my thesis, and I do not include them to support it. They are simply curiosities, which I have not yet found explained, and which I believe may have some meaning in connection with the dolorous stroke.

I.

Cuchulinn, famous young hero of Ireland, prefigured Gawain, Balin, Perceval, and Galahad.[60] He was a sun god, and, "when his battle fury was upon him he knew not friend from foe."[61] One day, before he was seven years old, his battle fury came upon him with such a vengeance that his neighbors were hard put for a means to subdue him. Finally, a marvelous bit of strategy reduced him to fashionable temperature. The ladies of the court appeared before him unclad. Modestly the raging child shut his eyes. Then, quickly, he was seized and passed through three vats of cold water. His fury caused the water to boil, but his rage departed from him.[62]

At one time, "among the clouds over his head were visible showers and sparks of ruddy fire, which the seething of his savage wrath caused to mount above him.... His hero's paroxysm thrust itself out of his forehead longer and thicker than a warrior's whetstone, taller, thicker, more rigid, longer than a ship's mast, was the upright jet of dusky blood which shot upwards from his scalp, and then was scattered to the four airts."[63]

Cuchulinn was killed by a thrust of his own spear: Lugaid transfixed him with it. Then Lugaid with a sword beheaded Cuchulinn. Even in death, however, the hero was avenged, for his sword fell from his right hand and smote off the right hand of Lugaid.

This twofold assault may be a confused vestige of the two fashions in which fertility gods were wont to give up their ghosts. It may be our earliest extant rendering of the two dolorous strokes which we have already considered. If it is, then it bespeaks a dolorous stroke dealt the young hero god.

2.

In the Welsh *Peredur* there is an interesting episode which retains traces of having been at one time a dolorous stroke:

Peredur slays a serpent which he finds lying upon a gold ring, and thus he wins the ring. For a long time thereafter, longing for his lady love, he speaks to no Christian, and loses all colour and aspect. He returns to Arthur's court, "but none of the household recognized him. 'Whence comest thou, chieftain?' said Kai. And this he asked him twice and thrice times, and he answered him not. And Kai thrust him through the thigh with his lance."[64]

In the French *Queste del Saint Graal* appears what I believe is a recurrence of this episode, somewhat awry:

Perceval "helps a lion against a snake and wins its service.... That night... [he] dreams of two women visiting him, one mounted on a lion, the second on a serpent; this one reproaches him for killing the serpent. On the morrow an old man comes ship-borne, comforts Perceval... and interprets his dream: The dame on the lion was Christ's new law, she on the serpent the old law...." A damsel then appears who warns Perceval against the old interpreter. She "prepares for him a rich banquet... and excited his passion. He is on the point of yielding, but seeing the cross-handled pommel of his sword crosses himself, and the damsel disappears in flames. Perceval pierces his thigh with his sword in his contrition."[65]

Here the allegory need not detain us. The *Queste*'s a late romance worked by a monk who was very much interested in temptation and virginity. We shall consider him more carefully in Part IV. The lion, however, and the thrust through the thigh are very interesting.

Professor Rhys, by a feat of dexterity, has related gold rings to romantic lions.[66] He has pointed out that a gold ring is a solar symbol, and consequently that it is to be associated with light. He has found, moreover, that in Welsh "lleu" means light, and "llew," lion. He believes, therefore, that in Welsh romance a lion may represent the confused version of a ring. The parallel is elusive, but perhaps significant nevertheless.

Peredur is certainly the Welsh rendering of the name Perceval, and these two lance thrusts may relate the two adventures. Support for the relationship may be furnished by the parallel rescues of ring or lion from a serpent, and by the subsequent musings upon a damsel. Both lance thrusts were immediately occasioned by emotional reactions to visions of the fair lady. In *Peredur* these reactions were chivalric, in the *Queste* they were monastic. Thus these incidents furnish a provoking echo of the dolorous stroke, as well as a neat example of ascetic reinterpretation. They may stand as relics of tales which explained how the young god grew old, and once suffered a dolorous stroke.

PART IV

We have considered the genesis of the dolorous stroke and must turn now to the metamorphosis. I should like to direct attention to the reinterpretation which the theme has suffered. Originally a serious attempt to explain nature, and to subject it to the will of man, the dolorous stroke, in time, lost its scientific value. Then, in light of Christian theory, it was revamped, and conscripted to the advertisement of the system which had displaced it.

Beliefs rejected by man's intelligence have very often lodged in his emotions, and there, with a coating of mildew to render them impressive, they have recommended themselves to his reverence. Associated with memories of childhood and sacred hearthstones, they have been sanctified, cherished as traditional, and passionately defended. Therefore it is not surprising to discover that the dolorous stroke, in spite of its barbaric character, survived to the glory of Christendom, and to its own baptized regeneration.

Finally, under the auspices of what many of us are pleased to call modern enlightenment, the dolorous stroke was transferred from the service of religion to that of art. But here, sad to say, it has steadily feebled. Drained of all meaning, it has survived as a fantastic, impossible adventure, which poets have been unable to treat enthusiastically. The dolorous stroke has run its course, and totters now at the edge of its grave.

I.

Before Chrétien, or Gautier, or Robert of Boron wrote their romances of the holy grail, some sophisticated practice must have brought to focus the savage theories with which we have lately been concerned, reinterpreting them according to its own peculiar purpose. Evidence of this reworking is to be found throughout grail literature, and we shall examine it in connection with the lance and cauldron which Gawain sees when he is left to the queasy fellowship of an unidentified corpse:

"Think ye that Sir Gawain was in no wise troubled when he found himself thus left alone? I tell ye he was much in doubt and right wrathful that he should be in such case. He commended himself humbly unto God, praying that He would guard him from mischance, sorrow, and enchantment, even as He had power to do. Right suddenly he beheld there a lance, the blade of which was white as snow, 'twas fixed upright at the head of the master dais, in a rich vessel of silver, and before it burned two tapers which shed a bright light all around. From the point of the lance issued a stream of blood, which ran down into the vessel, even unto the brim rose the drops of blood, which fell not save into the silver cup. Yet might it not be filled for a fair mouthpiece, wrought of a verdant emerald, through which the blood fell into a channel of gold, which by great wisdom and artifice ran forth without the hall, but Gawain might not see whither it led."[67]

This lance and cauldron are certainly related to the lance and cauldron of Balin and Pisear: but the lance bleeds, and thus confronts us with a genuine difficulty. Many careful scholars have recognized the formidable character of this difficulty, and, as a consequence, the grail lance has come to be the centre of a feverish and waxing vortex of learned controversy. Though my original purpose was to keep clear of skirmishes, I cannot overlook the discussion which has concentrated upon this problem.

Up to this point we have agreed with the inclination of Professor Brown to credit the grail lance with Celtic origin. When the lance of Pisear is added to the evidence which he carefully considers, it becomes very difficult to believe that the parallels can be accidental. The resemblance of the dolorous stroke to the Blinding of King Cormac, if they are not the consequences of relationship, are weird. Furthermore, Balin and Pellean, as I have tried to show, are probably fertility gods. It would be natural for them to be associated with the lightning weapon which the Luin of Celtchar seems to represent.

But, to combat the tendency of Celtic evidence, it has been urged that no Irish lance which bleeds has yet been found, and that it is consequently futile to argue for Celtic antecedents for the grail lance. As a probable source for the weapon, objectors have offered a Christian lance, which bleeds, indeed, but which never of its own accord appears in juxtaposition to a cauldron (as the Lun appears, and as the lances of the dolorous stroke and of this Gawain vision appear), or in a situation similar to that of the dolorous stroke (as the Luin of Celtchar twice appears).[68] This seems to me a poor offering indeed.

But, though we need not favor the substitution of Christian lance for Celtic, we must nevertheless, recognize the fact that it is a long step from a lance simply dipped in blood, to one emitting blood of its own.[69] Something more than a lightning shaft seems to find expression in the bleeding lance, and it will be the purpose of the next few paragraphs to suggest what that something may be.

At the conclusion of *Temair Breg*, Macalister has suggested that "in Crete and in Classical Greece we see the highest manifestations of the native civilization of Europe. Probably nowhere better than in Ireland can we study the crude materials of which that civilization was composed, and by which it can be interpreted."[70] Macalister has set Temair in its place "as the Irish example of a European cultus,"[71] and he feels that we may perhaps trace some relics of this European cultus in certain of the rites of the Eleusinian mysteries."[72] He has indicated evidence which suggests that a common background probably affected Greece and Ireland,[73] and he has certainly demonstrated parallel tendencies in Greek and Irish religious customs.[74] Finally, he has recognized trade connections between the Aegean culture-centres and the northern tribes,[75] and it is inevitable that these should have involved a commerce not in tin alone, but in practices besides.

Among the practices probably shared by Greece and Ireland were those magical rites designed to assist nature in its production of crops. These rites, associated in Greece with the worship of such popular deities as Attis, Adonis, Dionysius, Demeter, Hecate, and Cybele, exhibited an elaborate development which involved a good deal of phallic symbolism and erotic expression. Miss Weston has suggested that similar cults may stand at the source of the grail legend.[76] She has observed that the lance and cauldron "are sex symbols of immemorial antiquity and world-wide diffusion, the Lance or Spear, representing the Male, the Cup, or Vase, the Female, reproductive energy.

"Found in juxtaposition, the Spear upright in the Vase.... Their signification is admitted by all familiar with 'Life' symbolism, and they are absolutely in place as forming part of a ritual dealing with the processes of life and reproductive vitality."[77]

In the face of the evidence which identifies the lance as a lighting shaft, it is difficult for me to agree with Miss Weston that mystery cult influence may stand at the source of grail romances, but I believe that it probably stands toward the head of the course, and that it has played an important part in shaping the legend. In connection with the lance, I believe that some mystery cult devotee must have recognized, long ago, the susceptibility of the Irish lightning shaft and cauldron to the mystery cult purpose, and that by adapting it to the phallic role, he added characteristics which could not otherwise have become attached to a lightning symbol. I believe that before reaching Gautier the Irish lance and cauldron must have been adjusted to the mystery cult method of symbolizing the very situation which they were originally designed to represent, and that when the bleeding lance appears in Arthurian romance, it is probably a representation of this doubly charged symbol.

Professor Brown has not looked with favor upon the ritual theory of Miss Weston, and Miss Weston,[78] so far as I know, has never ascribed to the grail lance and cauldron any Celtic folklore connections. But the tendency of two representative critics to confine their enthusiasms to their own discoveries need not lead us to conclude that both are wrong. I do not know what objection there can be to recognizing validity in both causes, and to concluding that, before emerging as romance, the grail legend must have been affected by at least two important influences. The phase of the legend with which we are especially concerned seems, in its pristine form, to have been indigenous to the British Isles, and prefigured by such tales as the Blinding of King Cormac. But, during the course of its career, it appears to have been retouched and sophisticated by the mystery cults. A vivid result of this reworking appears in the bleeding lance.

2.

When we turn from the Gawain romances to those which deal with Perceval as hero, we find that our two typical versions of the dolorous stroke continue to play significant roles. It is evident, however, that their primitive character has been lost, and that they have taken on an aspect which is a curious mixture of mystery cult and Christian symbolism.

Chrétien de Troyes, in recounting the first visit of Perceval to the castle of the Fisher King, gives us, with his description of the grail procession, conclusive proof that the old mythological character of the lance has been obscured by a new, and decidedly less naïve, point of view. Professor Nutt gives the following summary of the incident:[79]

Perceval "comes to a river, upon which is a boat, and therein two men fishing. One of them, in reply to his questions, directs him for a night's shelter to his own castle hard by. Perceval starts for it.... Suddenly he perceives the castle before him, enters therein, is disarmed, clad in a scarlet mantle, and led into a great hall. Therein is a couch upon which lies an old man; near him is a fire, around which some four hundred men are sitting. Perceval tells his host he had come from Biau Repaire. A squire enters, bearing a sword, and on it is written that it will never break save in one peril, and that known only to the maker of it. 'Tis a present from the host's niece to be bestowed where it will be well employed.' The host gives it to Perceval, 'to whom it was adjusted and destined.' Hereupon enters another squire, bearing in his hand a lance, from the head of which a drop of blood runs down on the squire's hand. Perceval would have asked concerning this wonder, but he minds him of Gonemans' counsel not to speak or inquire too much. Two more squires enter, holding each a ten-branched candlestick, and with them a damsel, a 'graal' in her hands. The graal shines so that it puts out the light of the candles as the sun does that of the stars. Thereafter follows a damsel holding a (silver) plate. All defile past between the fire and the couch, but Perceval does not venture to ask wherefore the grail is used. Supper follows, and the grail is again brought, and Perceval, knowing not its use, had fain asked, but always refrains...and finally puts off his questions till the morrow. After supper the guest is led to his chamber, and on the morrow, awakening, finds the castle deserted. No one answers his calls. Issuing forth he finds his horse saddled and the drawbridge down. Thinking to find the castle dwellers in the forest he rides forth, but the drawbridge closes so suddenly behind him that had not his horse leapt quickly forward it had gone hard with steed and rider. In vain Perceval calls; none answer.

"He pricks on and comes to an oak, beneath which sits a maid holding a dead knight in her arms and lamenting over him. She asks him where he has passed the night, and on learning it tells him the fisher who had directed him to the castle and his host were one and the same; wounded by a spear thrust through both thighs his only solace is in fishing, whence he is called the Fisher King. She asks, has Perceval seen the bleeding lance, the grail, and the silver dish? Had he asked their meaning? No; then what is his name? He does not know it, but she guesses it: Perceval le Galleis; but it should be Perceval the Caitiff, for had he asked concerning what he saw, the good king would have been made whole again, and great good have sprung therefore.... She tells him about the sword, how it will fly in pieces if he have not care of it, and how it may be made whole again by dipping it in a lake, near which dwells its maker, the smith Trebucet."

It may be significant of their connections with fertility that grail romance swords should frequently be associated with bodies of water. Both Balin's sword and Arthur's are bound up closely with the Lady of the Lake, Excalibur being returned to her at Arthur's death. Perhaps the broken Perceval sword, plunged into a lake, represented a variant of the symbolism intended by the return of the sword to its native mere.

The grail procession witnessed by Perceval may represent a mystery cult ceremony. Here the bleeding lance appears in a form which is decidedly subdued. But, though it has been adapted to the refinements of a religious procession, this lance still retains clear suggestions of its "life" significance.

The Fisher King, "wounded by a spear thrust through both his thighs" is, beyond a doubt, in the same rule as Pellean. Perceval should have asked concerning the things he saw so that "the good king would have been made whole again, and great good have sprung therefrom." The primitive character of the king is explicit enough in that statement, and the object of the quest is clearly presented.

Manessier, another of Chrétien's continuators, describes a dolorous stroke which seems to attempt a combination of the versions represented in Gautier and in Chrétien:

"....In Quinquagrant dweld Goon Desert the (Fisher) King's brother. Beseiged by Espinogre he made a sally and slew him. Espinogre's nephew swore revenge; donning the armour of a knight of Goon Desert, he slew him, but the sword broke when the traitorous blow was struck. Goon Desert's body was brought to his brother's castle, whither came, too, his daughter with the broken sword, foretelling that a knight should come, rejoin the pieces, and avenge the foul blow. The Fisher King, taking up the fragments incautiously, was pierced through the thigh, and the wound might not be healed until his brother's death was avenged. The murderer's name is Partiniaus, Lord of the Red Tower. Perceval vows to avenge this wrong....

"Perceval rides on to Partinal's castle, before which stands a fir tree whereon hangs a shield. Perceval throws this down, whereupon Partinal appears and a desperate combat ensues, ended by the overthrow of Partinal, and, as he will submit to no conditions, his death. Perceval cuts off his head and makes for the Grail Castle, but only after a summer's seeking, lights upon it chancewise.

"As he nears the castle, the warders come to the King, telling him a knight is coming with a head hanging at his saddlebow; hereupon the King leaps to his feet and is straightaway made whole. Partinal's head is stuck on a pike on the highest tower of the castle. After supper, at which the...mystic procession of talismans takes place...the King learns Perceval's name, and thereby finds that he is his own sister's son. He would hand him his crown, but Perceval has vowed not to take it, his uncle living...."[80]

Here the murder of Goon Desert, the Fisher King's brother, resembles the murder of Garlon, Pellean's brother. Both victims were killed by avengers who broke their swords when the blows were struck. It is interesting to note that Partiniaus donned the armour of a knight of Goon Desert, just as Gawain donned the armor of the questing knight who sent him on his way to the grail castle. It is interesting, also, that Partiniaus should have been summoned to battle in a fashion similar to that employed by Griflet, who summoned Pellinore.

The Fisher King, like Pellean, was pierced through the thigh, but a sword pierced him rather than a lance. This is the first sword which I have been able to find, piercing the maimed king through the thigh.

A curious transformation of the revenge motif may be discerned in the fact that the mere slaying of Goon Desert's murderer releases the Fisher King from his painful plight. A vestige of the primitive idea survives, however, in the promise of Perceval to refuse the crown so long as his uncle lives. The young man could have no claim to divinity with the old god still intact.

In the German *Parzival* of Wolfram von Eschenbach, we find a new note. In this version the king is wounded in punishment for an unlawful love.

> And his battle cry was "Amor", yet it seemeth unto me
> Not all too well such cry suiteth with a life of humility
> One day as the king rode lonely, in search of some venture high
> (Sore trouble it brought upon us) with love's payment for victory,
> For love's burden lay heavy on him, in a joust was he wounded sore
> With a poisoned spear, so that healing may be wrought on him
>   nevermore.
> ...
> Then the knights of the Grail knelt lowly, and for help to the Grail they
>   prayed
> And, behold; the mystic writing, and a promise it brought of aid,
> For a knight should come to the castle, and so soon as he asked the king
> Of the woe that so sorely pained him his questions should healing bring.
> ...
> And in the first night of his coming must the healer his task fulfill,
> Or the question shall lose its virtue; but if at the chosen hour
> He shall speak, his shall be the kingdom, and the evil hath lost its power.
> So the hand of the Highest sendeth to Anfortas the end of woe,
> Yet King shall he be no longer tho' healing and bliss he knew.[81]

While Miss Weston, in her translation, has euphemized, for English eyes, the plight of the king, Wolfram clearly explains that the king was emasculated by the blow which felled him. This fact we have alluded to in our argument of Part I. It is a fact which is important as an indication of the primitive nature of the dolorous stroke.

With these few examples we shall turn from early versions of the dolorous stroke to those which appear in the late prose romances. In considering these we shall direct special attention to the *Queste del Saint Graal,* and to the *Grand Saint Graal.* These represent the climax of ecclesiastical revision, and serve best to illustrate the attitude which

worked its radical transformation upon these savage myths which we
have studied.

Let us approach them with a prologue.

3.

"In the Julian calendar the twenty-fifth of December was reckoned the
winter solstice, and it was regarded as the Nativity of the Sun, because
the day begins to lengthen and the power of the sun to increase from
that turning point of the year. The ritual of the nativity, as it appears
to have been celebrated in Syria and Egypt, was remarkable. The cele-
brants retired into certain inner shrines, from which at midnight they
issued with a loud cry, 'The Virgin has brought forth! The light is waxing!' The Egyptians even represented the new-born sun by the image
of an infant which on his birthday, the winter solstice, they brought
forth and exhibited to his worshippers.... Now Mithra was regularly
identified by his worshippers with the Sun...hence his nativity also
fell on the twenty-fifth of December. The Gospels say nothing as to
the day of Christ's birth, and accordingly the early church did not
celebrate it. In time, however, the Christians of Egypt came to regard
the sixth of January as the date of the Nativity, and the custom of
commemorating the birth of the Saviour on that day gradually spread
until by the fourth century it was universally established in the East.
But at the end of the third or the beginning of the fourth century the
Western Church, which had never recognized the sixth of January as
the day of the Nativity, adopted the twenty-fifth of December as the
true date, and in time its decision was accepted also by the Eastern
Church. At Antioch the change was not introduced till about the year
375 A.D.

"Thus it appears that the Christian Church chose to celebrate the
birthday of its Founder on the twenty-fifth of December in order to
transfer the devotion of the heathen from the Sun to Him who was
called the Sun of Righteousness. If that was so, there can be no intrinsic improbability in the conjecture that motives of the same sort may
have led the ecclesiastical authorities to assimilate the Easter festival
of the death and resurrection of their Lord to the festival of the death
and resurrection of another Asiatic god which fell at the same season. Now the Easter rites still observed in Greece, Sicily, and Southern Italy bear in some respects a striking resemblance to the rites of

Adonis, and…the Church may have consciously adapted the new festival to its heathen predecessor for the sake of winning souls to Christ. But his adaptation probably took place in the Greek-speaking rather than the Latin-speaking parts of the ancient world; for the worship of Adonis, while it flourished among the Greeks, appears to have made little impression on Rome and the West.… The place which it might have taken in the affections of the vulgar was already occupied by the similar but more barbarous worship of Attis and the Great Mother. Now the death and resurrection of Attis were officially celebrated at Rome on the twenty-fourth and twenty-fifth of March, the latter being regarded as the spring equinox, and therefore as the most appropriate day for the revival of a god of vegetation who had been dead or sleeping throughout the winter. But according to an ancient and widespread tradition Christ suffered on the twenty-fifth of March, and accordingly some Christians regularly celebrated the Crucifixion on that day without any regard to the state of the moon. This custom was certainly observed in Phrygia, Cappadocia, and Gaul, and there seem to be grounds for thinking that at one time it was followed also in Rome. Thus the tradition which placed the death of Christ on the twenty-fifth of March was ancient and deeply rooted. It is all the more remarkable because astronomical considerations prove that it can have had no historical foundation. The inference appears to be inevitable that the passion of Christ must have been arbitrarily referred to that date in order to harmonize with an older festival of the spring equinox.… When we remember that the festival of St. George in April has replaced the ancient pagan festival of Parilia; that the festival of Saint John the Baptist in June has succeeded to a heathen midsummer festival of water; that the festival of the Assumption of the Virgin in August has ousted the festival of Diana; that the feast of All Souls in November is a continuation of an old heathen feast of the dead; and that the Nativity of Christ himself was assigned to the winter solstice in December because that day was deemed the Nativity of the Sun; we can hardly be thought rash or unreasonable in conjecturing that the other cardinal festival of the Christian Church—the solemnization of Easter—may have been in like manner, and from like motives of edification, adapted to a similar celebration of the Phrygian god Attis at the vernal equinox."[82]

I believe that in the Gospels traces remain of early associations between popular ideas of the dead Christ and the dead fertility gods, Attis and Adonis:

"Now from the sixth hour there was darkness over the whole earth until the ninth hour....And Jesus again crying with a loud voice, yielded up the ghost. And behold the veil of the temple was rent in two from the top even to the bottom, and the earth quaked, and the rocks were rent....Now the centurion and they that were with him watching Jesus, having seen the earthquake, and the things that were done, were sore afraid, saying: Indeed this was the Son of God. And there were there many women afar off, who had followed Jesus from Galilee, ministering unto Him:"[83] "But one of the soldiers with a spear opened his side, and immediately there came out blood and water...these things were done that the scripture might be fulfilled: You shall not break a bone of him. And again another scripture saith: They shall look on him whom they pierced. And after those things, Joseph of Arimathea (because he was a disciple of Jesus, but secretly for fear of the Jews) besought Pilate that he might take away the body of Jesus. And Pilate gave leave. He came therefore, and took away the body of Jesus."[84]

I feel that this description of nature's sympathetic reaction to the death of Christ is distinctly reminiscent of the spectacular desolation wrought upon nature by the dolorous stroke dealt the fertility god incarnate. The multitude of weeping women, and the somewhat unnecessary lance thrust, augment, it seems to me, the evidence for parallel tradition.

But no matter what their origins may have been, it is clear that these curious parallels between tales of the Crucifixion and of the dolorous stroke were recognized by Mediaeval ecclesiastics, and employed to allegorical purpose. Discovering in the grail romances material susceptible to reinterpretation, good monks carefully set about reorganizing the legend, abridging here, interpolating there, explaining, allegorizing, and embellishing. The lance they connected with the lance of the Crucifixion. The grail they connected with the cup of the Last Supper. The maimed king they connected with Joseph of Arimathea, who preserved the holy relics of Christ's passion. The young fertility god, they renamed, finally, Galahad; and then they exalted him to the strangely incongruous role of celibate ideal. The women connected with the legend they transformed either into nuns or into temptations. The Celtic marvels they turned into Hebraic miracles. Still the ancient theme very often peers out through the folds of its sombre disguise. A cassock does not fit well upon the wild form of savage deity.

The *Queste del Saint Graal* was composed by a Cistercian monk who was blessed with a marvelous faculty for finding evil in the beautiful, and thrilling inspiration in what seems very silly to-day. He was prone to a morbid brooding upon the subject of virginity, and was blessed with a keen appetite for extravagant allegory. Throughout his writing he seems to have had no apprehension of the fact that his legends originally had been dedicated to the cause of fertility. In objects which would have terrified him could he have learned their significations he found delight and pious exaltation. Easily recognising a religious quality in the tales to which he was enthralled, he never understood that theirs was a piety which would have seemed to him wicked. His predecessors had glorified a function which he found redolent of Beelzebub; but he completely inverted the tendency of their meaning, and directed it to the credit of a celibate condition which he thought to be seraphic. Thus he effected a wizard-transformation comparable, for sheer dexterity, to the reinterpretation which his forbears wrought upon Solomon's Song of Songs.

The *Grand Saint Graal* is a kind of supplement to the *Queste*. It attempts to clarify apparent inconsistencies, and to gather together loose threads. Together with the *Queste* it works havoc upon the continuity of the dolorous stroke.

In Part III of this paper we discussed a brief episode from the *Queste* in connection with the Welsh *Peredur*. There we obtained a glimpse of the characteristic allegorizing, and of the aspersions to which the defenceless ladies were subjected. We shall not revert to those subjects, but shall proceed to a consideration of the manglings and reduplications of our beloved theme.

In the *Queste* I have found the following vestiges of dolorous strokes:

1. Galahad repairs a broken sword which pierced Joseph of Arimathea through the thighs.[85]
2. At a cross outside a little forest chapel Lancelot witnesses the lamentations of a sick knight who comes on a bier

drawn by two horses. The cause of the invalid's pain is unexplained. After easing his anguish by kissing the grail, the sick knight rides away on Lancelot's horse, and leaves our hero to be roundly rebuked by a disembodied voice. Because he had failed to speak while the grail was visible, Lancelot is "harder than stone, bitterer than wood, more despised than the fig tree—he must away, not pollute the spot where is the holy grail."[86]

3. Perceval pierces himself through the thigh.[87] This dolorous stroke (if it is one) was discussed in Part III.

4. Lancelot arrives at a castle guarded by two lions. "Entering, he comes to a room wherein are the Holy Vessel, and a priest celebrating Mass; Lancelot is warned not to enter, but when he sees that the priest about raise the body of God has a man put into his hands, he cannot refrain from pressing forward to his aid, but is struck down by a fiery wind and remains fourteen days dumb, food- and drinkless. He finds he is in Castle Corbenic, and a damsel tells him his quest is ended."[88]

5. At a monastery Perceval sees a sick man attending Mass. He is Mordrains, who, four hundred years ago, pressed forward too eagerly to see the Holy Grail, and was struck blind and helpless. Christ permitted him to survive until the good knight should come, and then he should be made whole, and receive the light of his eyes.[89]

6. King Lambar, father of the maimed king, was killed by King Urlain with a marvelous sword found in a ship and destined for Galahad. There came from that blow "such pestilence and destruction in the land of the two kingdoms that it was afterwards called the Waste Land. When Urlain re-entered the ship he fell down dead.[90]

7. Nasciens, brother-in-law of Mordrains, came to a Turning Isle where he found the same ship, "and therein bed and sword, this last he coveted, but had not the hardihood to draw it, though he stayed eight days food- and drinkless longing for it; on the ninth day a tempest drove him to another island, where, assailed by a giant, he

drew the sword, and though it snapped in two and thus fulfilled the inscription, yet he overcame the giant. He afterwards met Mordrains and told him of these wonders; Mordrains reunited the fragments, then, in obedience to a voice, they left the ship, but in going Nasciens was wounded for having dared to draw a sword of which he was not worthy."[91]

8. "King Pelles, called the Maimed King, once came to this ship on the shore of the sea over against Ireland, and entering it found the sword, drew but was wounded through the thighs by a lance. He will be healed by Galahad, who will end the wonders of Great Britain.[92]

9. At Castle Corbenic "four damsels bring in on a wooden bed a man, crowned, in evil plight, who greets Galahad as his long-expected deliverer."[93]

With variations in detail the *Grand Saint Graal* describes the strokes which I have numbered 1, 5, 6, 7, and 8. To these it adds six more, which include extra versions of the Lambor and Nasciens strokes. These dolorous strokes, surviving in the *Grand Saint Graal* but not in the *Queste*, are as follows:

10. Mordrains, having just been converted to Christianity, has enthusiastically ordered all his subjects either to be baptized or to leave his lands. "Many take the latter course and are met outside the town by a devil who wounds them grievously, whereupon Josephes (son of Joseph of Arimathea) hurries to their aid, but is met by an angel with a lance and smitten through the thigh... a voice is heard, 'After my vengeance my healing,' and an angel appears, touches Josephes' thigh with the lance shaft, whereupon the head comes out, and from it drop great drops of blood which the angel collects in a vessel, and wherewith he anoints Josephes' wounds, making it whole."[94]

11. "The Christians come to a house where burns a great fire out of which is heard a lamentable voice; it is that of Moys; at Josephes' prayer rain falls from heaven and quenches half the flames, but he may not be wholly delivered until the Good Knight, Galahad, come."[95]

12. "The Christians come into the land of King Escos....
     The Holy Grail refuses meat to Chanaan and to Symeu,
     Moys' father, whereat enraged Symeu attacks Pierre and
     wounds him, and Chanaan slays his twelve brethren.
     Symeu, is carried off by devils, whilst Chanaan's grave
     bursts out in flames, which may not quench till Lancelot
     come."[96]

These are curious inversions of the dolorous stroke theme for
which I cannot account. Instead of making the release of revivifying
waters depend upon the reclamation of the god, they seem to have
made the reclamation of the god depend upon the release of quenching
waters. I have included them as dolorous strokes in spite of their
exotic nature, because they imply that deliverance will be effected at
the consummation of the grail quest.

13. The King of Terre Foraine, sleeping in a castle, "beholds
     the holy vessel covered with crimson samite, and a man
     all flaming tells him no mortal may sleep where the Holy
     Grail rests, and wounds him through both thighs, and bids
     others beware of sleeping in the Palace Adventurous."[97]
14. Lambor has become Grail Keeper. Fighting with his
     enemy, Bruillant, he "pursues him to the sea shore, and
     Bruillant finds there Solomon's ship and enters it, and
     finds the sword with which he slays Lambor...and such
     great woes sprang therefrom that no laborers worked, nor
     wheat grew, nor fruit trees bore, nor fish was found in the
     waters, so that the land was known as the Waste Land.
     But Bruillant falls dead for drawing the sword."[98]
15. Nasciens has got himself marooned upon the Turning
     Isle. To this marvelous phenomenon a ship comes one
     day which Nasciens would enter "but for words warning
     him against it unless he be full of faith. However, crossing
     himself, he enters." Inside he finds the bed and sword,
     precisely as they appear in the *Queste*, and a history is
     told of them which agrees with the *Queste*'s recounting,
     "Nasciens deeming there must be magic in this, the ship
     splits in twain, and had well nigh drowned him...on the
     morrow as old man comes in a ship and gives him an
     allegorical explanation...."

Meanwhile, Calidoine, set adrift in a boat with a lion, by King Label, a heartless heathen, "after three days comes to Nasciens' island. The two rejoice on their meeting, and leave the island together in Solomon's ship, come after four days to another island, where Nasciens, attacked by a giant, seizes Solomon's sword, but it breaks in his hand, nevertheless, with another sword he overcomes the giant. He chides Solomon's sword, but Calidoine says it is some sin of his made it break. Thereafter they see a ship approaching wherein is Mordrains.... Nasciens shows the broken sword to Mordrains, who, taking it in his hands, joins it together, whereupon a voice bids them leave the ship; Nasciens, not obeying fast enough, is wounded in the shoulder by a fiery sword in punishment of his having drawn Solomon's sword."[99]

This catalogue presents us with some startling variations on our single theme. It produces a variety of caricatures which play upon distinctive details and magnify them splendidly.

The fiery wind in 4, the fires in 11 and 12, the man all flaming in 13, and the fiery sword in 15, point, perhaps, to the blazing origin of the solar sword and the lightning lance. The broken swords, thrusts through the thighs, wasted kingdoms, and ubiquitous invalids clearly speak for themselves.

Solomon's ship, which appears in connection with strokes 6, 7, 8, 14, and 15, is a misrepresentation of the grail castle wherein Pellean was injured. It is the vessel to which Galahad, Perceval, Bors, and Perceval's sister finally come in the magic, self-propelled craft which we have discussed in connection with the Children of Tuireann (Part I). In a chamber within Solomon's ship is "a rich bed with a crown at its head, and at its foot a sword six inches out of the scabbard, its tip a stone of all the colours in the world, its handle of the bones of two beasts, the serpent Papagast, the fish Orteniaus; it is covered with a cloth whereon is written that only the first of his line would grasp the sword. Perceval and Bors both essay vainly. Galahad, on being asked, sees written on the blade that he only should draw who could strike better than others."[100]

The dolorous strokes which this sword dealt (numbers 6, 7, and 14) bear characteristics suggestive of the dolorous stroke dealt Garlon. The languishing of the land is emphasized, and the tragical reaction upon the king who dealt the stroke is mentioned. The extra sword in the version which I have numbered 15, is the result, no doubt, of gemination.

In connection with our argument of Part II it is interesting that King Pelles—who is simply Pellean—should retain, even in this late text, his association with the marvelous sword, and his characteristic lance wound. The distinction between lance stroke and sword stroke is thus preserved.

One more brief adventure from the *Queste* will conclude this phase of our history:

One day Galahad and Perceval meet Bors, "who in the five years had not been in bed four times. The three come to Castle Corbenic where they are greeted by King Pelleas, and where Eliezer, King Pelles' son, brings the broken sword with which Joseph had been pierced through the thighs; Bors cannot rejoin the pieces, Perceval can only adjust them together, Galahad alone can make the sword whole, and it is given then to Bors.

"Four damsels bring in on a wooden bed a man, crowned, in evil plight, who greets Galahad as his long-expected deliverer. A voice orders out of the room him who has not been a companion of the Quest, and straightway King Pelles and Eliezer and the damsel depart....

"Then there appears a grail procession which includes a lance bleeding so hard that the drops run into a box held in the hand of the lance-bearer. The Resurrected Christ appears and to Galahad and his friends dispenses the Sacrament. He explains that the Grail is the dish of the Last Supper, and Galahad shall see it more fully in the City of Sarras, whither it is going, Britain being unworthy of it, and whither he is to follow it with Perceval and Bors; but as he must not leave the land without healing the Maimed King he is to take some of the blood of the lance and therewith anoint his legs... Galahad...heals the Maimed King, who goes into an abbey of white monks."[101]

This certainly is a linsey-woolsey medley of paganism and Christianity. Could the contemporaries of its good monk redactor have appreciated the situation into which he introduced the Resurrected Christ, they would, no doubt, have done some violence to his pietistical misdevotion. But, fortunately for all concerned, the phallicism involved was completely misunderstood, and the romance passed as a first-rate argument for celibate continence.

But to careful scrutiny this curious society of Maimed King, mystery procession, and Resurrected Christ, presents a vivid historical panorama. The Maimed King is distinctly in the role which we traced to its source through Pellean. He is the fertility god upon whom the whole course of nature depends, self-mutilated, and languishing for complete rejuvenation. Galahad, descendant of Cuchulinn, Gawain, and Perceval, is a personification of the rejuvenated god.

The Maimed King is cured in a fashion fundamentally similar to that by which the master huntsman was cured by Meriadeuc, and by which Josephes was cured by an angel (Stroke #10). In these cases the invalid recovers upon being touched by something associated with the bloody weapon which crippled him. In *Meriadeuc* the weapon itself is employed; in the *Queste*, blood from the weapon effects the cure; in the *Grand Saint Graal* both weapon and blood are required. These three healings are worked upon principles of what Frazer has called sympathetic magic,[102] and they are certainly quite barbarous.

The grail procession with its bleeding lance is transparent enough. It represents, I believe, the mystery cult phase of the dolorous stroke, and it is probably phallic in character.

The Resurrected Christ is a monastic innovation, and fits discordantly into this circle of broken-down gods. It is difficult to suppose that the Cistercian who introduced Him to these people intended that He should signify tolerance. The whitewash gleaming on Galahad and his companions betrays the solemn purpose which inspired the pious author of this most holy *Queste del Saint Graal.*

In some sequestered abbey, therefore, reading offices and psalms, praying with the white monks to a God who has deposed him, an immortal lives, who, in better days held floodtide, sunlight, and thunderbolt, subject to the wink of his eye. Let us leave him here, forgotten by this world, and glance at two very recent reports of his adversities.

4.

Tennyson and Swinburne have put the Tale of Balin into poetry, their versions being diverse in purpose and effect. Tennyson charged the tale with a moral; Swinburne developed its tragical aspect. Neither favored the dolorous stroke itself with complete understanding.

The poets recognized dramatic possibilities in the battle of Balin with his brother, and it is clear that they were attracted to the tale, not by the dolorous stroke, but by this fratricide. My own interest, however, is with the tragical history of the dolorous stroke, and therefore my consideration of Tennyson and Swinburne will have to turn upon their treatments of this venerable theme.

We have recognized, at the heart of Celtic mythology, a belief in the might of magic. The mystery cults, which impressed their notions upon the grail legend, were simply amplifications and systemizations of the older, magical principles. Under their influence the dolorous stroke flourished in its original character, and retained much of its native meaning.

With Christianity came a fresh kind of wonder seeking. Founded upon miracles, the Mediaeval Church dedicated a good deal of its attention to cultivating man's susceptibility to belief in miracles. As a consequence, the magic expressed in the dolorous stroke remained credible to good Christians. The pious business of referring the miracles to saintly sources was all that was needed to render them up to date. Accordingly, with the help of lively imaginations, Cuchulinn was passed through tempering vats and baptised.

After the Renaissance, however, a miracle had to be a bit subtle to slip into discerning credit. Thus the fantastic marvels of Celtic gods, branded as somewhat too quaint, went by the board. A god, wounded by a lance, whose injury entails the blight of his land, and the misery of his people, revived by a magic question, or salve of blood, or homeopathic blow, was incredible. He meant little that could possibly be intelligible to mankind.

But miracles of refined demeanor still enjoy civilized incense. Therefore it is not surprising that Tennyson should have substituted a sin of adultery for the dolorous stroke. In old romances the battle of Balin with his brother is the direct result of evil wrought by the dolorous stroke, but in Balin and Balan no dolorous stroke is mentioned. In its motivating role stands a growing, insinuating influence of the sin of Guinevere and Lancelot.

Tennyson has remodeled the tale of Balin completely. Poor Pellean, he has traduced. Arthur is told that this hoary man was

         once
A Christless foe of thine as ever dash'd
Horse against horse; but seeing that thy realm
Hath prosper'd in the name of Christ, the King
Took, as in rival heat, to holy things;
And finds himself descended from the Saint
Arimathean Joseph; him who first
Brought the great faith to Britain over seas;
He boasts his life as purer than thine own;
Eats scarce enow to keep his pulse abeat;
Hath push'd aside his faithful wife, nor lets
Or dame or damsel enter at his gates
Lest he should be polluted. This gray King
Show'd us a shrine wherein were wonders—yea—
Rich arks with priceless bones of martyrdom,
Thorns of the crown and shivers of the cross,
And therewithal (for thus he told us) brought
By holy Joseph hither, that same spear
Wherewith the Roman pierced the side of Christ.
He much amazed us; after, when we sought
The tribute, answer'd "I have quite foregone
All matters of this world: Garlon, mine heir,
Of him demand it," which this Garlon gave
With much ade, railing at thine and thee.[103]

Garlon, Tennyson has rationalized:

  in those deep woods we found
A knight of thine spear-stricken from behind.[104]

Of Balin and Balan, he has made "two strange knights"

Who sit near Camelot at a fountain side,
A mile beneath the forest, challenging
And overthrowing every knight who comes.

The plot, he has thoroughly revised:
  King Arthur overthrows Balin and Balan, and they follow him to
his court. Then Balan rides forth to avenge a knight killed by Garlon,
while Balin remains at Camelot to idolize Lancelot and the Queen.

Then chanced, one morning, that Sir Balin sat
Close-bower'd in that garden nigh the hall.
A walk of roses ran from door to door;
A walk of lilies crest it to the bower;
And down that range of roses the great Queen
Came with slow steps, the morning on her face;
And all in shadow from the counter door
Sir Lancelot as to meet her . . . .

Then Lancelot lifted his large eyes; they dwelt
Deep-tranced on hers, and could not fall: her hue
Changed at his gaze: so turning side by side
They past, and Balin started from his bower.

. . . .
in him gloom on gloom
Deepen'd: he sharply caught his lance and shield,
Nor stay'd to crave permission of the king,
But, mad for strange adventure, dash'd away.[105]

Then Balin ranged the skyless woods, taking the self-same track
as Balan. Suddenly the shadow of a spear, shot from behind him, ran
along the ground. He started, and saw a light of armor flash, and vanish into the woods. He followed. But in his rage Balin rode so blindly
that

       unawares
He burst his lance against a forest bough,
Dishorsed himself, and rose again, and fled
Far, till the castle of a King, the hall
Of Pellam, lichen-bearded, grayly draped
With streaming grass, appear'd, low-built but strong;
The ruinous donjon as a knoll of moss,
The battlement overtopt with ivytods,
A home of bats, in every tower an owl.[106]

Balin entered. Some while later, at the feast Garlon asked:

"Why wear ye that crown-royal?" Balin said.
"The Queen we worship, Lancelot, I and all,
As fairest, best and purest, granted me
To bear it!" Such a sound (for Arthur's knights

Were hated strangers in the hall) as makes
The white swan-mother, sitting, when she hears
A strange knee rustle thro' her secret reeds,
Made Garlon, hissing; then he sourly smiled.
"Fairest I grant her: I have seen: but best,
Best, purest? thou from Arthur's hall, and yet
So simple! hast thou eyes, or if, are these
So far besotted that they fail to see
This fair wife-worship cloaks a secret shame?
Truly, ye men of Arthur be but babes."

Balin, through dint of a gentle recollection, managed to withhold
his wrath until, in the castle court, Garlon asked: "What, wear ye still
that same crown-scandalous?" Then

Sir Balin with a fiery "Ha!
So thou be shadow, here I make thee ghost,"
Hard upon helm smote him, and the blade flew
Spintering in six, and clinkt upon the stones
Then Garlon, reeling slowly backward, fell.

There rang a hue and cry, and Balin was forced to seek cover in
King Pellam's chapel. Here he

Beheld before a golden altar lie
The longest lance his eyes had ever seen,
Point-painted red; and seizing thereupon
Push'd thro' an open casement down, lean'd on it,
Leapt in a semicircle, and lit on earth;
Then hand at ear, and harkening from what side
The blindfold rummage buried in the walls
Might echo, ran the counter path, and found
His charger, mounted on him and away.
An arrow whizz'd to the right, one to the left,
One overhead; and Pellam's feeble cry
"Stay, stay him! he defileth heavenly things
With earthly uses" made him quickly dive
Beneath the boughs, and race thro' many a mile
Of dense and open, till his goodly horse,
Arising wearily at a fallen oak,
Stumbling headlong, and cast him face to ground.[107]

Thus, at pathetic dotage our theme has arrived. The dolorous stroke has become a melodramatically executed pole-vault. The bleeding lance has become a painted trinket. Balin has become a gingerbread hero. Tennyson has perverted the feeling of his source, and developed little of its artistic potentiality.

With the feeble, greybeard king, amongst the owls and waving weeds of his crumbling walls, I can sympathize. I can understand his trembling cry to the woodland thickets, "Stay, stay him! he defileth heavenly things with earthly uses."

Swinburne, when he turned to the tale of Balin, has no moral to draw—only beauty to give. His efforts were devoted to recounting the story which appears in Malory, rather than to inventing a tale of his own. His treatment expresses something of nobility, and of enthusiasm for his subject.

Whether Swinburne understood the full significance of the tale, I do not know; but he seems to have had some inkling of its meaning, for, during the course of his poem, he records the progress of the seasons. Beginning with springtime, he progresses through summer, and arrives at autumn before describing the dolorous stroke. Then he chronicles wintertime.

Swinburne's *Tale of Balin* has not been popularly read, I believe, because it involves a theme which men of today find unintelligible. This century of science cannot be expected to thrill to the fate of fertility gods, or to understand the cosmic import of Pellean's woes.

Perhaps the type of treatment accorded the tale by Tennyson is the only type of treatment which men of today can relish. Perhaps poor Pellean must seem, henceforth, a mere fool. If that be the case, it is a pity; and I rejoice that my king-god, secluded in his cloister, never hears a sound of modern rumor.

If Tennyson has shown to what extent the dolorous stroke may be abused, Swinburne has shown how well it can survive poetic treatment. Let his stanzas be an epitaph to the adventure which we have traced from vague beginnings through many vicissitudes:

Then gat he leave to wear his sword
Beside the strange king's festal board
Where feasted many a knight and lord
In seemliness of fair accord:
And Balen asked of one beside,
"Is there not in this court, if fame

Keep faith, a knight that hath to name
Garlon?" and saying that word of shame,
Now scanned that place of pride.

"Yonder he goeth against the light,
He with the face as swart as night,"
Quoth the other: "but he rides to fight
Hid round by charms from all men's sight,
And many a noble knight he hath slain,
Being wrapt in darkness deep as hell
And in silence dark as shame." "Ah, well,"
Said Balen, "is that he? the spell
May be the sorcerer's bane."

Then Balen gazed upon him long,
And thought, "If here I wreak my wrong,
Alive I may not scape, so strong
The felon's friends about him throng;
And if I leave him here alive,
This chance perchance may life not give
Again: much evil, if he live,
He needs must do, should fear forgive
When wrongs bid strike and strive."

And Garlon, seeing how Balen's eye
Dwelt on him as his heart waxed high
With joy in wrath to see him nigh,
Rose wolf-like with a wolfish cry
And crossed and smote him on the face,
Saying, "Knight, what wouldst thou with me? Eat,
For shame, and gaze not: eat thy meat:
Do that thou art come for: stands thy seat
Next ours of royal race?"

"Well hast thou said: thy rede rings true;
That which I came for will I do,"
Quoth Balen: forth his fleet sword flew,
And clove the head of Garlon through
Clean to the shoulders. Then he cried
Loud to his lady, "Give me here
The truncheon of the shameful spear
Wherewith he slew your knight, when fear
Bade hate in darkness ride."

And gladly, bright with grief made glad,
She gave the truncheon as he bade,
For still she bare it with her, sad
And strong in hopeless hope she had,
Through all dark days of thwarting fear,
To see if doom should fall aright
And as God's fire-fraught thunder smite
That head, clothed round with hell-faced night,
Bare now before her here.

And Balen smote therewith the dead
Dark felon's body through, and said
Aloud, "With even this truncheon, red
With baser blood than brave men bled
Whom in thy shameful hand it slew,
Thou hast slain a nobler knight, and now
It clings and cleaves thy body: thou
Shalt cleave again no brave man's brow,
Though hell would aid anew."

And toward his host he turned and spake:
"Now for your son's long-suffering sake
Blood ye may fetch enough, and take
Wherewith to heal his hurt, and make
Death warm as Life." Then rose a cry
Loud as the wind's when stormy spring
Makes all the woodland rage and ring:
"Thou hast slain my brother," said the king,
"And here with him shalt die."

"Ay?" Balen laughed him answer. "Well,
Do it then thyself." And the answer fell
Fierce as a blast of hate from hell,
"No man of mine that with me dwell
Shall strike at thee but I their lord
For love of this my brother slain."
And Pellam caught and grasped amain
A grim great weapon, fierce and fain
To feed his hungering sword.

And eagerly he smote, and sped
Not well: for Balen's blade, yet red

With lifeblood of the murderous dead,
Between the swordstroke and his head
Shone, and the strength of the eager stroke
Shore it in sunder: then the knight,
Naked and weaponless for fight,
Ran seeking him a sword to smite
As hope within him woke.

And so their flight for deathward fast
From chamber forth to chamber passed
Where lay no weapon, till the last
Whose doors made way for Balen cast
Upon him as a sudden spell
Wonder that even as lightning leapt
Across his heart and eyes, and swept
As storm across his soul that kept
Wild watch, and watched not well.

For there the deed he did, being near
Death's danger, breathless as the deer
Driven hard to bay, but void of fear,
Brought sorrow down for many a year
On Many a man in many a land,
All glorious shone that chamber, bright
As burns at sunrise heaven's own height:
With cloth of gold the bed was dight,
That flamed on either hand.

And one he saw within it lie:
A table of all clear gold thereby
Stood stately, fair as morning's eye,
With four strong silver pillars, high
And firm as faith and hope may be:
And on it shone the gift he sought,
A spear most marvelously wrought,
That when his eye and handgrip caught
Small fear at heart had he.

Right on King Pellam then, as fire
Turns when the thwarting winds wax higher,
He turned, and smote him down. So dire
The stroke was, when his heart's desire

Struck, and had all its fill of hate,
That as the king fell swooning down
Fell the walls, rent from base to crown,
Prone as prone seas that break and drown
Ships fraught with doom for freight.
And there for three days' silent space
Balen and Pellam face to face
Lay dead or deathlike, and the place
Was death's blind kingdom, till the grace
That God had given the sacred seer
For counsel or for comfort led
His Merlin thither, and he said,
Standing between the quick and the dead,
"Rise up, and rest not here."

And Balen rose and set his eyes
Against the seer's as one that tries
His heart against the sea's and sky's
And fears not if he lives or dies,
Saying, "I would have my damosel,
Ere I fare forth, to fare with me."
And sadly Merlin answered, "See
Where now she lies; death knows if she
Shall now fare ill or well.

"And in this world we meet no more,
Balen." And Balen, sorrowing sore,
Though fearless yet the heart he bore
Beat toward the life that lay before,
Rode forth through many a wild waste land
Where men cried out against him, mad
With grievous faith in fear that bade
Their wrath make moan for doubt they had
Lest hell had armed his hand.

For in that chamber's wondrous shrine
Was part of Christ's own blood, the wine
Shed of the true triumphal vine
Whose growth bids earth's deep darkness shine
As heaven's deep light through the air and sea;
That mystery toward our northern shore
Arimathean Joseph bore

For healing of our sins of yore,
That grace even there might be.

And with that spear there shrined apart
Was Christ's side smitten to the heart,
And fiercer that the lightning's dart
The stroke was, and the deathlike smart
Wherewith, nigh drained of blood and breadth,
The king lay stricken as one long dead:
And Joseph's was the blood there shed,
For near akin was he that bled,
Near even as life to death.

And therefore fell on all that land
Sorrow: for still on either hand,
As Balen rode alone and scanned
Bright fields and cities built to stand
Till time should break them, dead men lay;
And loud and long from all their folk
Living, one cry that cursed him broke;
Three countries had his dolorous stroke
Slain, or should surely slay.[108]

BIBLIOGRAPHY

Brown, Arthur C. L., *The Bleeding Lance*, Publications of the Modern Language
    Association of America. Vol. 25, 1910.
————"Notes on Celtic Cauldrons of Plenty and the Land-beneath-the-Waves,"
    Anniversary papers, by colleagues and pupils of G. L. Kittredge, Boston, 1913.
Bruce, James D., *The Evolution of Arthurian Romance*, Baltimore, 1923.
Fisher, Lizette A., *The Mystic Vision in the Grail Legend and in the Divine Comedy*,
    New York, 1917.
Frazer, Sir James G., *The Golden Bough*, London: 1922. Published in twelve volumes
    as follows:
    Vols. 1 & 2: *The Magic Art and the Evolution of Kings*; ·
    Vol. 3: *Taboo and the Perils of the Soul*;
    Vol. 4: *The Dying God*;
    Vols. 5 & 6: *Adonis, Attis and Osiris*;
    Vols. 7 & 8: *Spirits of the Corn and of the Wild*;
    Vol. 9: *The Scapegoat*;
    Vol. 10 & 11: *Balder the Beautiful*;
    Vol. 12: *Bibliography and Index*.

Goldschmidt, Moritz, editor, *Sone von Nausay*, Gedruckt für den Litterarischen Verein in Stuttgart and Tübingen, 1899.

Guest, Lady Charlotte, trans., *The Mabinogion*, Everyman edition, London, 1924.

Hartland, E. S., *Folklore: What Is It and What Is the Good of It?* (#2 of Nutt's Popular Studies in Mythology Romance and Folklore), London, 1904.

———. *Mythology and Folktales, Their Relations and Interpretations* (#7 of Nutt's Popular Studies), London, 1900.

Holy Bible, Translated from the Latin Vulgate, New York, 1914.

Hull, Eleanor, *The Cuchulian Saga in Irish Literature*, London, 1898.

John, Ivor B., *The Mabinogion* (#11 of Nutt's Popular Studies), London, 1901.

Joyce, Patrick W., trans., *Old Celtic Romances*, translated from the Gaelic, London, 1894.

Jubainville, Arbois de, *The Irish Mythological Cycle and Celtic Mythology*, translated from the French by Best, Dublin, 1903.

Kempe, Dorothy, *The Legend of the Holy Grail, Its Sources, Character, and Development*, London, 1905.

Lang, Andrew, *Alfred Tennyson*, New York, 1901.

Lot-Borodine, Myrrha, et Gertrude Schoepperle, avec une introduction par Roger Loomis, *Lancelot et Galaad*, New York, 1926.

Lowie, Robert H., *Primitive Religion*, New York, 1924.

Macalister, R. A. S., *Temair Breg: A Study of the Remains and Traditions of Tara*, Proceedings of the Royal Irish Academy, Vol. 34, 1917–1919.

Malory, Sir Thomas, *Le Morte Darthur*, Everyman edition, London, 1919.

Martin, Ernst, editor, *Wolfram v. Eschenbach, Parzival und Titurel*, Halle A. S. verlag der Buchhandlung des Waisenhauses, 1900.

Maynadier, Howard, *The Arthur of the English Poets*, Cambridge, Mass., 1907.

Newell, W. W., *King Arthur and the Table Round*, Boston, 1905.

Nutt, Alfred, *Celtic and Mediaeval Romance* (#1 of Nutt's Popular Studies), London, 1904.

———. *Cuchulainn, the Irish Achilles* (#8 of Nutt's Popular Studies), London, 1900.

———. *Studies on the Legend of the Holy Grail*, London, 1888.

Nyrop, Kr., *Sone de Nasai et La Norvege*, Romania, 35e Année, Paris, 1906.

O'Curry, *The Fate of the Children of Tuireann*, in The Atlantis, or Register of Literature and Science of the Catholic University of Ireland, Vol. 4. London, 1863.

Paris, Gaston, et Jakob Ulrich, eds., *Merlin, Roman en prose du XIIIe Siecle*, Société des anciens texts francais, Paris, 1886.

Peebles, Rose J., *The Legend of Longinus in Ecclesiastical Tradition and in English Literature, and Its Connection with the Grail*, Baltimore, 1911.

Rhys, J., *Studies in the Arthurian Legend*, Oxford, 1891.

Scudder, Vida D., *Le Morte Darthur of Sir Thomas Malory and Its Sources*, New York, 1917.

Sommer, H. Oskar, *Le Morte Darthur* by Syr Thomas Malory Faithfully Reprinted from the Original Edition of William Caxton; Published in three volumes as follows: Vol. 1: Text; Vol. 2: Introduction; Vol. 3: Studies on the Sources. London, 1890.

Swinburne, Algernon Charles, *Collected Poetical Works*, William Heinemann, London, 1917.

Tennyson, Alfred, Lord, *Idylls of the King*, New York, 1926.

Tylor, Edward B., *Primitive Culture, Researches into the Development of Mythology, Philosophy, Religion, Language, Art, and Custom*, London, 1920.

Waite, Arthur E., *The Hidden Church of the Holy Grail, Its Legends and Symbolism Considered in Their Affinity with Certain Mysteries of Initiation and Other Traces of Secret Tradition in Christian Times*, London, 1909.

Weston, Jessie L., *The Legend of Sir Gawain*, London, 1897.

———. *The Legend of Sir Perceval*, London, 1909.

———. *Legends of the Wagner Drama*, Studies in Mythology and Romance, New York, 1896.

———, translator. *Sir Gawain at the Grail Castle*, London, 1903.

———. *From Ritual to Romance*, Cambridge, Eng., 1920.

———. *The Quest of the Holy Grail*, London, 1913.

———. *Parzival, A Knightly Epic by Wolfram v. Eschenbach*, translated into English, London, 1894.

———. *King Arthur and His Knights, A Survey of Arthurian Romance* (#4 of Nutt's Popular Studies), London, 1899.

APPENDIX B

———•———

Joseph Campbell's Library

Works on the Arthurian Romances of the Middle Ages from the Joseph Campbell Collection

Adam de La Halle. *Adam Le Bossu, trouvère artésien du XIIIe siècle: Le jeu de
la feuillée.* Edited by Ernest Langlois. Paris: Librairie Ancienne Honoré
Champion, 1923.

———. *Adam Le Bossu, trouvère artésien du XIIIe siècle: Le jeu de Robin et Marion,
suivi du jeu du Pèlerin.* Edited by Ernest Langlois. Paris: Librairie Ancienne
Honoré Champion, 1924.

———. "Le Jeu de Robin et Marion." Translated by Ernest Langlois. Paris: E. de
Boccard, 1923.

Signed, "Joseph Campbell"

Anglade, Joseph. *Anthologie des troubadours.* Paris: E. de Boccard, 1953.

Extensive translations, etymologies, conjugations for Arnaut Daniel, Giraut de
Borneil, Bertran de Born.

Arthurian Chronicles, Represented by Wace and Layamon. New York: E. P. Dutton,
1921.

Aucassin et Nicolette: Chantefable du XIIIe siècle. Edited by Mario Roques. Paris:
Librairie Ancienne Honoré Champion, 1925.

Marginal definitions in French.

Avalon to Camelot.

Journal issued quarterly in the 1980s on matters Arthurian. Sample issue titles
include "The Grail Legend," 1, no. 3 (1984); "Women and the Arthurian Tradition," 1, no. 4 (1984); "The Many Faces of Arthur," 2, no. 1 (1984). Articles
include Burne-Jones's "Beguiling of Merlin," sources of the Grail legends, etc.
No notes.

Article with graphics by Jean-Claude Lozachmeur, "Components for a
Solution to the Puzzle of the Grail," 2, no. 1 (1984).

Article by Barri C. DeVigne, "The Glastonbury Zodiac," 1, no. 2 (1983):
"hill has a secret entrance to the underworld" and is a "three-dimensional
maze" (with 7 visible concentric ridges): "world's largest labyrinth" (26);

"abode of Anud" of Celtic lore; the approach to the White Goddess or "Earth Mother" (26); Necrotypes: mountain, spiral, GG, underworld; St. Michael's Tor on top.

Article by Geoffrey Ashe, "Arthur-Riothamus," 1, no. 2 (1983): constellation Ursa Major and Arthur: "Parsifal/Parzival and Wagner/ Wolfram."

Article by Edward B. Haymes, "Parsifal/Palzival and Wagner/Wolfram," 1, no. 3 (1984): "Glastonbury = Isle of Glass = Isle of Apples: the isle to which the wounded Arthur was conveyed" (8).

Béroul. *Le Roman de Tristan, poème du XIIe siècle.* Edited by Ernest Muret. Paris: Librairie Ancienne Honoré Champion, 1922.

Of several Tristans, this one is extensively annotated and includes a long head note on the inside front cover:

"Comme la légende arturienne, la légende de Tristan et Iseut appartient à la 'matière de Bretagne': comme la légende arturienne, nous ne la connaisons que par des texts français. Ce sont le poème du trovère Anglo-Norman, Thomas, composé entre 1155 et 1170; celui de trouvère normand Béroul composé vers la fin du XIIe siècle; deux petits poèmes épisodiques de la *Folie Tristan*, écrits l'un vers 1170, l'autre au debut du XIIIe siècle; le Lai du Chèvre feuille de Marie de France; enfin un vaste roman en prose, qui fut écrit vers la 1230. Toutes les versions en des langues étrangères, le poème d'Eilhart d'Oberg, cel de Gottfried von Strasburg, Sir Tristram, etc., ne sont que des derivés l'un ou de l'autre de ces romans français.

"Le plus ancient poème parvenu jusqu'à nous où soit traité ce beau 'conte d'amour et de mort' est celui de Thomas. D'autre poètes ou tout au moins un autre la'avaent traité avant lui.... Thomas est un conte facile, elégant, agréable, et sa narration la mort des amants, par exemple, est belle et pathétique. Mais auteur mondain, entice de préciosité, il recherché des effets litteraires et donne à ses héros des attitudes qui jurent étrangement avec la rude simplicite impliquée par le thème. . . . C'est donc une legende déja célèbre, que selon toute apparence Thomas racontait, avant lui, elle a traite en un roman régulier duquel derive semble-t-il tous les texts que nous avons conservés e qui explique leurs éléments communs."

Bruce, James Douglas. *The Evolution of Arthurian Romance from the Beginnings Down to the Year 1300.* 2nd edition with a supplement by Alfons Hilka. 2 vols. Göttingen: Vandenhoeck & Ruprecht, 1928; Baltimore: Johns Hopkins Press, 1923.

Very few notes.

Cercamon. *Les Poésies de Cercamon.* Edited by Alfred Jeanroy. Paris: Librairie Ancienne Honoré Champion, 1922.

Chrétien de Troyes. *Arthurian Romances.* Translated by W. Wistar Comfort. New York: E. P. Dutton, 1914.

Underlinings and marginalia tracking the stories.

———. *Cligès; Textausgabe mit Variantenauswahl, Einleitung, Anmerkung und*

Vollstandigem Glossar. Edited by Wendelin Foerster. Halle: Max Niemeyer, 1910.
Marginal definitions in French and German in fine pencil.

———. *Erec und Enide.* Edited by Wendelin Foerster. Halle: Max Niemeyer, 1909.
Underlinings and marginal definitions in French.

———. *Guillaume d'Angleterre, roman du XIIe siècle.* Edited by Maurice Wilmotte. Paris: H. Champion, 1927.
"Mr. J. Campbell No 1." No notes.

———. *Der Karrenritter (Lancelot) und Das Wilhelmsleben (Guillaume d'Angleterre).* Edited by Wendelin Foerster. Halle: Max Niemeyer, 1899.
Marginal definitions in French (a few critical of the editor).

Cohen, Gustave. *Le théâtre en France au moyen âge.* Paris: Rieder, 1928.
Marginal notes for introduction; Plate XXXVII "Les Trois Marie au Tombeau," and Plate I from "Manuscrit Allemand Bibl. de Reichnau."
Lots on Dante, some on Chaucer, a bit of Beowulf, Chansons de Geste.

A Demanda do santo graal. Translated by Augusto Magne. 3 vols. Rio de Janeiro: Imprensa Nacional, 1944. Uncut pages.

Faral, Edmond. *Recherches sur les source latines des contes et romans courtois du moyen âge.* Paris: Édouard Champion, 1913.
No notes.

Geoffrey of Monmouth. *Histories of the Kings of Britain,* translated by Sebastian Evans. London and Toronto: J. M. Dent & Sons; New York: E. P. Dutton, 1920.
Underlining and notes in pencil.

Gottfried von Strassburg. *Tristan: Translated Entire for the First Time; with the Surviving Fragments of the Tristran of Thomas, Newly Translated.* With an Introduction by A. T. Hatto. Baltimore: Penguin Books, 1960.
Ruled underlinings and notes.

———. *Tristan und Îseult.* Edited by August Closs. Oxford: Basil Blackwell, 1958.
Middle High German. Introduction has notes and ruled underlinings.

———. *Tristan und Isold.* Herausgegeben von Friedrich Ranke. 4th edition. Berlin: Weidmannsche Verlagsbuchhandlung, 1959.
No notes.

Guénon, René. *L'Ésoterisme de Dante.* Deuxieme Édition Corrigée. Paris: Les Éditions Traditionnelles, 1939.
Ruled underlinings. Notes in French.

Guillaume de Lorris. *The Romance of the Rose by W. Lorris and J. Clopinel.* Translated by F. S. Ellis. Vol. 1. London: J. M. Dent, 1900.

Hartmann von Aue und Gottfried von Strassburg: Eine Auswahl mit Anmerkungen und Wörterbuch. Edited by Hermann Jantzen. Berlin and Leipzig: Walter de Gruyter, 1925.
With notes in fine pencil in French, German, and English. To "Der arme

Heinrich." Mostly translations of the text, some with grammatical notations
("prêt. of Kiesen"). Others ("What I dared to suffer / you dare not endure").
Longer notes in French to the introduction regarding Gottfried's sources.

Holland, Vyvyan. "The Medieval Courts of Love." Paper read before Ye Sette of Odd
Volumes at Ye 421st Meeting of Ye Sette, held at the Royal Adelaide Gallery
on February 22, 1927. London: Ye Caymre Press and sold by NO Booksellers,
1927. Signed by the author and with an inscription: "From [?] Mabs to Joseph
Campbell, 1957." Other signatures: Copy 55 presented to Margarie Leslie (?) by
Vyvyan Holland. From Shane Leslie to Mabs Mollke (?) 1952.

Huizinga, Johan. *The Waning of the Middle Ages.* New York: Doubleday, n.d.
Ruled underlining.

Jacobus de Voragine. *La Légende Dorée: Traduite du Latin d'après les plus anciens
manuscrits.* Edited by Teodor de Wyzewa. Paris: Perrin et C Libraires, 1925.
"Mr. Joseph Campbell #3" in pencil. No notes.

Jean Renart. *Galeran de Bretagne: Roman du XIIIe siècle.* Edited by Lucien Foulet.
Paris: Librairie Ancienne Edouard Champion, 1925.
Poem in couplets.
"Mr. J. Campbell No. 2." No notes.

———. *Le Lai de l'ombre.* Publié par Joseph Bédier. Paris: Librairie de Firmin-
Didot et cie, 1913.
With twelve "graphiques" to illustrate the "classement des Manuscrits. Pencil
"Stammbaum fur manuscripts" in Campbell's hand. Notes in French on the
couplets, underlinings.

Jenkins, Elizabeth. *The Mystery of King Arthur.* New York: Coward, McCann &
Geoghegan, 1975.
Picture book. No notes.

Kittredge, George Lyman. *A Study of Gawain and the Green Knight.* Cambridge,
MA: Harvard Univ. Press, 1916.
Extensive notes, underlinings, and checks. Another graph (57). Axeman and
"supernaturals whose heads return and their bodies after decapitation: a universal motif-associated with serpent (water) demons."

Lawrence, William Witherle. *Medieval Story and the Beginnings of the Social Ideals of
English-Speaking People.* 2nd ed. New York: Columbia Univ. Press, 1926.
Most notes on "The History of Reynard the Fox."

Locke, Frederick W. *The Quest for the Holy Grail: A Literary Study of a Thirteenth-
Century French Romance.* Stanford: Stanford Univ. Press, 1960.

Loomis, R. S. *Arthurian Tradition and Chrétien de Troyes.* New York: Columbia
Univ. Press, 1949.
Most of the notes and underlinings in book 5, "Le Conte del Graal."

———. *Celtic Myth and Arthurian Romance.* New York: Columbia Univ. Press,
1927.
Most of the extensive notes and underlinings in book 4, "Brides of the Sun."

——. *The Grail: From Celtic Myth to Christian Symbol.* New York: Columbia
Univ. Press, 1963.
Extensive notes and underlining throughout.

——. Introduction to *Lancelot et Galahad.* Mis en nouveau langage par Myrrha
Lot-Borodine et Gertrude Schoepperle. New York: Oxford Univ. Press, 1926.
No notes.

——. *Studies in Medieval Literature: A Memorial Collection of Essays.* New York:
Burt Franklin, 1970.
No notes.

——, ed. *Medieval Studies in Memory of Gertrude Schoepperle Loomis.* Paris:
Librairie Honoré Champions; New York: Columbia Univ. Press, 1927.
Notes and ruled underlinings, especially in "King Arthur and the Grail" and
"Tristan and Lancelot."

The Mabinogion. Translated by Lady Charlotte Guest. New York: E.P. Dutton, 1924.
Notes only for table of contents.

*Les Mabinogion du Livre Rouge de Hergest avec les variantes du Livre blanc de Rhyd-
derch.* Translated by J. Loth. 2 vols. Paris: Fontemoing et cie, 1913.

Malory, Thomas, Sir. *Le Morte Darthur, by Syr Thomas Malory.* Edited by H. Oskar
Sommer. Vol. 1, *Text.* Vol. 2, *Introduction.* Vol. 3, *Studies on Sources.* London:
David Nutt in the Strand, 1889–91.
No notes. Huge book.

——. *Le Morte D'Arthur by Sir Thomas Malory.* Edited by Ernest Rhys. 2 vols.
Everyman's Library, no. 45. New York: E.P. Dutton, 1917.
A few notes.

Marie de France. *French Mediaeval Romances from the Lays of Marie de France.*
Translated by Eugene Mason. New York: E.P. Dutton, 1924.

Mary, André. *La Chambre des Dames.* Paris: Boivin et cie, 1922.
Handwritten inscription: "A Joseph Campbell de son ami dévoué H.K.S.
Paris, Noël, 1927."
Only a couple of underlinings: "Seigneurs, c'est la nature de la femme d'age
toujours contre la raison" (181). And "'Le Lai de l'Ombre' est ici."

Maynadier, Howard. *The Arthur of the English Poets.* Boston and New York:
Houghton Mifflin, 1907.
Up to Tennyson. No notes.

Die Minnesinger in Bildern der Manessichen Handschrift. Mit einem Geleitwort von
Hans Neumann. Leipzig: Insel-Verlag, 1933–45.

Nitze, William A. *Perceval and the Holy Grail: An Essay on the Romance of Chrétien
de Troyes.* University of California Publications in Modern Philology, vol. 28,
no. 5. Berkeley: Univ. of California Press, 1949.
Heavily annotated. On Marie intro Lais: "art (escience) brings out meaning
(san) beneath obscure malerie."

Nutt, Alfred. *Studies on the Legend of the Holy Grail: With Especial Reference to the
Hypothesis of Its Celtic Origin.* London: David Nutt, 1888.
No notes.

Owens, Harry J., ed. *The Scandalous Adventures of Reynard the Fox*. New York: Alfred A. Knopf, 1945.
A few marginal notes.
The Oxford Book of Medieval Latin Verse. Chosen by Stephen Gaselee. Oxford: Clarenden Press, 1928.
Marginal notes in French, some in Latin.
Perlesvaus. *Le Haut Livre du Graal*. Edited by William A. Nitze and T. Atkinson Jenkins. Vol. 1, *Text, Variants, and Glossary*. Chicago: Univ. of Chicago Press, 1932.
No notes. Some interesting diagrams (Eagle, Man, Ox, Lion: Pater, Filius, Dei, Spiritus in downward pointed triangle).
———. *The High History of the Holy Graal*. Translated from the Old French by Sebastian Evans. New York: E. P. Dutton, 1921.
"Perlesvaus" written on first page. A few vertical marginal indicators.
Piramus et Tisbé: Poème du XIIe siècle. Edited by C. de Boer. Paris: Librairie Ancienne Honoré Champion, 1921.
Quite heavily annotated with marginal notes (translations, definitions).
La Queste del Saint Graal: Roman du XIIIe siècle. Edited by Albert Pauphilet. Paris: Librairie Ancienne Honoré Champion, 1923.
Two copies. Second 1949 reprint. Underlinings for introduction. Underlined passage (often quoted by Campbell):
"Si pristrent cele nuit conseil que il porroient fere: et a l'endemain s'accordent a ce qu'il se departiroient et si tendroit chascuns sa voie, par ce que a honte lor seroit atorné se lit aloient tuit ensamble" (26).
"Si issirent dou chastel et se departirent maintenant li uns de l'autre einsi come il l'avoient porparlé, et se mistrent en la forest li uns ça et lie autres la, la ou il la voient pluse espesse, en tous les leus ou il trovoient ne voie ne sentier" (26).
P. M. Matarasso, editor. *The Quest of the Holy Grail*. New York: Penguin, 1977.
Robert de Boron. *Le Roman de L'Estoire dou Graal*. Edited by William A. Nitze. Paris: Librairie Ancienne Honoré Champion, 1927.
Underlined: "A lui dedenz la prison vint/Et son veissel porta, qu'il tint, /Qui grant clartéseur lui gita, Si que la charter enlumina" (p. 25, vv. 717–20).
Extensive handwritten note on back page:
"La véritable signification du vase mysterieux, la grail, ni Chrétien ni Wauchier ne la laissaient entrevoir et il est probable qu'eux-mêmes ne savaient trop que penser à ce sujet. Notre auteur eût-il par ses seules forces réussi a opéres la transformation du mysterieux grail en relique sacrée? C'est possible mais il fut devanceé par un autre dont l'oeuvre a exercé sur lui une influence decisive. Robert de Boron imagina le premier que ce grail était un vase, le 'vaissel' où Joseph d'Arimathie avait recuelli le sang dégouttant des plaies du Crucifié; en même temps c'était dans ce vase que [péous?] avait célélere la Cénel [?] chez Simon.

"Robert eut l'idée de prendre l'histoire de cette rélique à ses débuts et de la mener jusqu'à sa conclusion ultime dans une serie de trois ouvrages: Joseph d'Arimathie, Merlin, Perceval (comprenant une Mort d'Arthur) (le premier en vers; le second en prose sauf un fragment du début qui est en vers; le troisième en prose = le Percival – Didot).

"L'oeuvre de Robert Boron affecte un caractère trés différent de celui des romans de ses prédécesseurs et de ses contemporains. Elle envelope l' aventure' dans une atmosphère de dévotion et de mysticism inconnue à Chrétien et aux émules celui-ci. Elle s'efforce en même temp...."

———. *Le Roman de Merlin, or The Early History of King Arthur.* Edited by H. Oskar Sommer. London: Privately Printed for Subscribers, 1894. French. No notes.

Le Roman de Renard. Principaux épisodes. Translated by Madame B.A. Jeanroy. Paris: E. De Boccard, 1926.

Le Roman de Renart. Publié par Ernest Martin. 3 vols. Strasbourg: K.J. Trubner. Paris: Ernest Leroux, 1882.

A few marginal definitions and translations early on.

Rutherford, John. *Troubadours: Their Loves and Their Lyrics.* London: Smith, Elder, 1873.

Schröder, Franz Rolf. *Die Parzivalfrage.* München: C.H. Beck'sche Verlagsbuchhandlung, 1928.

Lots of marginalia and underlining: "Gralsburg und Minnegrotte-mit dieser Antithese haben wir ungeheure Kluft bezeichnet über die Keine Brücke fuhrt noch fuhren kann" (78).

Also marginal diagrams: Arabern, Sizilien Provence?, Spanien, Europa. Notes on etymology of the word *gral* (Miraj Namah?) (40–41). "Wolframs *Parzival* als gnostisches Mysterium" (37–38).

Smythe, Barbara, ed. *Troubadour Poets.* London: Chatto & Windus, 1929.

Thomas of Britain. *The Romance of Tristram and Ysolt, by Thomas of Britain.* Translated from the Old French and Old Norse by R.S. Loomis. New York: E.P. Dutton, 1923.

Contains the tiles reproduced in *Creative Mythology.* No notes.

Tolkien, J.R.R., trans. *Sir Gawain and the Green Knight, Pearl, and Sir Ofeo.* Boston: Houghton Mifflin, 1975. Advance uncorrected proofs.

Tolkien, J.R.R., and E.V. Gordon, eds. *Sir Gawain and the Green Knight.* Oxford: Oxford Univ. Press, 1930.

Weigand, Hermann J. *Wolfram's Parzival: Five Essays with an Introduction.* Edited by Ursula Hoffman. Ithaca and London: Cornell Univ. Press, 1969.

Williamson, John. *The Oak King, The Holly King, and the Unicorn: The Myths and Symbolism of the Unicorn Tapestries.* New York: Harper & Row, 1986.

NOTES

———————————●———————————

All explications by the editors are marked in square brackets ([]). All other notes are either citations of source material or Campbell's own notes.

EDITOR'S FOREWORD

1. James Joyce, *Finnegans Wake* (Oxford: Oxford Univ. Press, 2012), 628.
2. [We are here and elsewhere using the geographic distinction that Campbell himself used in describing collectively the cultures of South and East Asia and North Africa. While Eurocentric, the terms *Oriental* and *Occidental* provide simple collective adjectives that tie in with Campbell's own schema of the world's high culture centers. For more on this schema, see the opening chapters of Joseph Campbell, *Masks of God: Oriental Mythology,* digital edition (San Anselmo, CA: Joseph Campbell Foundation, 2014), and *Goddesses: Mysteries of the Feminine Divine* (Novato, CA: New World Library, 2013). —Ed.]
3. [In fact, it could be argued that the Arthurian myths are not the first secularized mythology. The writings of the Roman poets Lucretius, Virgil, and Ovid predate them by over a thousand years and, in the case of Lucretius, develop an explicitly psychological view of the myths as images of what we all go through, right here and now, before we die. —Ed.]
4. Stephen and Robin Larsen, *A Fire in the Mind: The Life of Joseph Campbell* (New York: Doubleday, 1991), 105.
5. Denis de Rougement, *Love in the Western World,* 1st ed. (Princeton, NJ: Princeton Univ. Press, 1940).
6. See Henry and Renée Kahane, *The Krater and the Grail* (Urbana: Univ. of Illinois Press, 1965).
7. Larsen and Larsen, *Fire in the Mind,* 325.

8. Larsen and Larsen, *Fire in the Mind,* 63.
9. Larsen and Larsen, *Fire in the Mind,* 326.
10. [The archive numbers (for example, L181) correspond to items found in the Joseph Campbell Archive.—Ed.]
11. Robert O'Driscoll, ed., *The Celtic Consciousness* (New York: George Braziller, 1981).

Chapter 1. Neolithic, Celtic, Roman, and German Backgrounds

1. [For more on the religions and myths of Old Europe, see Campbell, *Goddesses,* chaps. 1–3 (see Editor's Foreword, n. 2), and Marija Gimbutas, *The Language of the Goddess* (San Francisco: Harper & Row, 1983), passim. —Ed.]
2. [See Marija Gimbutas, *The Goddesses and Gods of Old Europe, 6500–3500 BC, Myths and Cult Images* (Berkeley: Univ. of California Press, 1982), 17ff. —Ed.]

Chapter 2. Irish Christianity: Saints Brendan and Patrick

1. Kenneth H. Cooper, *Aerobics* (New York, 1968), 101.
2. [Campbell's telling of Brendan's legend follows the version of Lady Gregory, *A Book of Saints and Wonders* (London, 1920), 185–208. —Ed]
3. *The Gospel According to Thomas,* Coptic text established and translated by A. Guillaumont, H.-Ch. Puech, G. Quispel, W. Till, and Yassah 'abd al Masih (Leiden: E. J. Brill; New York: Harper, 1959).
4. [See, for example, Silas T. Rand, *Legends of the Micmac* (New York: Longmans, Green, 1894), 24, 35, 114; and for other North American examples, the bibliography in Stith Thompson, *Tales of the North American Indians* (Cambridge, MA: Harvard Univ. Press, 1929), 335n210. —Ed.]

Chapter 3. Theology, Love, Troubadours, and Minnesingers

1. Girhault de Borneilh, *"Tam cum los oills el cor...,"* from John Rutherford, *The Troubadours: Their Loves and Their Lyrics* (London: Smith, Elder, 1873), 34–35.

Chapter 4. Wolfram von Eschenbach's *Parzival*

1. Karl Lachmann, ed., *Wolfram von Eschenbach* (Berlin and Leipzig, 1926). There is an excellent English translation by Helen M. Mustard and Charles E. Passage, *Parzifal, by Wolfram von Eschenbach* (New York: Vintage Books, 1961).

2. Mustard and Passage, trans., *Parzival* 11. 177:6–8.
3. Richard Wagner, *Parsifal*, act 1 [Campbell's translation].
4. Mustard and Passage, trans., *Parzival* 15. 740: 26–29.
5. Mustard and Passage, trans., *Parzival* 16. 818: 25–30.
6. Mustard and Passage, trans., *Parzival* 13. 589: 8.
7. [See Hermann Goetz, "Der Orient der Kreuzzüge in Wolframs *Parzival*," *Sonderdrucke der Mitglieder* (Böhlau: Südasien-Institut der Universität Heidelberg), 36–37 and n. 59, citing *Fattsien*, ed. H. Giles (1923), 14, and Hsuan-tsang, *Buddhist Records of the Western World*, vol. 1, 98ff. and vol. 11, 278.]
8. Jeremiah Curtin, *Myths and Folk-Lore of Ireland* (Boston: Little, Brown, 1890), 327–32.
9. Sir James George Frazer, *The Golden Bough: A Study in Magic and Religion* (New York: Macmillan, 1922), 469–71.
10. [See Campbell, *Goddesses*, 199–200 (see Editor's Foreword, n. 2). —Ed]
11. Katha Upaniṣad 3.12.
12. Mustard and Passage, trans., *Parzival* 3. 140: 16–17.

CHAPTER 5. TRISTAN AND ISEULT

1. [See Joseph Campbell, *The Hero with a Thousand Faces*, 3rd ed. (Novato, CA: New World Library, 2008), passim, and *Pathways to Bliss: Mythology and Personal Transformation*, ed. David Kudler (Novato, CA: New World Library, 2004), chap. 6, "The Self as Hero." —Ed.]
2. Gottfried von Strassburg, *Tristan*, trans. A. T. Hatto (New York: Continuum, 2003), 234 [Campbell's translation].
3. Gottfried von Strassburg, *Tristan*, 207 [Campbell's translation].
4. [For more on the aspects of the Goddess, see Campbell, *Goddesses*, passim (see Editor's Foreword, n. 2). Seven-headed dragons or serpents appear frequently in myths worldwide. In the West such creatures are frequently associated with death and destruction (for example, the beast faced by the archangel Michael in Revelation 12:3). In Asian myth they are associated with transformation and illumination, as in Ananta (Sanskrit: "infinite"), on whom the dreaming Viṣṇu sleeps, and Mucalinda, who protects Gautama Buddha from the elements for seven days and seven nights immediately following his achieving *nirvāṇa*. —Ed.]
5. [See Joseph Campbell, *Myths to Live By*, ebook edition (San Anselmo, CA: Joseph Campbell Foundation, 2010), chap. 4. —Ed.]
6. Marie de France, "Chevrefoil," lines 66–74 [Campbell's translation].
7. Myrrha Lot-Borodine, *De l'amour profane à l'amour sacré: Études de psychologie sentimentale au Moyen Âge* (Paris: Nizet, 1979), 53 [Campbell's translation].
8. Gottfried von Strassburg, *Tristan*, 5.
9. Béroul, *Le roman de Tristan* (Paris: Fermin Didot, 1903), 42, line 1334.

10. Shōtoku, *Shomangyo-gisho*, translation following Shinsho Hanayama, "Japanese Development of Ekayana Thought," in *Religious Studies in Japan*, ed. Japanese Association for Religious Studies and Japanese Organizing Committee of the Ninth International Congress for the History of Religions (Tokyo: Maruzen, 1959), 373.

11. Gertrude Schoepperle Loomis, *Tristan and Isolt* (London: D. Nutt; Frankfurt a.m.: Joseph Baer, 1913), 227.

12. Gottfried von Strassburg, *Tristan*, prologue [Campbell's translation].

13. Campbell, *Hero with a Thousand Faces*, 190–94.

14. Joseph Campbell, *Masks of God: Oriental Mythology*, digital edition (San Anselmo, CA: Joseph Campbell Foundation, 2014), chap. 8.

15. Leo Frobenius, *Erythräa: Länder und Zeiten des heiligen Königsmordes* (Berlin and Zürich: Atlantis-Verlag, 1931), 155–60.

16. Campbell, *Myths to Live By*, chap. 4.

Chapter 6. The Knights of the Round Table

1. Katha Upaniṣad, 3.14.

Chapter 7. The Waste Land

1. T. S. Eliot, *The Waste Land*, "The Burial of the Dead," lines 19–20.

2. Oswald Spengler, *The Decline of the West*, 2 vols. (New York: Knopf, 1926, 1928), 2:290.

3. Gottfried von Strassburg, *Tristan*, 165 (see chap. 5, n. 2).

4. Meister Eckhardt, *The Works of Meister Eckhart*, trans. C. de B. Evans (London: J. M. Watkins, 1952), no. 96 ("Riddance"), line 239.

5. Lao-tzu, *Tao Te-ching*, 1.1–2.

6. Mustard and Passage, trans., *Parzival* 9. 491:1–3 [see chap. 4, n. 1].

7. Eliot, *The Waste Land*, "What the Thunder Said," line 340.

8. Gospel according to Thomas, logion 113.

9. [See Campbell, *Masks of God*, chap. 8.]

10. Matthew 4:19.

11. Kuno Meyer, trans., *The Voyage of Bran, Son of Febal, to the Land of the Living* (London, 1895), 1:2–34.

12. *Missale Romanum*, 1962, 67.

13. See Roger S. Loomis, *The Grail: From Celtic Myth to Christian Symbol* (New York: Columbia Univ. Press, 1927), 3–4, 228.

14. James Douglas Bruce, *The Evolution of Arthurian Romance from the Beginnings Down to the Year 1300* (Göttingen: Vandenboeck & Ruprecht, 1928), 1:423.

15. Bṛhadāraṇyaka Upaniṣad, 3.8.

16. Mustard and Passage, trans., *Parzival* 9. 453:1–454:30.

17. R. S. Loomis, *Grail,* 264.

Appendix A: A Study of the Dolorous Stroke

1. Sir Thomas Malory, *Le Morte D'Arthur,* bk. 2, chap. 3; Everyman's Library ed., 1:55; Sommer ed., 84.

2. G. Paris and J. Ulrich, eds., *Merlin, roman en prose du XIIIe Siècle,* Société des anciens texts francais (Paris: Firmin Didot, 1886), 1:1.

3. H. Oskar Sommer, ed., *Le Morte Darthur* (London: D. Nutt, 1889–91), 3:7n.

4. Arthur C. L. Brown, *The Bleeding Lance,* Publications of the Modern Language Association of America 25 (Baltimore: Modern Language Association of America, 1910), 46.

5. Malory, *Morte D'Arthur,* Everyman's Library ed., 1:64; Sommer ed., 93.

6. Brown, *Bleeding Lance,* 46–47. The French text for these adventures appears in Paris and Ulrich, eds., *Merlin,* 2:6–31. On p. 27 the gap is indicated, which we have filled with Prof. Brown's translation of the *Demanda del Sancto Grail.*

7. Malory, *Morte D'Arthur,* bk. 2, chap. 16; Everyman's Library ed., 1:65; Sommer ed., 94.

8. Jessie L. Weston, *From Ritual to Romance* (Cambridge, 1919), 19.

9. Brown, *Bleeding Lance,* 50.

10. Brown, *Bleeding Lance,* 49.

11. Brown, *Bleeding Lance,* 49.

12. Edward B. Tylor, *Primitive Culture: Researches into the Development of Mythology, Philosophy, Religion, Language, Art, and Custom* (London, 1920), 1:428–79.

13. Frazer, *Golden Bough,* 1:373f. (see chap. 4, n. 9).

14. Frazer, *Golden Bough,* 375.

15. Frazer, *Golden Bough,* 3:1–2.

16. Frazer, *Golden Bough,* 4:9–10.

17. Robert H. Lowie, *Primitive Religion* (New York: Boni and Liveright, 1924), 136ff.

18. R. A. S. Macalister, *Temair Breg: A Study of the Remains and Traditions of Tara,* Proceedings of the Royal Irish Academy, vol. 34 (Dublin: Hodges, Figgis, 1917–1919), 326, 383ff.

19. Macalister, *Temair Breg,* 324ff.

20. Macalister describes these ceremonies: *Temair Breg,* 328ff.

21. O'Curry, *The Fate of the Children of Tuireann,* in The Atlantis, or Register of Literature and Science of the Catholic University of Ireland, vol. 4 (London, 1863), 189.

22. O'Curry, *Fate,* 193–95.

23. O'Curry, *Fate,* 205.

24. O'Curry, *Fate,* 205.

25. Patrick W. Joyce, trans., *Old Celtic Romances* (London, 1894), 74. O'Curry translates the story almost literally; Joyce gives a less constrained version. My summary has been based upon the former and has drawn from Joyce simply this conclusion.

26. Malory, *Morte D'Arthur*, bk. 17, chaps. 1–2; Everyman's Library ed., 2:237–39. Sommer ed., 690–92.

27. Brown, *Bleeding Lance*, 18–19.

28. Brown, *Bleeding Lance*, 22.

29. Brown, *Bleeding Lance*, 22.

30. Brown, *Bleeding Lance*, 53–56.

31. Brown, *Bleeding Lance*, 54.

32. Macalister, *Temair Breg*, 320.

33. Macalister, *Temair Breg*, 318–20.

34. Frazer, *Golden Bough*, 5:264–65.

35. Frazer, *Golden Bough*, 8:22–24.

36. Weston, *From Ritual to Romance*, 41.

37. Ernst Martin, ed., *Wolfram von Eschenbach: Parzival und Titurel* (Halle a. S.: Verlag der Buchhandlung des Waisenhauses, 1900), 1:169.

38. Moritz Goldschmidt, *Sone von Nausay* (Tübingen: Litterarischen Verein, 1899), p. 123, lines 4775–76.

39. Alfred Nutt, *Studies on the Legend of the Holy Grail* (London: D. Nutt, 1888), 15–16.

40. Jessie L. Weston, trans., *Sir Gawain at the Grail Castle* (London: D. Nutt, 1903), 27.

41. Nutt, *Studies on the Legend*, 15–16.

42. Weston, *Sir Gawain*, 73.

43. Brown, *Bleeding Lance*, 51.

44. Weston, *Sir Gawain*, viii.

45. Malory, *Morte D'Arthur*, bk. 2, chap. 12; Everyman's Library ed., 1:60–61; Sommer ed., 90.

46. Malory, *Morte D'Arthur*, bk. 2, chap. 13; Everyman's Library ed., 1:61; Sommer ed., 90–91.

47. Malory, *Morte D'Arthur*, bk. 1, chaps. 19–24; Everyman's Library ed., 1:35–42; Sommer ed., 65–72.

48. The publication of Professor Loomis's studies is now in progress.

49. Lady Charlotte Guest, trans., *The Mabinogion*, Everyman's Library (New York: E. P. Dutton, 1924), 154–55, cf. also 158ff.

50. Frazer, *Golden Bough*, 1:247ff.

51. Guest, *Mabinogion*, 161.

52. Guest, *Mabinogion*, 164.

53. Bruce, *Evolution of Arthurian Romance*, 2:233 [see chap. 7, n. 14].

54. Bruce, *Evolution of Arthurian Romance*, 2:236.

55. Bruce, *Evolution of Arthurian Romance*, 2:236.

56. Malory, *Morte D'Arthur*, bk. 4, chap. 18; Everyman's Library ed., 1:114; Sommer ed., 142–43.

57. Malory, *Morte D'Arthur*, bk. 20, chap. 21; Everyman's Library ed., 2:375–76; Sommer ed., 835.

58. Weston, *Legend of Sir Gawain*, 7ff.

59. Weston, *Legend of Sir Gawain*, 17.

60. Weston, *Legend of Sir Gawain*, 110.

61. Alfred Nutt, *Cuchulainn, the Irish Achilles*, Popular Studies in Mythology, Romance, and Folklore 8 (London: D. Nutt, 1899), 9.

62. Nutt, *Cuchulainn*, 9.

63. Nutt, *Cuchulainn*, 41.

64. Guest, *Mabinogion*, 198.

65. Nutt, *Studies on the Legend*, 44.

66. John Rhys, *Studies in the Arthurian Legend* (Oxford: Clarendon, 1891), 97.

67. Weston, *Sir Gawain*, 21–22.

68. Rose J. Peebles, *The Legend of Longinus in Ecclesiastical Tradition and in English Literature, and Its Connection with the Grail* (Baltimore: J. H. Furst, 1911), 171–72, and Bruce, *Evolution of Arthurian Romance*, 1:272ff.

69. Peebles, *Legend of Longinus*, 174.

70. Macalister, *Temair Breg*, 398.

71. Macalister, *Temair Breg*, 397.

72. Macalister, *Temair Breg*, 397.

73. Macalister, *Temair Breg*, 383ff.

74. Macalister, *Temair Breg*, 361ff.

75. Macalister, *Temair Breg*, 385.

76. Jessie L. Weston, *The Legend of Sir Perceval: Studies upon Its Origin, Development, and Position in the Arthurian Cycle* (London: D. Nutt, 1906–1909), 2:252ff.

77. Weston, *From Ritual to Romance*, 71.

78. Brown, *Bleeding Lance*, 59n.

79. Nutt, *Studies on the Legend*, 11–12.

80. Nutt, *Studies on the Legend*, 20–22.

81. Jessie L. Weston, trans., *Parzival, A Knightly Epic by Wolfram von Eschenbach* (London: D. Nutt, 1894), 1:275–78.

82. Frazer, *Golden Bough*, 5:303–8.

83. Matthew 27:45–55.

84. John 19:34–38.

85. Nutt, *Studies on the Legend*, 50.

86. Nutt, *Studies on the Legend*, 42.

87. Nutt, *Studies on the Legend*, 44.

88. Nutt, *Studies on the Legend*, 49–50.

89. Nutt, *Studies on the Legend*, 43–44.

90. Nutt, *Studies on the Legend*, 47.

91. Nutt, *Studies on the Legend,* 48.

92. Nutt, *Studies on the Legend,* 39.

93. Nutt, *Studies on the Legend,* 50.

94. Nutt, *Studies on the Legend,* 56–57.

95. Nutt, *Studies on the Legend,* 62.

96. Nutt, *Studies on the Legend,* 62–63.

97. Nutt, *Studies on the Legend,* 63.

98. Nutt, *Studies on the Legend,* 63, 64.

99. Nutt, *Studies on the Legend,* 59.

100. Nutt, *Studies on the Legend,* 47.

101. Nutt, *Studies on the Legend,* 50–51.

102. Frazer, *Golden Bough,* 1:52ff.

103. Alfred, Lord Tennyson, "Balin and Balan," *Idylls of the King* (New York, 1926), lines 94–116.

104. Tennyson, "Balin and Balan," lines 117–18.

105. Tennyson, "Balin and Balan," lines 235–84.

106. Tennyson, "Balin and Balan," lines 323–31.

107. Tennyson, "Balin and Balan," lines 387–91, 404–20.

108. Algernon Charles Swinburne, "The Tale of Balan," pt. 6, *Collected Poetical Works* (London: W. Heinemann, 1917), 4:208–13.

ILLUSTRATION SOURCES

FIGURE 1: Dora Curtis, from *Stories from King Arthur and His Round Table* by Beatrice Clay (1905). Public domain.

Figure 2: Artist unknown. Used through Creative Commons license: Johnbod / Wikimedia Commons.

Figures 3 and 4: Artist unknown. Public domain.

Figure 5: Artist unknown. Copyright © Biblioteca Monasterio del Escorial, Madrid, Spain. Used through license with Bridgeman Images.

Figure 6: William Russell Flint, from Thomas Malory's *Le Morte D'Arthur*, edited by Alfred W. Pollard (1911). Public domain.

Figure 7: Artist unknown. From *Mythos III: The Shaping of the Western Tradition* (DVD). Copyright © 2011 by Joseph Campbell Foundation.

Figures 8, 9, 10, 11, 12, and 13: Willy Pogány, from *Parsifal or the Legend of the Holy Grail: Retold from Ancient Sources with Acknowledgment to Richard Wagner* by T. W. Rolleston. (1912). Public domain.

Figure 14: William Ernest Chapman, from *The Story of Parzival, the Templar, Retold from Wolfram von Eschenbach* by Mary Blackwell Sterling (1911). Public domain.

Figures 15 and 16: Willy Pogány, from *Parsifal or the Legend of the Holy Grail: Retold from Ancient Sources with Acknowledgment to Richard Wagner* by T. W. Rolleston (1912). Public domain.

Figure 17: Howard Pyle, from *The Story of the Champions of the Round Table* by Howard Pyle (1905). Public domain.

Figures 18 and 19: Willy Pogány, from *Parsifal or the Legend of the Holy Grail: Retold from Ancient Sources with Acknowledgment to Richard Wagner* by T. W. Rolleston (1912). Public domain.

Figures 20 and 21: Howard Pyle, from *The Story of the Grail and the Passing of Arthur* by Howard Pyle (1910). Public domain.

Figure 22: Howard Pyle, from *The Story of King Arthur and His Knights* by Howard Pyle (1903). Public domain.

Figure 23: Artist unknown. Used through Creative Commons license: The Walters Museum, www.walters.org.

Figure 24: William Russell Flint, from Thomas Malory's *Le Morte D'Arthur*, edited by Alfred W. Pollard (1911). Public domain.

Figure 25: Howard Pyle, from *The Story of Sir Launcelot and His Companions* by Howard Pyle (1907). Public domain.

Figures 26 and 27: Artist unknown. Copyright © Bibliotheque des Arts Decoratifs, Paris, France / Archives Charmet. Used through license with Bridgeman Images.

Figure 28: Willy Pogány, from *Parsifal or the Legend of the Holy Grail: Retold from Ancient Sources with Acknowledgment to Richard Wagner* by T. W. Rolleston (1912). Public domain.

Figure 29: Artist unknown. Used through Creative Commons license: Heinrich Damm / Wikimedia Commons.

Figure 30: Artist unknown. Used through Creative Commons license: Chaithanya Krishnan / Wikimedia Commons.

Figure 31: Albrecht Dürer, *The Crucifixion* (1498). Public domain.

Figure 32: Artist unknown. Public domain.

Figures 33, 34, and 35: John L. Mackay, from *Masks of God: Creative Mythology* (1968). Copyright © 1968 by Joseph Campbell.

Figure 36: Artist unknown. Public domain.

Figure 37: Artist unknown. Digital image used courtesy of the Getty's Open Content Program. Public domain.

Figure 38: Howard Pyle, from *The Story of the Champions of the Round Table* by Howard Pyle (1905). Public domain.

Figure 39: Artist unknown. Copyright © Bayerische Staatsbibliothek, Munich, Germany / De Agostini Picture Library. Used through license with Bridgeman Images.

Figure 40: Artist unknown. Used courtesy of the British Library. Public domain.

Figures 41 and 42: Al Burkhardt. Copyright © 1968 by Joseph Campbell.

Figure 43: Artist unknown, from *Prolegomena to the Study of Greek Religion* by Jane Ellen Harrison (1908). Public domain.

Figure 44: Artist unknown. Used through Creative Commons license: G. Garitan / Wikimedia Commons.

Figure 45: Artist unknown. Public domain.

Figure 46: Artist unknown. From *Mythos III: The Shaping of the Western Tradition* (DVD). Copyright © 2011 by Joseph Campbell Foundation.

Figure 47: Artist unknown. Copyright © De Agostini Picture Library. Used through license with Bridgeman Images.

Figure 48: Artist unknown. Used through Creative Commons license: The Walters Museum, www.walters.org.

Figure 49: Howard Pyle, from *The Story of Sir Launcelot and His Companions* by Howard Pyle (1907). Public domain.

Figures 50 and 51: Gerald McDermott, from *The Knight of the Lion* by Gerald McDermott (1979). Copyright © 1979 by Gerald McDermott. Used with permission.

Figures 52 and 53: Artist unknown. Copyright © British Library Board. Used through license with Bridgeman Images.

Figures 54, 55, and 56: Willy Pogány, from *Parsifal or the Legend of the Holy Grail: Retold from Ancient Sources with Acknowledgment to Richard Wagner* by T. W. Rolleston (1912). Public domain.

Figure 57: Artist unknown. Public domain.

Figures 58 and 59: John L. Mackay, from *Masks of God: Creative Mythology* by Joseph Campbell (1968). Copyright © 1968 by Joseph Campbell.

Figure 60: Alfred Kappes, from *The Boy's King Arthur* by Sidney Lanier (1880). Public domain.

Figure 61: Joseph Campbell, from "A Study of the Dolorous Stroke" (1927). Copyright © 2015 by Joseph Campbell Foundation.

CHART 278–79: *Chart of Sources for Arthurian Legends* by David Jones (1943). Copyright © 1943 by the estate of David Jones. Used through permission of Tate Images.

A JOSEPH CAMPBELL BIBLIOGRAPHY

———————◆———————

Following are the major books authored and edited by Joseph Campbell. Each entry gives bibliographic data concerning the first edition or, if applicable, the original date of publication along with the bibliographic data for the edition published by New World Library as part of the Collected Works of Joseph Campbell. For information concerning all other editions, please refer to the Complete Works of Joseph Campbell on the Joseph Campbell Foundation website (www.jcf.org).

Author

Where the Two Came to Their Father: A Navaho War Ceremonial Given by Jeff King. Bollingen Series I. With Maud Oakes and Jeff King. Richmond, VA: Old Dominion Foundation, 1943.

A Skeleton Key to Finnegans Wake: Unlocking James Joyce's Masterwork. With Henry Morton Robinson. 1944. Second edition, Novato, CA: New World Library, 2005.*

The Hero with a Thousand Faces. Bollingen Series xvii. 1949. Third edition, Novato, CA: New World Library, 2008.*

The Masks of God, 4 vols. New York: Viking Press, 1959–1968. Vol. 1, *Primitive Mythology,* 1959. Vol. 2, *Oriental Mythology,* 1962. Vol. 3, *Occidental Mythology,* 1964. Vol. 4, *Creative Mythology,* 1968.

The Flight of the Wild Gander: Explorations in the Mythological Dimension—Selected Essays 1944–1968. 1969. Third edition, Novato, CA: New World Library, 2002.*

Myths to Live By. 1972. Ebook edition, San Anselmo, CA: Joseph Campbell Foundation, 2011.

The Mythic Image. Bollingen Series c. Princeton, NJ: Princeton University Press, 1974.

The Inner Reaches of Outer Space: Metaphor as Myth and as Religion. 1986. Reprint, Novato, CA: New World Library, 2002.*

The Historical Atlas of World Mythology:

Vol. 1, *The Way of the Animal Powers.* New York: Alfred van der Marck Editions, 1983. Reprint in 2 pts. Part 1, *Mythologies of the Primitive Hunters and Gatherers.* New York: Alfred van der Marck Editions, 1988. Part 2, *Mythologies of the Great Hunt.* New York: Alfred van der Marck Editions, 1988.

Vol. 2, *The Way of the Seeded Earth,* 3 pts. Part 1, *The Sacrifice.* New York: Alfred van der Marck Editions, 1988. Part 2, *Mythologies of the Primitive Planters: The Northern Americas.* New York: Harper & Row Perennial Library, 1989. Part 3, *Mythologies of the Primitive Planters: The Middle and Southern Americas.* New York: Harper & Row Perennial Library, 1989.

The Power of Myth. With Bill Moyers. Edited by Betty Sue Flowers. New York: Doubleday, 1988.

Transformations of Myth Through Time. New York: Harper & Row, 1990.

The Hero's Journey: Joseph Campbell on His Life and Work. Edited by Phil Cousineau. 1990. Reprint, Novato, CA: New World Library, 2003.*

Reflections on the Art of Living: A Joseph Campbell Companion. Edited by Diane K. Osbon. New York: HarperCollins, 1991.

Mythic Worlds, Modern Words: On the Art of James Joyce. Edited by Edmund L. Epstein. 1993. Second edition, Novato, CA: New World Library, 2003.*

Baksheesh & Brahman: Asian Journals—India. Edited by Robin Larsen, Stephen Larsen, and Antony Van Couvering. 1995. Second edition, Novato, CA: New World Library, 2002.* [Reissued in paperback, together with *Sake & Satori,* in 2017; see *Asian Journals* entry below.]

The Mythic Dimension: Selected Essays 1959–1987. Edited by Antony Van Couvering. 1997. Second edition, Novato, CA: New World Library, 2007.*

Thou Art That. Edited by Eugene Kennedy. Novato, CA: New World Library, 2001.*

Sake & Satori: Asian Journals—Japan. Edited by David Kudler. Novato, CA: New World Library, 2002.* [Reissued in paperback, together with *Baksheesh & Brahman,* in 2017; see *Asian Journals* entry below.]

Myths of Light. Edited by David Kudler. Novato, CA: New World Library, 2003.*

Pathways to Bliss: Mythology and Personal Transformation. Edited by David
  Kudler. Novato, CA: New World Library, 2004.*
Mythic Imagination: Collected Short Fiction. Novato, CA: New World
  Library, 2012.*
Goddesses: Mysteries of the Feminine Divine. Edited by Safron Rossi. Novato,
  CA: New World Library, 2013.*
Romance of the Grail: The Magic and Mystery of Arthurian Myth. Edited by
  Evans Lansing Smith. Novato, CA: New World Library, 2015.*
Asian Journals: India and Japan. Combined paperback reissue of *Baksheesh
  & Brahman* and *Sake & Satori.* Book I: *Baksheesh & Brahman*—edited
  by Robin Larsen, Stephen Larsen, and Antony Van Couvering; book
  II: *Sake & Satori*—edited by David Kudler. Novato, CA: New World
  Library, 2017.*
The Ecstasy of Being: Mythology and Dance. Edited by Nancy Allison, CMA.
  Novato, CA: New World Library, 2017.*

* Published by New World Library as part of the Collected Works of Joseph Campbell.

EDITOR

Books edited and completed from the posthuma of Heinrich Zimmer:
Myths and Symbols in Indian Art and Civilization. Bollingen Series vi. New
  York: Pantheon, 1946.
The King and the Corpse. Bollingen Series xi. New York: Pantheon, 1948.
Philosophies of India. Bollingen Series xxvi. New York: Pantheon, 1951.
The Art of Indian Asia. Bollingen Series xxxix, 2 vols. New York: Pantheon,
  1955.

Other books edited:
The Portable Arabian Nights. New York: Viking Press, 1951.
Papers from the Eranos Yearbooks. Bollingen Series xxx, 6 vols. Edited with
  R. F. C. Hull and Olga Froebe-Kapteyn. Translated by Ralph Manheim.
  Princeton: Princeton University Press, 1954–1969.
Myth, Dreams and Religion: Eleven Visions of Connection. New York: E. P.
  Dutton, 1970.
The Portable Jung. By C. G. Jung. Translated by R. F. C. Hull. New York:
  Viking Press, 1971.
My Life and Lives. By Rato Khyongla Nawang Losang. New York: E. P. Dut-
  ton, 1977.

INDEX

Page references followed by *fig.* indicate illustrations or material contained in their captions.

ABOUT THE AUTHOR

———————•———————

JOSEPH CAMPBELL WAS AN AMERICAN author and teacher best known for his work in the field of comparative mythology. He was born in New York City in 1904, and in early childhood became interested in mythology. He loved to read books about American Indian cultures and frequently visited the American Museum of Natural History in New York, where he was fascinated by the museum's collection of totem poles. Campbell was educated at Columbia University, where he specialized in medieval literature, and, after earning a master's degree, continued his studies at universities in Paris and Munich. While abroad he was influenced by the art of Pablo Picasso and Henri Matisse, the novels of James Joyce and Thomas Mann, and the psychological studies of Sigmund Freud and Carl Jung. These encounters led to Campbell's theory that all myths and epics are linked in the human psyche, and that they are cultural manifestations of the universal need to explain social, cosmological, and spiritual realities.

After a period in California, where he encountered John Steinbeck and the biologist Ed Ricketts, Campbell taught at the Canterbury School, and then, in 1934, joined the literature department at Sarah Lawrence College, a post he retained for many years. During the 1940s and '50s, he helped Swami Nikhilananda to translate the Upaniṣads and *The Gospel of Sri Ramakrishna*. He also edited works by the German scholar Heinrich Zimmer on Indian art, myths, and philosophy.

In 1944, with Henry Morton Robinson, Campbell published *A Skeleton Key to Finnegans Wake*. His first original work, *The Hero with a Thousand Faces,* came out in 1949 and was immediately well received; in time, it became acclaimed as a classic. In this study of the "myth of the hero," Campbell asserted that there is a single pattern of heroic journey and that all cultures share this essential pattern in their various heroic myths. In his book he also outlined the basic conditions, stages, and results of the archetypal hero's journey.

Joseph Campbell died in 1987. In 1988 a series of television interviews with Bill Moyers, *The Power of Myth,* introduced Campbell's views to millions of people.

ABOUT THE
JOSEPH CAMPBELL FOUNDATION

———————●———————

THE JOSEPH CAMPBELL FOUNDATION (JCF) is a nonprofit corporation that continues the work of Joseph Campbell, exploring the fields of mythology and comparative religion. The foundation is guided by three principal goals.

First, the foundation preserves, protects, and perpetuates Campbell's pioneering work. This includes cataloging and archiving his works, developing new publications based on his works, directing the sale and distribution of his published works, protecting copyrights to his works, and increasing awareness of his works by making them available in digital formats on JCF's website.

Second, the foundation promotes the study of mythology and comparative religion. This involves implementing and/or supporting diverse mythological education programs, supporting and/or sponsoring events designed to increase public awareness, donating Campbell's archived works, and utilizing JCF's website as a forum for relevant cross-cultural dialogue.

Third, the foundation helps individuals enrich their lives by participating in a series of programs, including our global, Internet-based Associates program, our local international network of Mythological Roundtables, and our periodic Joseph Campbell–related events and activities.

www.jcf.org

For more information on Joseph Campbell
and the Joseph Campbell Foundation, contact:

Joseph Campbell Foundation
www.jcf.org
P.O. Box 1836
New York, NY 10026
Email: info@jcf.org

Celtic & pre-celtic

Pre-celtic

PREHISTORIC BRITAIN
AD 60 ROMAN OCCUPATION to 5th Cat.
— Druidic Gnosis

Emigrations to BRITTANY   c. 450 & also
c. 550

537, trad. date of ARTHUR's death   Irish & Saxon
at Camlann.   Annals
Gildas 500-570

Histories of
Eusebius
Jerome
Isidore
Prosper

— Bede

NENNIUS 800 AD
(Arthur already
a marvel-worker)

MYTH + HISTORY + PSEUDO-HISTORY IN
NORTH BRITAIN WALES & S.W. BRITAIN

GERMANIC
Weltanschauung

IRELAND

Urien   Gawain   King
* Drystan Peredur   Grail?   March
Owain   of Meirion

Welsh-Irish
Non-Arthurian
Mythology

①
*

CORNWALL
WALES   (isolated from 685)
The Welsh Saints

1150
FRENCH
ROM

N.B.
refugees
Ireland in?
pseudo

Pedeir Keinc
Mabinogi
many other
correspondences

Ecclesiastical Legend
Gallo-Roman
(from district of Lyons)
Irish & Welsh
in 5th Century, proved.

'Life of Gildas'
c. 1100

Norse
influence
?

WELSH MSS.
in the earliest
strata Arthur
appears as a
quasi-mythological
figure in association
with historical and
mythological
characters.
in two poems &
two prose-tales he
is a central figure
& tends to be associated
with the Dumnonian
peninsular, but
North Britain
is associated with
some of the most
important figures.

②
Archdeacon Walter's "book from Brittany"
Geoffreys avowed source

"Blehiri" "Bledri" "Bréri"

Blehe16ricus
ille fabulator

'famosus'

Other Direct Welsh influences on G.o.M ?

Very Great influence of G.o.M from before 1200. on Wales

GEOFFREY of

The Hist. Reg. Brit. was in
(also similar popular
Notes conviction in Brittany)
① * Riot in Bodmin, Cornwall
in 1113 because a French
monk said Arthur would
never return.
② Existence not proved

Wace
(a pr

Laye

Metamorphosis of the characters.
Prose-tales in the new
European Romance
style.
(e.g. 'Geraint son of Erbin'
'The Lady of the Fountain'
'Peredur son of Evrawc')

The Early Engli

Subsequent Welsh
MSS. & tradition
Tudor & later
pseudo-bardic invention,
antiquarian & literary
influences.

? ?
??

Red, thus:
= Celtic
Channels AD.

N.B. Arthur present in, but not central to main primitive

ARYAN MYTH
India (Wasteland motif?) Rig Veda
Non-Aryan Myth?

C MEDITERRANEAN CULTURES

PERSIA

NB
3rd Cent A.D. Jewish & Arabian knights & troubadours at the Courts of the Ghassanids. (Peto-Capjonits)

CE & ROME
ANTIVM
& Literature

Magian Gnosis

Manichees

Arabian-Spanish complex

Late Empire mounted Knights

Cathars

PROVEÇAL COURTS of LOVE

Madonna WORSHIP

Eleanor of Poitou (1122-1204) The Crusades
1095 onwards

Marie de Champagne
(patroness of Chrétien)

RMAN

Western Catholic-Xtian Influences.
ascetical and mystical.
The Cistercians.
Development of Eucharistic cultus (Corpus Xti 12-6)
& its effect on the Western imagination & symbol.

Metrical followed by prose Romances

Chrétien de Troyes
Béroul : Thomas de Bretagne
Eilhart von Oberge
Hartmann von Aue
Gottfried von Strassburg
Wolfram von Eschenbach
and other French & German versions (Metrical) of the separate stories.

(a pseudomorphosis in, e.g., Grail material
i.e. the immemorial themes given forms
of Xtian significance.)

1190
1200
100

Norwegian 1226 (Tristan)

Italian 1300 (Tristan)

Czech 1350 circa (Tristan)

Torigni copy in form from Bec in Normandy
139

German Prose circa 1450
Tristrant und Isalde

H. Hist. Reg. Britanniae
(present form before 1150)

Vita Merlini
Bretuns de Brut
eux)

Rhyming of as glossies dedicated to Eleanor of Aquitaine
1155 (first mention of Round Table.)
(in French)

t 1160 English translated

Round Table themes developed
& Arthur as English King
English folk-lore elements

1469
MALORY is a
synthesis of French material
(Suite du Merlin &c & insular material

& the Grene Knyghte
14th Cent

of Syr Gawayne

Cent poem Mort Arthure
a proveat saing for Malory

Chroniclers etc.

XIX Cent.

Richard Wagner
(Tristan 1859)
1809-1872 Tennyson

Late English Tradition
Drayton, Camden, Spenser,
Milton, Dryden, Blake, etc.